THE
GRANDDAUGHTERS
OF EDWARD III

THE GRANDDAUGHTERS OF EDWARD III

KATHRYN WARNER

PEN & SWORD
HISTORY

AN IMPRINT OF PEN & SWORD BOOKS LTD.
YORKSHIRE – PHILADELPHIA

First published in Great Britain in 2023 by
PEN AND SWORD HISTORY
An imprint of
Pen & Sword Books Ltd
Yorkshire – Philadelphia

ISBN 978 1 52677 925 0

A CIP catalogue record for this book is available from the British Library.

Typeset in Times New Roman 11.5/14 by
SJmagic DESIGN SERVICES, India.
Printed and bound in the UK by CPI Group (UK) Ltd.

Pen & Sword Books Limited incorporates the imprints of Atlas, Archaeology,
Aviation, Discovery, Family History, Fiction, History, Maritime, Military, Military
Classics, Politics, Select, Transport, True Crime, Air World, Frontline Publishing,
Leo Cooper, Remember When, Seaforth Publishing, The Praetorian Press,
Wharncliffe Local History, Wharncliffe Transport, Wharncliffe True Crime and
White Owl.

For a complete list of Pen & Sword titles please contact
PEN & SWORD BOOKS LIMITED
47 Church Street, Barnsley, South Yorkshire, S70 2AS, England
E-mail: enquiries@pen-and-sword.co.uk
Website: www.pen-and-sword.co.uk

Or
PEN AND SWORD BOOKS
1950 Lawrence Rd, Havertown, PA 19083, USA
E-mail: Uspen-and-sword@casematepublishers.com
Website: www.penandswordbooks.com

Contents

Family Trees

Table 1: Edward III's Granddaughters

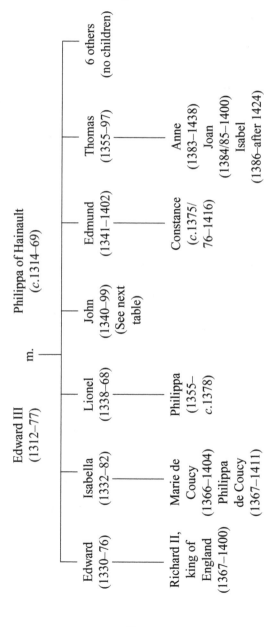

Edward III (1312–77) m. Philippa of Hainault (c.1314–69)

- Edward (1330–76)
  - Richard II, king of England (1367–1400)
- Isabella (1332–82)
  - Marie de Coucy (1366–1404)
  - Philippa de Coucy (1367–1411)
- Lionel (1338–68)
  - Philippa (1355–c.1378)
- John (1340–99) (See next table)
- Edmund (1341–1402)
  - Constance (c.1375/76–1416)
- Thomas (1355–97)
  - Anne (1383–1438)
  - Joan (1384/85–1400)
  - Isabel (1386–after 1424)
- 6 others (no children)

Table 2: John of Gaunt's Daughters

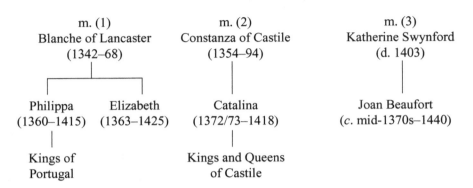

John of Gaunt, second duke of Lancaster
(1340–99)

m. (1)
Blanche of Lancaster
(1342–68)

m. (2)
Constanza of Castile
(1354–94)

m. (3)
Katherine Swynford
(d. 1403)

Philippa
(1360–1415)

Elizabeth
(1363–1425)

Catalina
(1372/73–1418)

Joan Beaufort
(*c*. mid-1370s–1440)

Kings of
Portugal

Kings and Queens
of Castile

Table 3: Royal House of Portugal

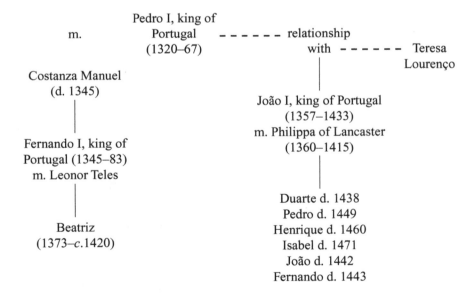

m.

Pedro I, king of
Portugal
(1320–67)

– – – – – relationship
with – – – – – – Teresa
Lourenço

Costanza Manuel
(d. 1345)

João I, king of Portugal
(1357–1433)
m. Philippa of Lancaster
(1360–1415)

Fernando I, king of
Portugal (1345–83)
m. Leonor Teles

Beatriz
(1373–*c*.1420)

Duarte d. 1438
Pedro d. 1449
Henrique d. 1460
Isabel d. 1471
João d. 1442
Fernando d. 1443

Table 4: Royal House of Castile

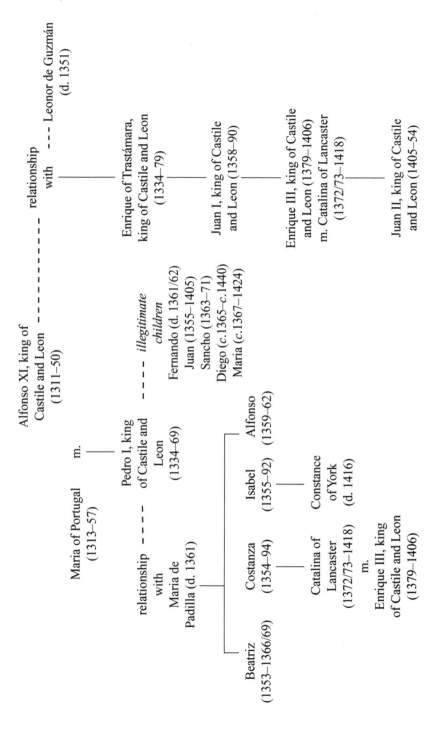

Introduction

The Catedral Primada Santa María de Toledo, usually known in English simply as Toledo Cathedral, dominates the skyline of the central Spanish city of Toledo. Inside the cathedral, on the north side, stands the *Capilla de los Reyes Nuevos*, the 'Chapel of the New Kings'. It was built in the 1530s to house the mortal remains of the Trastámaras, the dynasty which ruled the mighty kingdom of Castile, and the much smaller kingdom of Leon in the north of Spain, from 1369 onwards. One effigy, which stands close to the altar of San Hermenegildo or Saint Hermenegild, depicts a woman wearing a wimple covering her neck, a tunic and a cloak and clutching a small prayer-book in her left hand. This tomb and effigy particularly capture the attention, especially as the inscription on the tomb describes the person in question as the 'Lady Queen Doña Catalina, granddaughter of the righteous kings, King Edward of England and King Don Pedro of Castile' and daughter of 'the most noble prince Don Juan, duke of Alencastre', i.e. John, duke of Lancaster.

Three hundred and twenty miles away, in the Founders' Chapel inside the monastery of Batalha in central Portugal, stands another effigy of a woman holding a small prayer-book in her left hand, while her right clasps the right hand of her husband's effigy. Their tomb, built in the 1430s, is the first joint tomb of a couple ever constructed in Portugal, and was almost certainly influenced and inspired by the woman herself, Queen Philippa, who was the older half-sister of Queen Catalina. These English women, lying for all eternity far from their homeland, are two members of a generation of women who were the granddaughters of a famous warrior king of England. Edward III reigned from January 1327 until June 1377, and married Philippa of Hainault in January 1328 when he was 15 and she, according to a chronicler, was almost 14.[1] Of the king and queen's twelve children born between June 1330 and January 1355, six lived long enough to marry and have children of their own. Eleven of the king and queen's granddaughters survived infancy, ten married, and eight had children. Two, as noted, became queens in the Iberian peninsula; two married three times; one was the mother of three duchesses, an earl, a countess, and a bishop; one became an abbess in London; one saw her husband leave her for a Bohemian lady; one rebelled against her cousin the king and was imprisoned, and had an affair with a nobleman a few years her junior which resulted in an illegitimate daughter; one had her first marriage hastily annulled in order to marry her second husband, then married her third husband without the permission of her brother the king; and another married two of her three husbands without royal permission. This book tells the story of the eleven granddaughters of Edward III and Queen Philippa.

A Note on Names

To avoid the confusion of constantly changing names, I refer to some of Edward III's granddaughters by their fathers' ducal titles even before their fathers received those titles, e.g. Philippa of Clarence, Philippa of Lancaster, Constance of York and Anne of Gloucester, and use their cousins' maiden names even after they married, e.g. Marie and Philippa de Coucy and Joan Beaufort. I also use the modern spelling of given names, e.g. Philippa, Eleanor and Joan, rather than the usual fourteenth-century spelling, Phelip or Philippe, Alianore and Johane. I refer to John of Gaunt and Costanza of Castile's daughter as Catalina of Lancaster, not Katherine, both to avoid possible confusion with Gaunt's long-term mistress Katherine Swynford and because Catalina moved to Castile when she was about 13 years old, and would probably have come to think of herself by the Spanish form of her name. The Portuguese, Spanish and Catalan forms of given names have been used for members of the Portuguese, Castilian and Aragonese royal families, e.g. João, Duarte, Enrique, María, Martí.

Who's Who: Edward III and Queen Philippa's Children

Edward of Woodstock (1330–1376), prince of Wales and Aquitaine, duke of Cornwall, earl of Chester; married Joan of Kent in 1361; one son who lived into adulthood, no daughters; his son Richard II, often called Richard of Bordeaux (b. 1367), succeeded his grandfather Edward III as king of England in 1377.

Isabella of Woodstock (1332–1382), countess of Bedford and Soissons, Lady Coucy; married Enguerrand (or Ingelram or Ingram), Lord de Coucy, later earl of Bedford and count of Soissons, in 1365; two daughters, no sons.

Joan of Woodstock (1334–1348), died as a teenager on her way to marry Pedro, future king of Castile and Leon; no children.

William of Hatfield (b. and d. 1337), died in infancy.

Lionel of Antwerp (1338–1368), duke of Clarence, earl of Ulster; married 1) Elizabeth de Burgh in 1342 and 2) Violante Visconti in 1368; one daughter from his first marriage, no sons.

John of Gaunt (1340–1399), titular king of Castile and Leon, duke of Lancaster, earl of Richmond, Lincoln, Leicester and Derby; married 1) Blanche of Lancaster in 1359, 2) Costanza of Castile in 1371, and 3) his long-term mistress Katherine Swynford in 1396; four daughters and four sons, plus a number of other children who died young, of whom four were born outside marriage and later legitimised; his and Blanche of Lancaster's only surviving son (b. 1367) became King Henry IV of England in 1399.

Edmund of Langley (1341–1402), duke of York, earl of Cambridge; married 1) Isabel of Castile in 1372 and 2) Joan Holland in 1393; one daughter, two sons from his first marriage.

Blanche of the Tower (b. and d. 1342), died in infancy.

Mary of Waltham (1344–1361/62), married John de Montfort, later Duke John IV of Brittany (b. 1339), and died as a teenager, no children.

Margaret of Windsor (1346–61/62), married John Hastings, heir to the earldom of Pembroke (b. 1347), and died as a teenager, no children.

William of Windsor (b. and d. 1348), died in infancy.

Thomas of Woodstock (1355–1397), duke of Gloucester, earl of Buckingham and Essex; married Eleanor de Bohun in *c.* 1374; one son, three daughters.

Who's Who: Edward III and Queen Philippa's Granddaughters

Philippa of Clarence, countess of March and Ulster, born 16 August 1355, died before 6 December 1379, possibly as early as the end of 1377 or the beginning of 1378; only child and heir of Lionel of Antwerp and Elizabeth de Burgh; married Edmund Mortimer, third earl of March (b. February 1352) in or before December 1358.

Philippa of Lancaster, queen of Portugal, born 31 March 1360, died 19 July 1415; first daughter of John of Gaunt and Blanche of Lancaster; married João of Aviz, king of Portugal (b. 1357), in February 1387.

Elizabeth of Lancaster, duchess of Exeter, countess of Pembroke and Huntingdon, born *c.* February 1363, died 24 November 1425; second daughter of John of Gaunt and Blanche of Lancaster; married 1) John Hastings, heir to the earldom of Pembroke (b. November 1372), in June 1380, though the marriage was annulled before consummation; 2) John Holland (b. *c.* 1353), later earl of Huntingdon and duke of Exeter, probably in June 1386; 3) John Cornwall (b. *c.* late 1360s or early 1370s), created Baron Fanhope after Elizabeth's death, in or before early April 1400.

Marie de Coucy, countess of Soissons and lady of Coucy, Marle and Oisy, born April 1366, died in or not long after mid-October 1404; elder daughter of Isabella of Woodstock and Enguerrand de Coucy; married Henri de Bar, son and heir of Robert, duke of Bar, not long after 26 November 1383.

Philippa de Coucy, duchess of Ireland and countess of Oxford, born on or shortly before 18 November 1367, died 24 September 1411; younger daughter of Isabella of Woodstock and Enguerrand de Coucy; married Robert de Vere (b. 1362), earl of Oxford and later marquess of Dublin and duke of Ireland, before 5 October 1376.

Catalina (or Katherine) **of Lancaster**, queen of Castile and Leon, born sometime between early June 1372 and 31 March 1373, died 2 June 1418; third daughter of John of Gaunt, only child and heir of her mother Costanza of Castile, and also heir of her grandfather Pedro I 'the Cruel' of Castile and Leon; married Enrique, prince of Asturias, later King Enrique III of Castile and Leon (b. October 1379), in September 1388.

Constance of York, countess of Gloucester and Lady Despenser, probably born *c.* 1375/76, died 28 November 1416; only daughter of Edmund of Langley and Isabel of Castile; married Thomas Despenser, later lord of Glamorgan and earl of Gloucester (b. 1373), in November 1379; as a widow in the early 1400s, had a relationship with Edmund Holland, earl of Kent (b. 1382 or 1383).

Joan Beaufort, countess of Westmorland, Lady Ferrers and Neville, born *c.* mid-1370s, died 13 November 1440; fourth and youngest daughter of John of Gaunt, born to Katherine Swynford and legitimised after her parents' marriage in 1396; married 1) Robert, Lord Ferrers of Wem (b. early 1370s) in *c.* March 1392; 2) Ralph Neville, later earl of Westmorland (b. *c.* 1364), in or before November 1396.

Anne of Gloucester, countess of Stafford and Eu, born shortly before 6 May 1383, died 16 October 1438; eldest daughter and ultimately the sole heir of Thomas of Woodstock and Eleanor de Bohun; married 1) Thomas Stafford, earl of Stafford (b. 1369) in *c.* 1390/91; 2) his brother Edmund, earl of Stafford (b. *c.* late 1370s) in or before June 1398; 3) William Bourchier (b. 1370s), later count of Eu, in or before November 1405.

Joan of Gloucester, Lady Talbot, born *c.* 1384/85, died 16 August 1400; second daughter of Thomas of Woodstock and Eleanor de Bohun; married Gilbert Talbot (b. *c.* 1383/84) after May 1392.

Isabel of Gloucester, born 23 April 1386; third and youngest daughter of Thomas of Woodstock and Eleanor de Bohun; entered the convent of the Minoresses in London as a child and professed as a nun on her sixteenth birthday in April 1402; appointed abbess of the convent in or before 1421; still alive in February 1424; date of death unknown.

Who's Who: Kings of England in the Later Middle Ages

Edward III, born 1312, reigned 1327–77; married Philippa of Hainault (*c.* 1314–1369) in 1328.

Richard II, b. 1367, r. 1377–99; second but only surviving son of Edward III and Queen Philippa's eldest son the prince of Wales; married Anne of Bohemia (1366–1394) in 1382, and secondly Isabelle de Valois (1389–1409) in 1396; no children.

Henry IV, b. 1367, r. 1399–1413; son of Edward III and Queen Philippa's fourth son John of Gaunt; married Mary de Bohun (*c.* 1370–1394) in 1381, and secondly Juana of Navarre, dowager duchess of Brittany (*c.* 1368/70–1437), in 1403.

Henry V, b. 1386, r. 1413–22; son of Henry IV and Mary; married Katherine de Valois (1401–37) in 1420.

Henry VI, b. 1421, r. 1422–61 and 1470–71; son of Henry V and Katherine; married Marguerite of Anjou (1430–1482) in 1445.

Who's Who: Kings of France in the Later Middle Ages

John II, b. 1319, r. 1350–64, son of Philip VI (r. 1328–50); married Bonne of Bohemia (1315–1349).

Charles V, b. 1338, r. 1364–80, eldest son of John II and Bonne; married Jeanne de Bourbon (1338–1378).

Charles VI, b. 1368, r. 1380–1422, elder son of Charles V and Jeanne; married Isabeau of Bavaria (*c.* 1370–1435).

Who's Who: Kings of Portugal in the Later Middle Ages

Pedro I, b. 1320, r. 1357–67, son of Afonso IV (r. 1325–57); married Costanza Manuel of Peñafiel and Villena (d. 1345); also had relationships with Inês de Castro and Teresa Lourenço.

Fernando I, b. 1345, r. 1367–1383, son of Pedro I and Queen Costanza Manuel; married Leonor Teles de Meneses (d. sometime between 1390 and 1406); their only child Beatriz (b. 1373) died in obscurity in about 1420.

João I, called 'of Aviz', b. 1357, r. 1385–1433; illegitimate son of Pedro I and Teresa Lourenço, half-brother of Fernando I, and ultimately his successor; married Philippa of Lancaster (1360–1415) in 1387.

Who's Who: Kings of Castile and Leon in the Later Middle Ages

Alfonso XI, b. 1311, r. 1312–50, son of Fernando IV (r. 1295–1312); married Maria of Portugal (1313–1357); also had a long-term relationship with his mistress Leonor de Guzmán (*c.* 1310–1351).

Pedro I 'the Cruel', b. 1334, r. 1350–69, son of Alfonso XI and Queen Maria; married Blanche de Bourbon (d. 1361) in 1353, but his mistress María de Padilla (d. 1361) was the mother of his daughter and heir Costanza of Castile (1354–1394), duchess of Lancaster; also had relationships with María González de Henestrosa, Juana de Castro, Isabel de Sandoval and Teresa de Ayala. (See below for a list of his illegitimate children.)

Enrique II, called 'of Trastámara', b. 1334, r. 1369–79, eldest surviving illegitimate son of Alfonso XI and Leonor de Guzmán; half-brother, usurper and killer of Pedro I; married Juana Manuel of Peñafiel and Villena (1339–1381).

Juan I, b. 1358, r. 1379–90, son of Enrique II and Juana Manuel; married Leonor of Aragon (1358–1382).

Enrique III, b. 1379, r. 1390–1406, son of Juan I and Leonor; married Catalina of Lancaster (1372/73–1418), granddaughter and heir of Pedro I.

Juan II, b. 1405, r. 1406–54, son of Enrique III and Catalina; married María of Aragon (1403–1445) and secondly Isabel of Portugal

(1428–1496); by his second marriage, father of Isabel la Católica, queen-regnant of Castile.

Who's Who: Illegitimate Children of Pedro I 'the Cruel' of Castile and Leon

Beatriz, b. *c*. March 1353, d. between September 1366 and March 1369; eldest child of María de Padilla; betrothed to Fernando of Portugal, later King Fernando I.

Costanza, b. July 1354, d. March 1394; married John of Gaunt, duke of Lancaster, in September 1371; mother of Catalina of Lancaster, queen-consort of Castile and Leon; second child of María de Padilla.

Isabel, b. summer or autumn 1355, d. December 1392; married Edmund of Langley, earl of Cambridge and later duke of York, in June 1372; third child of María de Padilla.

Alfonso, b. 1359, d. October 1362; fourth and youngest child of María de Padilla.

Juan, b. January 1355, d. 1405; only child of Juana de Castro, and nephew of Inês de Castro; married Elvira de Eril; father of Pedro (d. 1461), bishop of Osma and Palencia, and Costanza (d. 1478), prioress of Santo Domingo el Real in Toledo.

Fernando, lord of Niebla, birth date unknown, d. in the early 1360s; only child of María de Padilla's cousin María González de Henestrosa.

Sancho, b. September 1363, d. 1371; elder child of Isabel de Sandoval.

Diego, b. *c*. 1365, d. after 1424; younger child of Isabel de Sandoval.

María de Ayala, b. *c*. 1367, d. 1424; only child of Teresa de Ayala (d. 1424), who later became prioress of Santo Domingo el Real in Toledo.

Chapter 1

The First Granddaughter

Eltham Palace, Kent, Sunday the day after the feast of the Assumption in the twenty-ninth year of King Edward III's reign (16 August 1355)

Philippa of Clarence, the first and, as it turned out, only child of Lionel of Antwerp and Elizabeth de Burgh, earl and countess of Ulster and later the first duke and duchess of Clarence, was born at the royal palace of Eltham in Kent on 16 August 1355. The infant was named after her paternal grandmother, Philippa of Hainault, queen of England (b. *c.* 1314). The queen attended her granddaughter's baptism at Eltham on the day of her birth, and, with her daughter-in-law Elizabeth, 'lifted her from the sacred font'. This means that Philippa of Hainault was the little girl's godmother as well as her grandmother, and William Edington, bishop of Winchester and chancellor of England (d. 1366), conducted the baptism.

When little Philippa proved that she had come of age fourteen years later, three local men remembered her date of birth because the River Thames 'broke the pool called "Le Brech" at Grynewych [Greenwich] and flooded a very great number of acres of arable land' there in the summer Philippa was born. Ralph Pesekod, in his late twenties in 1355, remembered Philippa's birth because on the same day he sold his house near the bridge of Deptford, and John of Durham, then in his mid-fifties, remembered it because he married his wife Denise Depeslade on the same day. Three men at the proof of age in 1369 remembered Philippa's date of birth because her grandfather King Edward III set out on a military campaign to Calais in the same year that she was born, and another four remembered it because the king travelled to Scotland the following year.[1]

Little Philippa was born the day after her parents' thirteenth wedding anniversary, yet, rather astonishingly, her father was still only 16 years old at the time of her birth. Lionel of Antwerp, earl of Ulster, was the third son of Edward III and Philippa of Hainault, though was the second eldest of their seven sons to survive childhood. The king and queen's eldest son Edward of Woodstock, prince of Wales, duke of Cornwall and earl of Chester, heir to the throne, was born in the palace of Woodstock near Oxford on 15 June 1330, and their second, William of Hatfield, was born in early 1337 but died soon after his birth. Lionel was born on 29 November 1338 in the city of Antwerp in modern-day Belgium, during his parents' long sojourn on the Continent while Edward III sought allies against the king of France, Philip VI, whose throne he had begun to claim in 1337. Lionel's younger brother John of Gaunt was born in Ghent (which was known as 'Gaunt' to English people of the era and for centuries afterwards, hence his name) also in modern-day Belgium on 6 March 1340, a few months before King Edward, Queen Philippa and their young family returned to England. Philippa was then already pregnant again with her fifth son, Edmund of Langley, born in early June 1341, and bore another three daughters and two sons between 1342 and 1355.

To his contemporaries, Lionel of Antwerp was often known as 'Leo' or 'Lion', and in his own lifetime, his unusual Arthurian name was usually spelt 'Lyonell' or 'Leonell'. This latter spelling reveals its correct fourteenth-century pronunciation; as in Lionel Messi, not Lionel Ritchie. [2] The name of his mother and his daughter, Philippa, was spelt Phelip, Phelippe, Philippe or Phellipe in the fourteenth century, and was a unisex name, serving both for men called Philip and women called Philippa. The name was only very rarely given to women in England before Philippa of Hainault married Edward III in 1328, and thereafter became common. It was borne by three of the king and queen's eleven granddaughters.

Lionel of Antwerp married on 15 August 1342, when he was aged only 3 years and $8^1/_2$ months and could hardly have been old enough to have any memories of his own wedding. The ceremony took place in the Tower of London, and the mayor and aldermen of the city sent 10 tuns of wine for the guests to consume during the festivities. [3] Lionel's bride, Elizabeth de Burgh, was almost six and a half years older than he, born on 6 July 1332, and was 10 when they married. She was the only surviving child and heir of the influential Anglo-Irish nobleman William de Burgh, earl of Ulster (1312–1333) and Maud of Lancaster, and was also heir to her wealthy paternal grandmother, Elizabeth de Burgh, née de Clare, who inherited a third of the earldom of Gloucester from her brother Gilbert de Clare (d. 1314). The elder Elizabeth de Burgh was still alive, aged not quite 60, in August 1355 when her great-granddaughter Philippa of Clarence was born.[4]

Despite the age gap between them, Lionel of Antwerp and Elizabeth de Burgh the younger spent much time together over the years, and seem genuinely to have enjoyed each other's company. Elizabeth had to wait many years for her young husband to reach maturity and to be able to consummate their marriage, and it may not be a coincidence that their daughter was born thirty-seven weeks after Lionel's sixteenth birthday, which fell on 29 November 1354. Elizabeth was 23 when she bore Philippa, and although she lived for another eight years, she would have no more children; perhaps it was a difficult birth. Elizabeth's brother-in-law Edward of Woodstock, prince of Wales, gave her servant John Priour £20 for bringing him news of the birth of her daughter.[5] On 5 March 1356 when she was half a year old, Edward III sent his granddaughter Philippa of Clarence to the priory of Campsea Ashe in Suffolk to live for a while with her maternal grandmother Maud of Lancaster, dowager countess of Ulster, who had retired from the secular world in the late 1340s following the death of her second husband and became a canoness there. The king sent carpenters, masons and other workmen to repair the houses within the priory where Philippa would live.[6]

King Edward arranged Philippa's marriage to Edmund Mortimer, heir to his father Roger's earldom of March, and the young couple wed in or before December 1358. Philippa was then 3 years old, and Edmund, born in Llangoed, Wales on 1 February 1352, was 6. The king spent well over £200 for 2,000 pearls for the weddings of his granddaughter and his fifth and youngest daughter Margaret of Windsor (b. July 1346), who married John Hastings (b. August 1347), heir to his late father's earldom of Pembroke, around the same time.[7] Remarkably, Philippa's great-grandmother, the elder Elizabeth de Burgh, lived long enough to see her wedding; Elizabeth did not die until November 1360. Philippa's new husband Edmund Mortimer had been betrothed to Alice Fitzalan or Arundel, second daughter of Richard, earl of Arundel and Surrey, in October 1354 when he was 2 years old and she was probably a little older, but this planned marriage did not take place.[8] After her wedding, little Philippa returned to her mother's care, and Edward III granted his daughter-in-law £400 a year for the sustenance of herself and her daughter.[9]

Lionel of Antwerp had only recently turned 20 years old when his daughter married in late 1358, and evidently Edward III expected that his son and Elizabeth would have more children: he gave the Mortimer family a huge dowry of 5,000 marks or £3,333 for his granddaughter, which indicates that he believed Philippa would not ultimately inherit her parents' (and her great-grandmother's) lands. Had he known that she would be a great heiress, he would not have given the Mortimers such a large marriage portion.[10] Edmund's marriage to Philippa of Clarence ultimately resulted in a far better outcome for the Mortimer family than his planned union with Alice Arundel would have; Alice had three brothers and a sister who lived into adulthood, and would never have become the sole or even co-heir to her father's lands, earldoms and wealth. And although no-one could have guessed it in the late 1350s, the Clarence/Mortimer marriage would give Philippa and Edmund's son an excellent claim to the throne decades later as the senior descendant of Edward III's second eldest surviving son, when Richard II, the only surviving legitimate descendant of the king's eldest son, produced no offspring.

Edward III, just past his eighteenth birthday, had executed Edmund Mortimer's great-grandfather Roger Mortimer, first earl of March, on 29 November 1330. Roger's eldest son Edmund outlived him by only a few months, and thus the Mortimer heir was Edmund's son Roger the younger, born in Ludlow, Shropshire on 11 November 1328.[11] King Edward was never a man to punish a son (or grandson) for the sins of his father, and he found a great deal to admire in the younger Roger Mortimer, who distinguished himself in a joust held in Hereford in September 1344 before he even turned 16, and fought alongside the prince of Wales at the battle of Crécy in August 1346 at 17 years old. As a result of his 'laudable service' in the battle, and 'wishing to do him favour', Edward III allowed Roger to have full possession of his late father's lands on 6 September 1346, though he was well underage.[12] In 1354, Edward even permitted Roger to hold his namesake grandfather's contentious earldom of March, which the elder Roger had created for himself during his period of power as co-ruler of England with the king's mother Queen Isabella from 1327 to 1330. The younger Roger Mortimer (b. 1328) married Philippa Montacute, who was one of the

4

daughters of the king's friend William Montacute, earl of Salisbury (1301–1344), and who, given her name, might well have been another of the queen's goddaughters. The marriage of Roger Mortimer and Philippa Montacute's son to the king's eldest granddaughter was a great honour which confirmed the Mortimer family's triumphant return to royal favour.

Chapter 2

John and Blanche

Philippa of Clarence was the first grandchild of King Edward and Queen Philippa, and was only a few months younger than her uncle Thomas of Woodstock, youngest child of the king and queen. Thomas was born on 7 January 1355 when the queen was in her early forties, and was many years younger than his eleven older siblings. After his sisters Mary of Waltham and Margaret of Windsor died in the early 1360s, the sibling nearest to Thomas in age was Edmund of Langley, thirteen and a half years older than he, and his eldest brother the prince of Wales was a quarter of a century his senior.

In the late 1350s, with eight living children (Edward of Woodstock, Isabella of Woodstock, Lionel of Antwerp, John of Gaunt, Edmund of Langley, Mary of Waltham, Margaret of Windsor and Thomas of Woodstock) yet only one married child and only one legitimate grandchild, King Edward III decided that it was high time he arranged marriages for his other children. That none of them except Lionel was married was not entirely a matter of the king's own choice, however. He had arranged Edward of Woodstock's marriage to Leonor, daughter of King Afonso IV of Portugal, in 1347, but his envoys arrived in Leonor's homeland a few months later than planned and discovered that she had just married the king of Aragon instead. He arranged several marriages for his eldest daughter, Isabella of Woodstock, but she either refused them or the potential bridegrooms refused her. Finally, the king had arranged an excellent match with the future king of Castile and Leon in Spain for his second daughter Joan of Woodstock, but 14-year-old Joan died of the plague in southern France in the summer of 1348, on her way to her wedding.

The king and queen's fourth, though third eldest surviving, son John of Gaunt, earl of Richmond, married in Reading Abbey on 19 May 1359, aged 19. His bride was one of the greatest heiresses in the country, and

6

John's distant kinswoman: Blanche of Lancaster, born in March 1342 and the younger daughter and co-heir, with her sister Maud, of their partly royal father Henry of Grosmont, first duke of Lancaster and earl of Leicester, Lincoln and Derby. Maud of Lancaster herself had left England in 1352, aged barely 12, after she married Wilhelm von Wittelsbach, duke of Lower Bavaria and count of Hainault and Holland, the second son of the late Holy Roman Emperor, Ludwig of Bavaria (d. 1347), and Queen Philippa's eldest sister Margaretha of Hainault. The unfortunate Wilhelm became insane in 1357/58 and had to be incarcerated for the remaining thirty years of his life, and although he and Maud had a daughter in 1356, she died in infancy and they were unable to have more children. Duchess Maud was named as co-heir with her sister Blanche to their father when Duke Henry died in March 1361, but she died just over a year later in her early twenties, and was buried in a monastery near Leiden in Holland. Blanche therefore carried the entire enormous Lancastrian inheritance, a dukedom and three earldoms with lands in thirty-four English counties and across much of Wales, to her husband John of Gaunt and, later, their son.

Blanche became pregnant just weeks after her wedding, and gave birth to her and John's first child, a daughter named Philippa of Lancaster, on 31 March 1360. Philippa, the second granddaughter of Edward III and Philippa of Hainault, was not an heiress, and her place of birth was not recorded, as she did not have to prove her age as her older Clarence cousin did. It is likely that her paternal grandmother Queen Philippa was also her godmother, and gave the little girl her name. John of Gaunt referred to his daughter as 'Phellipe de Lancastre', and in a letter sent to Gaunt a few years later by Philippa of Lancaster's former nurse Maud (last name not given), Maud called her *Dame Phelip* or 'Lady Philippa'.[1]

Blanche and John of Gaunt's next oldest surviving child was Elizabeth of Lancaster, born in or around February 1363. The name 'Elizabeth' was a rather unusual one in the royal family at the time, and Elizabeth of Lancaster might have been named after a godmother, perhaps her aunt-in-law Elizabeth de Burgh, duchess of Clarence and countess of Ulster, or Elisabeth von Jülich, dowager countess of Kent, a German cousin of King Edward and Queen Philippa's children who lived in England from 1348 to 1411.[2] Alternatively, it might have been intended as a variant name of Blanche's mother, Isabella de Beaumont (d. 1359/60), duchess of Lancaster. Blanche and John had two or perhaps three sons who died in infancy, and their only surviving son was Henry, born in Bolingbroke Castle, Lincolnshire on 15 April 1367 (and often known to posterity as Henry of Bolingbroke, the name Shakespeare used for him). He was his parents' sole heir, and could look forward to receiving the entire Lancastrian inheritance after their deaths.

The king and queen's eldest daughter was Isabella of Woodstock, born in June 1332, and their second was Joan of Woodstock, probably born in January 1334. The third royal daughter Blanche of the Tower died shortly after she was born in 1342, and the fourth and fifth were Mary of Waltham and Margaret of Windsor, born in October 1344 and July 1346, who married the future duke of Brittany and the future earl of Pembroke respectively but died childless in 1361/62, perhaps in the second pandemic of the Black Death that killed their sister Joan in 1348. As of the early 1360s, 30-year-old Isabella of Woodstock was the only daughter of the king and queen still alive, and, most unusually for a royal woman of the Middle Ages, was not yet married.

Edward III celebrated his fiftieth birthday in November 1362 by raising his middle three sons to higher titles: Lionel of Antwerp became the first duke of Clarence, John of Gaunt became the second duke of Lancaster, and Edmund of Langley became the second earl of Cambridge. The king's eldest son Edward of Woodstock, prince of Wales, married his kinswoman Joan of Kent, a granddaughter of Edward I and countess of Kent in her own right, in 1361. The couple moved to the south of France in 1362 after Edward was made prince of Aquitaine, the large French territory ruled by the kings of England from the middle of the twelfth century until the fifteenth. Joan gave birth there to their two sons: Edward of Angoulême, who died young, in January 1365, and Richard of Bordeaux in January 1367. Richard became heir to the English throne behind his father after his elder brother's death in the early 1370s.

Lionel of Antwerp was widowed in December 1363 when Elizabeth de Burgh died in Ireland, leaving their daughter Philippa of Clarence, now 8 years old, as her heir. Other than her stay at Campsea Ashe Priory as an infant with her grandmother Maud of Lancaster, and her return to her mother's care in or before 1360, nothing is known of Philippa's upbringing. Perhaps she lived with her husband's mother, Philippa Mortimer née Montacute, dowager countess of March, after she lost her own mother.

Chapter 3

Isabella and Enguerrand

The king and queen's only living daughter Isabella of Woodstock finally married on 27 July 1365 at the age of 33, decades later than would normally have been expected for royal girls and women to wed in the fourteenth century. Her groom was Enguerrand de Coucy, or Ingelram or Ingram de Coucy, as his name often appeared in English documents of the era. He was a dashing young French nobleman about eight years Isabella's junior, born around 1340; his parents married in 1338. Enguerrand was the son and heir of Enguerrand the elder, lord of Coucy in Picardy in northern France, and Katharina, born in 1320 as the daughter of Leopold, duke of Austria. Enguerrand the elder was perhaps killed at the battle of Crécy in August 1346, the great victory of Isabella of Woodstock's father and eldest brother over Philip VI of France (though this is not certain), and his Austrian widow was briefly married to the count of Hardegg in Germany before dying of plague in 1349. Via his paternal grandmother Isabelle de Châtillon, Enguerrand de Coucy the younger was descended from Henry III, king of England (d. 1272), and therefore was a distant relative of his wife.

Enguerrand was sent to England in 1360 to join the retinue of King John II of France (r. 1350–64), whom the prince of Wales had captured at the battle of Poitiers in 1356, another famous English victory over the French, and who spent the remaining few years of his life as a prisoner in England. To at least some degree, Enguerrand and Isabella's marriage was a love match or lust match, and the English chronicler Ranulph Higden stated that Isabella wished to marry the Frenchman 'only for love' (*solum prae amore sibi voluit desponsari*). It is, however, not entirely fair to Isabella to suggest that she was only motivated by her own feelings and desires, as there is no doubt that her marriage to a great French lord served her father's political ambitions as well.[1] Although Enguerrand's father was not a prince, a duke or even a count, he came from a prestigious background. As far back as July 1334 when Edward of Woodstock was 4 years old, Edward III had tried to arrange a marriage for his eldest son and heir with Marie de Coucy, who was the daughter of Guillaume, lord of Coucy and the aunt of Isabella of Woodstock's future husband.[2] Edward III made his Coucy son-in-law the first earl of Bedford on 11 May 1366, and Enguerrand was also made count of Soissons in his homeland on 9 July 1367.[3]

The king bought a gold crown with sapphires and diamonds at a cost of 1,000 marks (£666.66) for his beloved daughter to wear during her wedding, and purchased an even more expensive one for Enguerrand at £733. In total, over £4,500 was spent on goldsmiths' work for the lavish royal wedding, far more than was spent on the weddings of any of Isabella's many siblings.[4] She became pregnant immediately, and gave birth to a daughter, Marie de Coucy, in April 1366 nine months after the wedding. 'Marie' was a Coucy name, and made a refreshing change from all the Philippas in the English royal family.

Edward III had given Isabella and Enguerrand permission to travel to France on 26 November 1365. Obviously aware that his daughter was pregnant when she departed from her homeland and that she might give birth in her husband's territories in France, Edward proclaimed that Isabella and Enguerrand's children, whether male or female and wherever they were born, 'shall enjoy their inheritance in England as if born in the realm'.[5] Although it is often stated that Marie de Coucy was born in her father's lands in France, specifically in his castle of Coucy in Picardy, Enguerrand was in England when his father-in-law made him earl of Bedford on 11 May 1366, and he was at Leeds Castle in Kent with Edward III on 26 May 1366. That seems rather soon after giving birth for Isabella of Woodstock to have crossed the Channel and returned to England from France. It would seem, therefore, that either Enguerrand travelled to Isabella's homeland, visited her family, and enjoyed the ceremony that made him an earl without her; or she gave birth to Marie in England, not in France. The French historian Jean-Joseph Carlier, an expert on the fourteenth-century de Coucy family, has stated that Marie was born in England. Sir Thomas Tyrell took the news of her birth to her royal English grandfather and was paid 100 marks (£66, 13s and 4d); this payment was recorded in the king's accounts on 28 July 1366. A few months later, the king paid only £5 to the messenger who informed him that his daughter-in-law

Blanche of Lancaster had borne a son, Henry, at Bolingbroke Castle in Lincolnshire.[6]

Isabella of Woodstock became a countess twice over in 1366/67, and gave birth to her second daughter, inevitably named Philippa, at the royal palace of Eltham in Kent on or a little before 18 November 1367. Philippa de Coucy was the fourth granddaughter of the king and queen, and the third who bore the queen's name. Her cousin Philippa of Clarence was also born at Eltham, and it is likely that Philippa of Hainault acted as Philippa de Coucy's godmother, as she had for her first granddaughter and probably also her second, John of Gaunt's eldest daughter. She and Edward III certainly attended the baptism, and the royal couple spent over £324 on gifts for the little girl on the occasion.[7] Isabella and Enguerrand were to have no more children, though Enguerrand had another much younger daughter, Isabelle de Coucy, with his second wife Isabelle of Lorraine, whom he married in *c.* 1386. His eldest daughter Marie de Coucy was to spend all or almost all her life in France and was heir to her father's French estates, while Marie's younger and certainly English-born sister spent all her life in England and inherited their parents' lands there. According to Jean-Joseph Carlier, Marie was taken to France in 1368 and grew up there.[8] If this was indeed the case, she was far too young to remember anything about her early life in England, and whether she had much contact with the English side of her family throughout her life is uncertain.

Chapter 4

Many Losses

John of Gaunt's daughters Philippa and Elizabeth of Lancaster lost their mother Duchess Blanche on 12 September 1368 when they were 8 and 5 years old and their brother Henry was not yet 18 months. Blanche of Lancaster was only 26, and her death was probably related to pregnancy or childbirth (it was once thought that she died of plague, but this theory was based on the erroneous belief that Blanche passed away in 1369, a year when there was a third pandemic of the Black Death in England). Blanche's only surviving son Henry was sole heir to her enormous Lancastrian inheritance, though her widower John of Gaunt was, because they had children together, entitled to hold all her lands until his own death thanks to a medieval custom called the 'courtesy of England'. Blanche's vast inheritance in thirty-four English counties and across Wales made John the richest man in England for the remaining thirty years of his life, with an annual gross income estimated at around £12,000. Lionel of Antwerp also benefited from this custom, and held all Elizabeth de Burgh's lands in England and Ireland after his wife died.

In the spring of 1368, Lionel travelled to Italy with a large retinue, and married his second wife Violante Visconti, the teenaged daughter of Galeazzo Visconti, lord of Milan and Pavia. Lionel did not live long after his splendid Italian wedding: he died in his father-in-law's house in Alba on 17 October 1368, a few weeks before his thirtieth birthday. He had been ill for a good while before death, and Pope Urban V asked his (Lionel's) kinsman Sir Hugh Despenser to send him news of the duke's welfare in August 1368. Lionel dictated his will before his death, and appointed his wife Violante, young though she was, as one of his executors.[1] The royal English duke was buried in the church of St Peter in the Sky of Gold (*San Pietro in Ciel d'Oro*) in Pavia twenty miles from Milan, though his remains were later returned to England and buried with Elizabeth de Burgh at Bruisyard Priory in Suffolk, which Lionel himself had founded some years before. News of Lionel's death only reached chancery clerks in England on 1 March 1369, and his inquisition post mortem was held in June and July that year. His 13-year-old daughter Philippa of Clarence was his and Elizabeth de Burgh's sole heir to their lands in England, Wales and Ireland, and Philippa inherited her mother's and her maternal grandfather's earldom of Ulster.[2] Lionel's dukedom of Clarence was not, however, given to his daughter and son-in-law Edmund Mortimer, and the title lapsed until Lionel's nephew Henry IV revived it in 1412 for his second son, Thomas.

Philippa of Hainault, queen of England, attempted to arrange a second marriage for her son John of Gaunt as early as 1 December 1368, just a few weeks after Blanche of Lancaster's death, when she sent an envoy to Louis, count of Flanders.[3] Louis's only child and heir was Margarethe of Flanders, born in 1350, who was set to inherit the counties of Flanders, Artois, Rethel and Nevers on Louis's death. It transpired, however, that she was already betrothed to Philip (b. 1342), youngest son of King John II of France and the brother of Charles V (r. 1364–80), and the couple married in 1369. Queen Philippa's envoy brought her the news at Windsor Castle, where the royal English family spent the festive season of 1368, and it was surely a rather muted occasion owing to the recent deaths of the duke of Clarence and the duchess of Lancaster.

It would be the last Christmas of the queen's life. At Windsor Castle on 15 August 1369, Philippa of Hainault died in her mid-fifties, after a decade of pain and immobility; she fell from her horse in 1358 and broke a shoulder-blade, and spent much of the 1360s as an invalid. Just nine days after her death, on 24 August 1369, the queen's eldest granddaughter Philippa of Clarence proved her age at Deptford in Kent, four miles from her birthplace of Eltham Palace. When a tenant in chief (the men and women who held lands directly from the king) died with her or his heir underage, when the heir came of age, s/he had to prove that s/he was now old enough to receive the lands. As Philippa was already married, she was allowed to enter her lands at 14; men came of age at 21, and women at 14 if married or 16 if not. Twelve jurors confirmed that Philippa was 'fourteen years of age on 16 August last' and was born and baptised in Eltham on that date in 1355.[4]

Philippa's grandfather the king was at the palace of Eltham on 24 August, and as soon as Philippa had legally proved her age, took the fealty of her husband Edmund Mortimer and ordered royal officials in fifteen English counties and in Wales and Ireland to give the young couple the lands of Philippa's late parents.[5] Edmund himself, now 17, would not be able to enter his own lands, inherited from his late father Roger, until he turned 21 in February 1373, and Philippa's uncle-in-law Enguerrand de Coucy, earl of Bedford and count of Soissons, was appointed as the custodian of the Mortimer lands during Edmund's minority. In the end, Edward III allowed Edmund possession of his inheritance on 6 January 1373, though, as that was less than four weeks before he turned 21, it was hardly a great favour to his grandson-in-law.[6]

On 1 September 1369, King Edward sent a letter ordering black cloth and fur for all the people he expected to attend Queen Philippa's funeral.[7] Among them were his granddaughters Philippa and Elizabeth, 'the daughters of Lancaster', and one of Isabella of Woodstock's two de Coucy daughters, almost certainly Philippa, not yet 2 years old; her sister Marie does not seem to have visited England often, if at all. The little de Coucy girl was to be accompanied to the funeral by her wet-nurse, nurse, and three damsels, while her older Lancaster cousins had three damsels and no fewer than ten 'under-damsels' (*souzdamoiselles*) to attend them, one of whom bore the excellent name of Billion Quaret. Philippa of Clarence and her husband Edmund Mortimer were also provided with fur and black cloth. The king and queen's sons John of Gaunt, Edmund of Langley and Thomas of Woodstock, who was still only 14 and was many years younger than his siblings, were all expected to attend as well, but their eldest son Edward of Woodstock and his wife and children were in Aquitaine, and their only surviving daughter Isabella of Woodstock was not mentioned and was probably in France with her husband Enguerrand. The queen's funeral finally took place on 9 January 1370, almost five months after her death, in Westminster Abbey; her tomb and life-like effigy, with a rather plump figure and kindly face, can still be seen there.

Chapter 5

Doña María's Daughter and the Duke

Philippa of Clarence, countess of March and Ulster, was just 15½ years old when she gave birth to her first child, Elizabeth Mortimer, in the Welsh lordship of Usk on 12 February 1371 (and therefore was only 14 when she conceived in or about May 1370; her husband was 18). She must surely have named her daughter in honour of her late mother Elizabeth de Burgh, and Elizabeth Mortimer was the eldest great-grandchild of Edward III, who was 58 years old when he became a great-grandparent. Over three years were to pass before Philippa gave birth again: her first son, who immediately became both her and Edmund Mortimer's heir, was born also in Usk on 11 April 1374, and was named Roger after his paternal grandfather, the second earl of March (1328–1360). Two more children quickly followed. Philippa Mortimer was born at her father's manor of Ludlow in Shropshire on 21 November 1375, and less than a year later on 9 November 1376, also in Ludlow, came Edmund Mortimer, the youngest.[1]

Thomas de Vere, earl of Oxford, born around Christmas 1336, died on 18 September 1371 at his manor of Bentley in Essex. On 16 October, Edward III granted the marriage rights of Thomas's son and heir Robert to Isabella of Woodstock and Enguerrand de Coucy, and they arranged Robert's marriage to their younger daughter Philippa de Coucy some years later (presumably selecting Philippa instead of her older sister Marie as Marie lived in France).[2] The de Veres were not as rich or influential as some of the other English comital families, but had an excellent pedigree; the family had held the earldom of Oxford since as far back as 1141. Robert de Vere was 9 years old when his father died: he was born in the Benedictine priory of Earls Colne, Essex on 16 January 1362, and was named after his godfather and maternal great-uncle, Robert Ufford, earl of Suffolk (1298–1369). His other godfather was Simon Sudbury (b. c. 1316), then bishop of London and later archbishop of Canterbury, who would be murdered in London during the Great Uprising or Peasants' Revolt of June 1381, and his godmother was Alice, widow of Sir Andrew Bures.[3]

Robert's mother was Maud Ufford (b. late 1345 or early 1346), a much younger half-sister of the late Elizabeth de Burgh, duchess of Clarence and countess of Ulster. Maud, only in her mid-twenties when she lost her husband in September 1371, became seriously ill from the shock of bereavement and was still 'too feeble to travel' two months after Thomas de Vere's death, though she recovered and outlived him by forty-two years.[4] She never remarried, though in July 1374 Edward III had to take her under his protection as 'certain persons ... purpose to ravish and carry off the countess against her will', which must surely refer to an attempt to force the rather well-off and well-connected Maud into a second marriage.[5] Robert de Vere's birthplace, Colne Priory, was the mausoleum of the de Vere family, and would be Robert's own burial place as well as his father's. The village of Earls Colne was given to Maud in 1371 as part of her dower from her late husband, and a few years later she feuded badly with the prior, Henry. He accused her and several dozen of her male servants of breaking into the priory at night, assaulting and imprisoning him, and taking him to various places in Essex and detaining him there 'shamefully clad' (by which he presumably meant his nightwear). For her part, Maud claimed that some of the Earls Colne monks broke into her mansion in the village and stole her goods, and also stole game and fish from her park. On another occasion, she said, the monks besieged her in her mansion and threatened her with arson 'and other evils', so that for a long time she dared not leave her home.[6] Maud Ufford, who was quite a character, became very close in later years to her daughter-in-law Philippa de Coucy.

Far away in the south of France, Philippa de Coucy's uncle John of Gaunt, duke of Lancaster, married his second wife Costanza of Castile in the town of Roquefort in Les Landes, in the English-ruled area of southern France called Aquitaine or Gascony, in early September 1371. There were great feasts and celebrations to mark this important royal wedding, and afterwards John took his new wife to Bordeaux, a city ruled by his brother the prince of Wales and the birthplace of John's nephew Richard, the future king of England, a few years earlier in January 1367.[7] John was 31 and Costanza was 17 when they wed. She and her younger sister Isabel had been living in Aquitaine since

16

the autumn of 1366 as hostages of the prince of Wales, albeit hostages treated with honour and consideration. They were the daughters of the late King Pedro 'the Cruel' of Castile, who had been defeated at the battle of Montiel in March 1369 and then stabbed to death by his illegitimate half-brother Enrique of Trastámara, who subsequently made himself King Enrique II of Castile. Edward of Woodstock and John of Gaunt had helped King Pedro to defeat Enrique at the battle of Nájera in 1367, but Enrique returned to Castile a couple of years later with French aid, and took his revenge on the half-brother he loathed.

By his marriage to the late Pedro's elder daughter, John of Gaunt became the rightful king of Castile and Leon, at least in name. John and Costanza were distantly related via common descent from Fernando III, king of Castile and Leon (d. 1252), whose daughter Leonor or Eleanor (d. 1290) married Edward I of England and was John's great-grandmother. Although Costanza was born in the north of her father's kingdom, she might have grown up in the Alcázar, the royal palace in her father's favourite city of Seville in southern Spain. Pedro himself had the Alcázar built, using many Muslim craftsmen; the words 'Only Allah is victorious' in Arabic can still be seen on the facade of Pedro's palace. Freshwater baths which can also still be seen in the Alcázar are called *Los Baños de Doña María de Padilla* after Costanza's mother, a Castilian noblewoman who was the daughter of Juan García de Padilla and María González de Henestrosa.

King Pedro and Doña María de Padilla met during a series of peregrinations the 17-year-old king made through Castile in the spring and summer of 1352, which were, in part, a campaign against his illegitimate half-brother Enrique of Trastámara. Enrique, also a teenager himself and almost exactly the same age as the king, had already rebelled against Pedro with his younger twin Fadrique, master of the military and religious Order of Santiago, whom Pedro would execute in 1358, and their brother Tello. Enrique, Fadrique and Tello's mother Doña Leonor de Guzmán had been the beloved and influential mistress of Alfonso XI, who was also the father of King Pedro by his marriage to Maria of Portugal. After Alfonso died of the plague in 1350, Queen Maria took her revenge on her husband's mistress by imprisoning and executing her, which made Maria's son a mortal enemy in the person of Leonor de Guzmán's eldest son Enrique.

Pedro (b. August 1334) had been betrothed to Edward III of England's second daughter Joan of Woodstock (b. *c*. January 1334), but she died of the plague on her way to their wedding, and he married the French noblewoman Blanche de Bourbon instead, in Valladolid on or around 3 June 1353. Earlier that same year, however, Pedro's mistress María de Padilla had borne their first child, Beatriz, in Córdoba in southern Spain, and Pedro abandoned the unfortunate Blanche two days after their wedding and went off with María. Their second child, Costanza, future duchess of Lancaster, was born in Castrojeriz near Burgos in the north of Castile in July 1354, and hence was conceived about four months after her father's wedding to another woman. Next came Isabel, future countess of Cambridge and duchess of York, born sometime in the summer or autumn of 1355 in Tordesillas in central Spain, where her grandfather and father had built a palace and where Pedro founded the Royal Monastery of Santa Clara some years later. King Pedro and Doña María de Padilla also had a son whom they named Alfonso after Pedro's late father, several years younger than his three sisters and born also in Tordesillas in 1359. Three-year-old Alfonso died in Seville on 18 October 1362, and his eldest sister Beatriz died as a teenager sometime after the autumn of 1366. Beatriz's fate is unclear; some modern writers claim that she became a nun at Santa Clara de Tordesillas, others that she died in Bayonne while a hostage of the English. It seems beyond doubt, however, that she was dead by the end of the 1360s. Her father had intended for her to marry his cousin Fernando (1345–1383), who succeeded his father as king of Portugal in 1367, and for Fernando to become king of Castile as well, but Beatriz died before the wedding could take place. If she had outlived her father, she would have been the rightful heir to Castile. Assuming that Beatriz survived, and married Fernando of Portugal as her father planned, it seems unlikely that the ambitious John of Gaunt would have wed Costanza, who in this scenario would have been merely a younger sister with little chance of inheriting her father's throne.

In spite of his undoubted devotion to his long-term lover María de Padilla, King Pedro was not faithful to her, and had an affair with her cousin María González de Henestrosa (who bore the same name as her aunt, María de Padilla's mother), which produced a son named Fernando. Pedro made his son lord of the town of Niebla forty-five miles west of Seville, and Fernando was still alive in the early 1360s but died young.

In 1354, Pedro became involved with his kinswoman Doña Juana de Castro, who, like Pedro himself, was a great-grandchild of Sancho IV of Castile (r. 1284–95) and was the widow of Diego López de Haro, whose family were lords of Biscay. Juana was the younger sister or half-sister of Doña Inês de Castro, the famous mistress and possibly the wife of Pedro's namesake maternal uncle Pedro I of Portugal (b. 1320, r. 1357–67). Inês was posthumously recognised as queen of Portugal after her assassination on the orders of her lover's father, deeply concerned about her relationship with his son, on 7 January 1355.

King Pedro of Castile claimed to have wed Juana de Castro in Cuéllar near Valladolid in early April 1354, even though he had already married Blanche de Bourbon ten months earlier and even though he was also involved in an intense relationship with María de Padilla; their second child Costanza was born about three months after her father's wedding ceremony with Juana. Pedro, who made a habit of abandoning women just after he married them, left Juana the day after their wedding and never saw her again, though their relationship resulted in a son named Juan born nine months later in early January 1355, who was a few months younger than his half-sister Costanza and a few months older than his half-sister Isabel. Juana de Castro died in 1374, and is known in Spanish as *La Desamada*, 'the Unloved'. Finally, Pedro's relationships with Isabel de Sandoval and Teresa de Ayala resulted in three more illegitimate children: sons Sancho (b. 1363) and Diego (b. *c.* 1365), and a daughter María de Ayala (b. *c.* 1367), a nun of Santo Domingo el Real in Toledo, who in later years was closely associated with her niece, John of Gaunt and Costanza of Castile's English-born daughter.

Having claimed in 1354 to have wed Juana de Castro, King Pedro was to claim in 1362 that he had married María de Padilla in Seville in 1352 before his official wedding to Blanche de Bourbon the following year. In the interests of political expediency, several biased witnesses confirmed his tale, including Doña María's brother Don Diego García de Padilla and their uncle Don Juan Fernández de Henestrosa. The Castilian *Cortes* duly legitimised Pedro and Doña María's daughters Beatriz, Costanza and Isabel, and four years later the girls were sent as hostages to Edward of Woodstock. After Pedro's death in 1369, his three living illegitimate sons, Juan, Sancho and Diego, were imprisoned by their half-uncle Enrique of Trastámara (Juan, the eldest at 14, sought refuge in Aquitaine, but was eventually handed over to the Trastámaras). Had Costanza and

Isabel not been in Aquitaine beyond Trastámara's reach when their father was killed, they would surely have suffered the same fate; they had been declared legitimate and therefore were Pedro's rightful heirs. As such, the two girls were a threat to Enrique of Trastámara, despite their youth and sex. In his will of 18 November 1362, made a month after the death of his and María de Padilla's 3-year-old son Alfonso, King Pedro named their three daughters as his heirs in birth order, followed by his and Juana de Castro's 7-year-old son Juan – whom he always acknowledged as his child despite the brevity of his and Juana's relationship – in case his daughters died and left no legitimate children. The Castilian chronicler, historian and statesman Don Pero López de Ayala (1332–1407), uncle of Pedro's mistress Teresa de Ayala and a man who fought for Enrique of Trastámara against King Pedro at the battle of Nájera in 1367, wrote that later on, Pedro intended Sancho, born in September 1363 as the elder of his two illegitimate sons with Isabel de Sandoval, to be his heir. Pedro's biographer Clara Estow disputes this claim, pointing out that as of 1361, Pedro was a widower, yet made no attempt in the 1360s to marry any other woman, including Isabel de Sandoval.[8]

María de Padilla, great-great-grandmother of the English kings Edward IV (d. 1483) and Richard III (d. 1485) and the Castilian queen-regnant Isabel la Católica (d. 1504), died in July 1361, still only in her twenties. For all his complicated associations with other women, King Pedro deeply loved María and grieved for her sincerely. He held a state funeral for her as though she were his wife and the rightful queen of Castile – in his will of November 1362, he referred to her repeatedly as 'the queen, Doña María, my wife' – and buried her in the monastery of Santa Clara de Astudillo in the province of Palencia, which María herself had founded in the mid-1350s. Her remains were later moved to the royal chapel in Seville Cathedral, and there is evidence that in the late 1380s their daughter Costanza had Pedro's body buried there as well. Blanche de Bourbon, meanwhile, Pedro's lawful wife, died in prison in Medina Sidonia in the same year as María de Padilla, and was buried in Jerez; she was only about 22 when she passed away. Pedro had not set eyes on his French wife since he abandoned her for María shortly after their wedding in 1353. Whether the king had a hand in the death of the unfortunate and tragic Blanche, who had done nothing wrong yet whom he kept in captivity for eight years, is still debated, though as she was the sister of the queen-consort of France, Pedro's harsh treatment of Blanche played an important role in his downfall when the French supported Enrique of Trastámara against him in the late 1360s.[9] In his 1362 will, Pedro left a 'French crown' which had belonged to Blanche to his and María de Padilla's third daughter, Isabel, later duchess of York. He refused to acknowledge Blanche as his wife and queen, and referred to her instead as 'Doña Blanca, daughter of the duke of Bourbon'.[10]

Chapter 6

Spanish Weddings

John of Gaunt, his 17-year-old bride Costanza, and her 16-year-old sister Isabel sailed to England in a ship called the *Gaynpayn*, which usually transported salt, and landed in Cornwall in early November 1371.[1] While John had been overseas in 1370/71, his children Philippa, Elizabeth and Henry of Lancaster stayed at Deeping in Lincolnshire and Ware in Hertfordshire with their great-aunt Lady Wake, eldest sister of their late maternal grandfather, Duke Henry. Lady Wake was a widow and had no children of her own, though evidently was a woman with strong maternal and familial feelings; she also looked after the Mowbray brothers John (b. 1365) and Thomas (b. 1367), orphaned grandchildren of her sister Joan of Lancaster (d. 1349).[2]

Isabel of Castile was betrothed to Gaunt's brother Edmund of Langley, earl of Cambridge, who, born in early June 1341, was fourteen years her senior; the same age gap as the one between John and Costanza. Edward III had tried for years to arrange either Edmund's or John's marriage to the great heiress Margarethe of Flanders, but it was not to be, and Edmund's marriage to Isabel was intended to cement the alliance between the English royal family and the deposed Castilian royal family. It brought Edmund himself no benefits whatsoever; no lands, no wealth, no powerful in-laws. Unlike his four brothers, Edmund did not marry an heiress, and had a tiny income of only £500 a year. He had problems accessing even this small amount, and by comparison, the gross annual income of his brother Gaunt, only fifteen months his senior, was about £12,000.[3] A few years later, Edmund and Isabel complained that Gaunt had unjustly set aside Isabel's rights to her late father's throne, so it seems that relations between the two Anglo-Castilian couples were not always particularly cordial, an impression probably confirmed by the fact that Isabel failed to mention her sister at all in her will but did leave valuable items to a few other family members. Costanza, meanwhile, made a ceremonial entry into London, as rightful queen of Castile and Leon, on 9 February 1372. The ceremony was hosted by her brother-in-law Edward of Woodstock, prince of Wales, now permanently returned to England from Aquitaine with his wife Joan of Kent and their 5-year-old son Richard of Bordeaux, and suffering recurring bouts of the unknown but obviously serious medical condition that would kill him in 1376.[4]

Edmund of Langley and Isabel of Castile married at Wallingford Castle a few miles from Oxford on 11 July 1372. Presumably Costanza was there, assuming that her physical condition – if she was pregnant with her and John of Gaunt's daughter, or recovering from childbirth – permitted her to travel. John attended the wedding, but was back at his London palace of the Savoy by 14 July 1372, so did not spend much time with his brother and sister-in-law.[5] He bought some splendid wedding gifts for Isabel: a gilded silver tripod 'in the shape of a monster with three supports and three mace-bearers standing on a green background', and a silver cup which matched the tripod; a silver ewer 'in parts enamelled with various grotesque figures'; another silver tripod 'with growing trees'; and a silver ewer decorated with vines and roses.[6]

Chronicler Thomas Walsingham called Isabel a 'pampered and voluptuous lady' and Costanza an 'exceptionally innocent and pious lady'. The Spanish sisters were very different, and Isabel probably took after their mother María de Padilla, a king's mistress and called 'beautiful and small of body' and 'a very beautiful young woman' by Castilian chroniclers, far more than Costanza did. Costanza, however, was also called 'a beautiful young lady' and 'a woman of great beauty' by a chronicler in the north of England, so was evidently far more attractive than is often supposed by modern writers, who tend to compare her unfavourably with her husband's long-term mistress.[7]

It is possible that Isabel of Castile had an affair with Sir John Holland, second son of Joan of Kent, princess of Wales and Aquitaine, from her previous marriage to Sir Thomas Holland (d. December 1360). A note in a fifteenth-century manuscript of Geoffrey Chaucer's poem *Compleynt of Mars*, written by the manuscript copyist John Shirley, states that the work was inspired by John Holland's love for Isabel of Castile. It is probably significant in this context that Shirley had a decades-long and successful career as the chief scribe of Richard Beauchamp, earl of Warwick, whose second wife Isabelle Despenser (1400–1439) was the granddaughter of Edmund of Langley and Isabel. As John Shirley was born in *c.* 1366, he was only a few years younger than John Holland (b. *c.* 1353) and Isabel of Castile (b. 1355) and was an adult in their lifetimes. Although one twentieth-century writer suggested that the *Compleynt of Mars* in fact referred to Holland's love for and marriage to John of Gaunt's daughter Elizabeth of Lancaster in 1386, Isabel of Castile left valuable items to John Holland in her will, and, other than the servants to whom she left bequests, he was the only beneficiary who was not a close relative of hers by blood or marriage. Isabel's will also mentions some high-value possessions which had been gifts to her from Holland and which she left to her first son Edward of York, including a gold brooch and a gold cup engraved with her arms (this presumably meant the royal arms of Castile).[8] This gives the impression that something went on between Isabel and John Holland; whether she had an affair with him is impossible to say for sure, but certainly there was a strong connection between the two.

Sometime before 31 March 1373, perhaps as early as the beginning of June 1372, Costanza of Castile gave birth to a daughter, Katherine or Catalina of Lancaster. On 6 June 1372, John of Gaunt told his receiver in Leicestershire to send *la sage femme*, i.e. the midwife (literally 'the wise woman'), Ilote, to Costanza at Hertford Castle as quickly as possible. Ilote was to be given a cart or a horse to speed her ninety-mile journey to Hertford, and almost certainly is the same person as the *Elyot la middewyf de Leycestre* or 'Elyot the midwife of Leicester' mentioned again by John in August 1375.[9] Either Duchess Costanza herself or Gaunt sent Katherine Swynford, whose sister Philippa Chaucer was one of Costanza's attendants, to Edward III to give him the news of his granddaughter's birth, and a payment of 20 marks (£13 33*d*) from the king to Katherine was recorded on 31 March 1373 (the date on which the payment was recorded in the royal accounts might have been a few weeks or months after it was made to Katherine).[10] If Costanza did give birth to her daughter Catalina on or shortly after 6 June 1372, she must have conceived on her wedding night or very soon afterwards.

In 1375, according to chronicler Jean Froissart, Duchess Costanza gave birth again while in the Continental town of Ghent, her husband's birthplace, after she returned there from a pilgrimage to the abbey of Saint Adrian in Grammont. She bore a son named John of Lancaster, who was, one assumes, either stillborn or died soon after birth.[11] John of Gaunt went to Bruges in the spring of 1375 and again that autumn to take part in negotiations regarding a truce between England and France, and evidently his wife travelled to the Continent with him. Costanza bore no more children, so Catalina was, as her only surviving child, her heir, and inherited Costanza's claim to the Castilian throne. A contemporary Spanish chronicler described Catalina of Lancaster much later in her life as 'very heavyset, fair, rosy and blonde. From the size of her body and the way she moved, she looked as much like a man as a woman'. As Catalina's biographer Ana Echevarría has pointed out, however, this description was written near the end of her life, when she suffered badly from palsy and was ill, stressed and tired.[12] It should not be taken as a general commentary on her lack of physical attractiveness throughout her life, or for that matter as a useful commentary on her mother Costanza's presumed lack of attractiveness. Catalina's rosy blonde fairness came from her Spanish and Portuguese ancestors: her grandfather King Pedro the Cruel and great-grandfather Alfonso XI of Castile, both of whom had Spanish fathers and Portuguese mothers, were blond-haired, blue-eyed and fair-skinned. Catalina's future husband and second cousin Enrique III of Castile, who was of entirely Spanish descent (he was the grandson of two Spanish kings, Enrique of Trastámara of Castile and Pere IV of Aragon), was called 'fair and blond' by a contemporary. The *Crónica del Rey Don Pedro* states of Pedro the Cruel that he 'was quite tall of body, was pale and blond, and spoke with a slight lisp ... he slept little and loved many women'.[13] This latter fact was something Catalina came to know well when she moved to her mother's homeland: she was on close terms with several of her mother Costanza's half-siblings and with at least one of her grandfather's former lovers.

Catalina was known in England in her own lifetime as *Katerine d'Espaigne* or Catalina of Castile; somewhat confusingly, *Espaigne* or 'Spain' almost always meant the kingdom of Castile in fourteenth-century English usage rather than the entire country of Spain, and Catalina's father the duke of Lancaster was addressed as *Monseigneur d'Espaigne* after his marriage to Costanza. Catalina was a rather fascinating cultural hybrid, and almost certainly grew up trilingual in English (the majority language of the country of her birth), French (the language most often spoken and written by the English elite during her childhood) and Castilian (her mother's native tongue). There is evidence that John of Gaunt also learnt some Castilian during his marriage to Costanza: Jean Froissart states that when Costanza's cousin King Juan

I sent an ambassador to the couple, Gaunt could not understand all that the man said (*ne les avoit toutes entendues*). This reveals that the duke could in fact follow at least some of the ambassador's Spanish speech.[14] It seems likely that Gaunt and Costanza, as well as his brother and her sister Edmund and Isabel, mostly spoke to each other in French, which Costanza and Isabel would have learnt during their years-long sojourn in Aquitaine, if not before.

The woman in charge of Catalina's household in the 1370s was an English noblewoman, the long-lived Joan née Burghersh, Lady Mohun, who was born in the early or mid-1320s and died in 1404. In late 1374, Catalina's father sent Juana Martyns from Castile to work in his daughter's household as well, and Juana probably spoke in Castilian to her young charge. Catalina's nurse early in life was Agnes Bonsergeant, who was probably English, and another of her servants was named Simond Templer. Her household was based in the village of Melbourne near Derby, which had belonged to the heiress Maud Chaworth (1282–1322), great-grandmother of Catalina's older half-siblings Philippa, Elizabeth and Henry, and was held by their father until his death then passed to Henry as the Lancastrian heir.[15] Philippa and Elizabeth, meanwhile, each received two fillets, i.e. headbands made of interlaced wire, from their father as their New Year present in 1373, and each fillet had three balas rubies and twenty-eight pearls.[16] Between April 1372 and early 1373, John of Gaunt contemplated the future marriage of his eldest child Philippa of Lancaster, who turned 12 at the end of March 1372. If he had a candidate in mind, he did not commit the man's identity to writing, but merely referenced the 'aid granted to us for marrying our eldest daughter' in various letters, and in 1374, he contemplated a match for her with the count of Foix in southern France.[17]

Chapter 7

The Beauforts and the Yorks

As she grew up, Catalina of Lancaster surely became aware that her mother was not the only woman in her father's life, and that she had a half-brother, John Beaufort, who was about the same age as she was. John of Gaunt was involved in a long-term, passionate and intense relationship with Katherine Swynford, née Roet; she was the widow of Sir Hugh Swynford of Lincolnshire, the sister-in-law of the great poet Geoffrey Chaucer, and was the woman who took news of Catalina of Lancaster's birth to the king in 1372 or 1373. John and Katherine's relationship appears to have begun in the spring or early summer of 1372, a few months after both John's marriage to Costanza in September 1371 and Hugh Swynford's death on 13 November 1371; Katherine, who previously had never been mentioned in Gaunt's register, suddenly appeared in it six times in May and June 1372. John of Gaunt and Katherine Swynford had four children in the 1370s: three boys, John, Henry and Thomas Beaufort, and one girl, Joan Beaufort. Gaunt probably used the name of one of the French lordships which had once belonged to his first wife Blanche of Lancaster for his illegitimate offspring, intending to give his and Katherine's children a name which emphasised that they were not in the Lancastrian line of succession. It is also possible that he chose the name of the French nobleman Sir Roger Beaufort, brother of Pope Gregory XI (born Pierre-Roger Beaufort), whom Gaunt kept in honourable captivity in England in the 1370s. Roger Beaufort was the godfather of Roger Deyncourt, the son of one of Gaunt's retainers, who was born at Gaunt's castle of Kenilworth in Warwickshire in May 1377 and was given his godfather's first name.[1]

The four Beauforts' dates of birth are not known, though John the eldest, the future earl of Somerset and marquis of Dorset, was born in the last few months of 1372 at the earliest and probably in 1373, and Henry, later Cardinal Beaufort, perhaps in January 1375. John Beaufort's entry in the *Oxford Dictionary of National Biography* gives his date of birth as *c.* 1371, as does the *Complete Peerage*. As Beaufort's mother's first husband Sir Hugh Swynford was alive until November 1371, this is impossible; had John been born or conceived in Hugh's lifetime he would have been given Hugh's family name and would legally have been Hugh's son and recognised as such, even if he was John of Gaunt's biological child. John Beaufort was never claimed or recognised as Hugh Swynford's son, which almost certainly proves that he was born sometime after August 1372, nine months after Hugh's death.[2] If Gaunt and Katherine's relationship really did begin in *c.* May or June 1372, John cannot have been born earlier than *c.* February or March 1373.

On 14 January 1375, Gaunt ordered his receiver in Lincolnshire to purchase a cask of Gascon wine and to send it to Katherine Swynford 'as hastily as you can'.[3] Given that Katherine gave birth to John's four Beaufort children throughout the 1370s, and that their second son Henry Beaufort is often assumed to have been born in 1375, it may be that this gift of wine was sent to Katherine shortly before or after she gave birth to Henry. It is surely also significant that there are only three entries relating to Katherine in the duke's register for the year 1373, only one in the whole of 1374, then suddenly four entries in one month, January 1375.

Joan Beaufort was perhaps the third child of John of Gaunt and Katherine Swynford, born between Henry and the third son, Thomas. Although modern writers always place her last in the birth order of the four siblings, there is no real evidence for the inevitable assumption that the three Beaufort boys were all older than Joan. As Joan married her first husband in *c.* March 1392 and gave birth to her first child at the end of that year or in the first few months of 1393, it is exceedingly unlikely that she was the youngest Beaufort child and born in 1379, as modern writers usually claim.[4] She was illegitimate at the time of her birth and wedding and would never become an heiress, and therefore there was no reason whatsoever for Gaunt to see her married and producing children at the beginning of her teens. Contrary to popular modern belief, it was not normal or usual in the Middle Ages for girls to give birth at 13 or 14, and although a handful unfortunately did, they were outliers, and were almost always wealthy heiresses. The system called the 'courtesy of England', which entitled a man who married an heiress to hold all her lands for the rest of his life even if she died many years before him, as long as the couple had at least one child together, gave such men an incentive to produce offspring with their wives as soon as possible. For everyone else, this motivation did not exist.

Joan Beaufort was probably, therefore, born in *c.* 1376/77 at the latest, though unfortunately her father's register, which might provide some clues as to the date of her birth, does not exist for those years. Thomas Beaufort, later duke of Exeter, was perhaps the youngest child of Gaunt and Katherine, and might have been born in November 1379, when the duke of Lancaster rushed from his castle of Kenilworth in Warwickshire to Kettlethorpe, a village and a Swynford manor a few miles from Lincoln held by Katherine from 1371 until her death in 1403. Gaunt spent at least three days in the village on that occasion.[5] On the other hand, perhaps Henry Beaufort, who outlived all his siblings, was the youngest child of Katherine Swynford and John of Gaunt and was born in November 1379, and the infant who appears to have been born to Katherine in January 1375 was either Joan or Thomas Beaufort. We know for certain that John, later earl of Somerset, was the eldest of the three brothers and was most probably the eldest Beaufort child overall, but otherwise the birth order of the siblings is uncertain.

As well as her four Beaufort half-siblings, Catalina of Lancaster had three cousins via the marriage of her father's brother Edmund of Langley and her mother's sister Isabel of Castile. The dates of birth of the three York siblings – Edmund of Langley, earl of Cambridge, later became the first duke of York – are not recorded, but Edward, their first son, was probably the eldest of the three, born around 1373/74 as his father's heir, followed by Constance in about 1375/76. Constance was surely named after her Castilian aunt the duchess of Lancaster, who was most probably her godmother as well. The youngest York sibling was Richard, later earl of Cambridge and the grandfather of Edward IV and Richard III, who according to his entry in the *Oxford Dictionary of National Biography* was not born until the summer of 1385. He was named after his cousin and godfather, the young king, Richard II (r. 1377–99), and Isabel of Castile's will of late 1392 asked King Richard to 'take and keep his humble godson to heart'.

Edward of Woodstock, prince of Wales and Aquitaine, who had been heir to the English throne since the moment he was born in June 1330, died on 8 June 1376, a week before his forty-sixth birthday. His 9-year-old son Richard of Bordeaux became heir to his grandfather the king, now over 60, and received his late father's titles in November 1376. Edward III set out his wishes regarding the succession to his throne sometime late that year. He clarified that Richard was his heir, followed by his fourth and now oldest living son John of Gaunt and John's male issue (which meant his only legitimate son, 9-year-old Henry of Lancaster); his fifth son Edmund of Langley and Edmund's male issue (his toddler son Edward); and his seventh and youngest son Thomas and Thomas's male issue (his only son Humphrey was not born until 1382).[6] The king thus, rather puzzlingly, excluded his granddaughter Philippa of Clarence and her Mortimer children, the only descendants of his third son Lionel, from the succession. This perhaps points to John of Gaunt exercising influence over his unwell and grieving father, and persuading him to favour himself and his son over his niece Philippa. The rightful order of succession to the English throne, and which descendants of Edward III should or should not have precedence, was to become a pressing matter in later decades, and particularly in the fifteenth century.

Sometime before 24 August 1376 when they were first certainly recorded as a married couple, Thomas of Woodstock, who turned 21 and thus came of age in January 1376, married Eleanor de Bohun. The wedding took place on 1 June in an unstated year, probably 1374, when a wedding gift of a silver cup to Eleanor from her brother-in-law John of Gaunt was recorded in his register in the middle of other documents dating to 1374.[7] Eleanor was the elder daughter and co-heir of Humphrey de Bohun and Joan Fitzalan or Arundel, earl and countess of Hereford, Essex and Northampton, and was born not long before 8 May 1366. She was only a child when she married Thomas, and first gave birth in April 1382 when she was 16 or almost. Her father Humphrey died in January 1373 at the age of 30, and her mother Joan outlived her husband by forty-six years and never remarried. Eleanor's younger sister Mary (b. *c.* December 1370) married John of Gaunt's son and heir Henry of Lancaster in February 1381 and was the mother of his six legitimate children, including King Henry V.[8] Confusingly, therefore, two sisters married an uncle and a nephew.

Chapter 8

A Coronation and an Early Death

As had been the case with her cousin Philippa of Clarence, her uncle Lionel of Antwerp, and her mother-in-law Maud Ufford, Isabella of Woodstock's younger daughter Philippa de Coucy married in childhood. The date of Philippa's wedding is not recorded, but she and Robert de Vere, heir to his late father's earldom of Oxford, were certainly already married by 5 October 1376, when Robert was 14 and Philippa not yet 9. Philippa remained in the custody of her mother for the time being, and Edward III granted his daughter £200 a year to look after her.[1] Philippa's older sister Marie de Coucy, resident in France, married a few years after Philippa: she wed Henri de Bar in 1383 when she was 17 (see below). Marie joined the household of the queen-consort of France, Jeanne de Bourbon, wife of her future husband's maternal uncle Charles V (r. 1364–80), in or about 1376 when she was 10, and was educated alongside the royal children of France.[2] Of the nine children borne by Queen Jeanne, only two lived into adulthood: Charles VI of France, born in December 1368, and Louis, duke of Orléans, born in March 1372. The queen died in February 1378 three days after her fortieth birthday, after giving birth to her daughter Catherine de Valois, who died young.

Marie and Philippa de Coucy's father returned to his native France permanently after the death of his father-in-law King Edward, and gave up his English allegiance, titles, and lands. Enguerrand was in fact already in Paris on 25 March 1377, three months before Edward III's death.[3] By returning to his homeland, Enguerrand forfeited all his lands in England, though in November 1377 most of them were restored to his wife Isabella of Woodstock 'in consideration of her noble birth and for her honourable maintenance'. If, however, 'she voluntarily, or otherwise by her husband's command, passes beyond the realm' to join Enguerrand in France, the lands would be confiscated from her.[4] Enguerrand and Isabella's 15-year-old son-in-law Robert de Vere was one of the boys and young men knighted by King Edward alongside Richard of Bordeaux, Henry of Lancaster and Thomas of Woodstock on 23 April 1377, during the annual celebrations held at Windsor to honour the feast day of Saint George.

Just two months later on 21 June, Edward III died at the age of 64, six months into the fifty-first year of his reign. Ten-year-old Richard of Bordeaux succeeded as Richard II, and his coronation took place in Westminster Abbey on a blazingly hot day in mid-July 1377. The English nobility petitioned to serve the king during the lavish banquet in Westminster Hall afterwards, these rituals being seen as of profound significance. Robert de Vere performed the office of chamberlain, served the king with water 'before and after meat' and removed Richard's basins and towels, while 10-year-old Henry of Lancaster stood in front of Richard, holding the sword of mercy, Curtana. Richard's uncle Thomas of Woodstock finally received a title and was made earl of Buckingham on the day of the coronation; Henry Percy (b. 1341), from a great northern family, became the first earl of Northumberland; and young John Mowbray (b. 1365) became the first earl of Nottingham, though was destined to die in his teens in 1383, leaving his brother Thomas as his heir.[5]

Philippa of Clarence, countess of March and Ulster, died early in the reign of her cousin Richard II, only in her early twenties. Given her youth, and given that she had borne children in 1371, 1374, 1375 and 1376, it seems possible or even likely that she died of complications during pregnancy or after childbirth. She was alive on 18 February 1377, and passed away sometime before 6 December 1379, when Edmund Mortimer appointed two chaplains to celebrate divine service daily for the souls of his father Roger, second earl of March, and 'Philippa, late the wife of the said Edmund'. The chaplains were also to pray for the good estate of Edmund himself and his mother while alive. According to an entry in the journal *Notes and Queries* in 1872, Philippa might have died as early as the end of 1377 or beginning of 1378: this entry states that a man named Geoffrey Styuecle or Stuckley was sent to Philippa's uncle John of Gaunt on 7 January 1378 to inform him of 'the death of the countess of March'.[6] No inquisition post mortem – which would reveal at least the approximate date of Philippa's death – was held for her, because Edmund had the right to keep all her lands for the rest of his life by the 'courtesy of England', and his own inquisition post mortem of 1382 lists all of his wife's lands which he held after her death. Philippa was the eldest granddaughter of a king and was a great heiress, and it is sad that we do not know the date of her death for certain. It is also rather sad that Philippa of Clarence, countess of March and Ulster, has often been confused with her mother-in-law, Philippa Mortimer née Montacute, countess of March, daughter of William Montacute, earl of Salisbury (d. 1344) and widow of Roger Mortimer, second earl of March (d. 1360).[7]

Philippa of Clarence's widower Edmund Mortimer, third earl of March, died on 27 December 1381, and his mother the dowager countess, Philippa Mortimer née Montacute, died a few days later on 5 or 6 January 1382. Their inquisitions post mortem both specified that Edmund's elder son Roger (b. April 1374) was heir to the massive joint inheritance of the Mortimer family and Roger's late mother Philippa of Clarence, including the earldom of Ulster and the lands of one-third of the old earldom of Gloucester.[8] Philippa Mortimer née Montacute had probably been ill for quite some time, as she made her will on 21 November 1378 more than three years before she died, and perhaps the news of her son's demise at the age of only 29 hastened her own. She bequeathed to Edmund numerous items including a bed of blue taffeta embroidered with 'asses branded on the shoulder with a rose', tapestries and coverlets, a gold ring containing a fragment of the True Cross (*la vraie croyce*) and inscribed with the words *In Nomine Patris et Filii et Spiritus Sancti*, another gold ring with a ruby, a gold cup with the arms of Mortimer, and a cup and matching jug of beryl decorated with gold. She did not update the will in the nine or ten days between her son's death and her own, and all the goods she had bequeathed to him presumably passed to her grandson Roger Mortimer (b. 1374) instead, as Edmund's heir.[9]

Edmund Mortimer made his own will on 1 May 1380, at a time when he was making preparations to travel to Ireland.[10] In it, he mentioned 'the body of my wife, whom God absolve' (*le corps de ma feme qe Dieu assoile*), a formulation which was a conventional way of referring to a dead person. Although she had died sometime before 6 December 1379, Philippa of Clarence had not yet been buried; if she did indeed pass away at the end of 1377 or the beginning of 1378, this seems a very odd and unusually long time for a body to lie above ground. A delay of three or four months between a royal person's death and their burial was usual in the fourteenth century; a delay of two or three years was not. Edmund asked for his body and Philippa's to be buried together in the church of Wigmore Abbey, Herefordshire and charged his executors to make no unnecessary expense at their joint funeral. The Mortimer children Elizabeth, Roger, Philippa and Edmund were still very young when they lost their parents and their grandmother the countess of March, and all their other grandparents (Roger Mortimer, Lionel of Antwerp and Elizabeth de Burgh) died before they were born. Their father left all four of them generous bequests in his will.

Roger, aged 7 when his father died at the end of 1381, received a gold cup with a cover, called *Benesonne* (which means 'Blessing' or 'Benediction' in medieval French), a sword decorated with gold which had belonged to his great-grandfather Edward III, and a 'great gold horn'. He was also bequeathed a large bed of black satin embroidered with white lions, gold roses and the arms of Mortimer and Ulster, a gilded, enamelled silver cup decorated 'with children's games' (*ove joeux des enfantz*), a silver salt-cellar in the shape of a dog, two gold spoons 'with the heads of ladies', and numerous silver pots, plates and vessels. Finally, Edmund left his heir 'our smaller gold horn with the strap'. These items were highly valuable, and Edmund requested that they should all remain in the Mortimer family forever and that if Roger had no heirs of his body, they should pass to Roger's younger brother Edmund.

Edmund, born in late 1376 and just 5 years old when his father died, and as the youngest Mortimer/Clarence child, was to receive 300 marks of land when he came of age. Like his brother, he received numerous silver plates and pots, a silver salt-cellar in the shape of a lion, a large cup with a matching jug, a gilded spice dish, two gold spoons, though these ones did not have 'heads of ladies', and a bed of white sendal (expensive cloth) powdered with red roses. The eldest child, Elizabeth, was given a salt-cellar in the shape of a dog, a gold cup, and a chaplet with 'fine red roses all around and 200 large pearls'. Finally, the younger Mortimer daughter, 6-year-old Philippa, received a gold coronet with precious stones, a circlet with roses, which had emeralds and 'rubies from Alexandria' in the roses, a red bed with red curtains, and a gold jug with two sapphires. Her loving father also left her £1,000 in money, adding the proviso that she would only get the cash 'in case she is not our heir', which Philippa would only become if both her brothers and her older sister died childless.

Elizabeth Mortimer, though only 9 years old when her father made his will in 1380, was already married to Henry 'Hotspur' Percy (b. 1364), son and heir of the earl of Northumberland; Edmund referred to Hotspur as 'our dear son Sir Henry Percy' and left him a small brooch 'in the shape of a stag with the head of an eagle'. Young Henry was present when his father-in-law made the will, and witnessed it. The earl of Northumberland himself was appointed as one of Edmund Mortimer's executors, and received a cup with a star in the base and a brooch 'with a bear'. Elizabeth, who probably received no money from her father as her younger sister did because she was already married, presumably went to live in the north of England with her husband and his family. She and 'Hotspur' (a nickname given to him by the Scots) were in no apparent hurry to produce children: their only son, inevitably also called Henry Percy, was born on 3 February 1393 when Elizabeth was in her early twenties.[11]

Another child-couple was Philippa of Clarence's much younger cousin Constance of York and Thomas Despenser, heir of the wealthy and influential Despenser family: they wed in early November 1379 when Thomas was 6 and Constance even younger.[12] Thomas was descended from Edward I so was a distant cousin of Constance, and was the only surviving son and heir of Edward, Lord Despenser, who died in November 1375 when Thomas was an infant. It was a grand match for the Despenser boy, as Constance was the granddaughter of two kings, whereas he was not even in line to inherit an earldom. He would, however, come into a large and rich inheritance across the south of England and in South Wales, where the Despensers owned no fewer than ten castles, when he came of age. Thomas had been granted an annual income of 100 marks (£66.66) in May 1378, and in January 1384 Constance herself was granted an annuity of 80 marks 'for her maintenance', payable by her mother-in-law Elizabeth, dowager Lady Despenser, out of the dower lands she held from her son's large inheritance.[13] In modern terms, 80 and 100 marks are both in excess of £100,000, exceedingly generous amounts for children, so evidently the young couple lived in fine style.

Chapter 9

The Young Bridegroom

The wedding of John of Gaunt's second daughter Elizabeth of Lancaster and John Hastings, heir to the earldom of Pembroke, took place at the duke's mighty Warwickshire castle of Kenilworth on 24 June 1380. Gaunt gave his daughter a gold ring as a wedding gift, and had perhaps been planning young John's marriage to Elizabeth for a while: his father granted him the rights to the boy's marriage on 16 September 1376.[1] The advantages of the marriage to Gaunt and his family were obvious. John Hastings was not only the heir to an earldom and to a wealthy inheritance from his late father (1347–75), he was the maternal grandson and co-heir, with his cousin John Mowbray the earl of Nottingham, of Margaret, countess of Norfolk. As a great-great-grandson of Edward I, John was of royal descent and well-connected to most of the English nobility.[2] Unfortunately for Elizabeth of Lancaster, however, John Hastings was born on or around 11 November 1372 and was almost a decade younger than she was. He was just 7 years old when he married Elizabeth; she was 17.[3]

That the duke arranged John Hastings' marriage to Elizabeth rather than to her half-sister Catalina, who was exactly the same age as the boy, surely confirms that Gaunt foresaw a marriage into Castile for his half-Castilian daughter. Gaunt's need for allies in England and his desire to hold his third daughter in reserve to benefit his Iberian affairs had condemned his second daughter to remain a virgin until she was at least 24, perhaps 26 years old. Time would reveal that Elizabeth was unwilling and unable to wait this long, and for a fourteenth-century noblewoman to be married to someone so many years her junior was unusual. It was also unusual for the duke of Lancaster's eldest child Philippa to be still unmarried at the age of 20, but the age gap between Philippa and John Hastings was almost thirteen years, so she was even more unsuitable than her younger sister to be the boy's bride. Gaunt also intended to use the marriage of his eldest daughter to further his and England's interests, and in the early 1380s entered into various negotiations for Philippa's marriage (see below).

After the June 1380 wedding, Gaunt referred to Elizabeth as 'our daughter of Pembroke', and continued to pay £100 annually for the 'expenses of her chamber and wardrobe'. He also paid 40 marks a year to stable and feed Elizabeth's horses, and after her marriage, Elizabeth's servants included Agneys Sallowe and Nicholas Pyne.[4] Her little husband, meanwhile, almost certainly remained in the care of his mother Anne Manny, dowager countess of Pembroke, for the time being; Anne and her mother Countess Margaret of Norfolk had been granted joint custody of John in early 1376, a few months after his father's death. On 8 July 1384 a few weeks after Anne died, Margaret was granted sole custody of her grandson, still only 11 years old then though a husband for four years.[5]

The following year, in June 1381, the south-east of England exploded into chaos and rebellion as thousands of people, unhappy at their living conditions and at the imposition of the ludicrously unfair poll tax (which fell most heavily on the poor), poured into London during the Great Uprising, or Peasants' Revolt as it was once called. The main targets of the rebels' rage were the chancellor and treasurer of England, Robert Hales and Simon Sudbury, archbishop of Canterbury and the godfather of Philippa de Coucy's husband the earl of Oxford, and another was John of Gaunt, the wealthiest and most powerful man in England and the most loathed. The whereabouts of Gaunt's daughters in June 1381 are unclear, but Philippa was perhaps with her stepmother Duchess Costanza, to whom she was very close, in Yorkshire. One hopes that Philippa, Elizabeth and Catalina were not in their father's great London palace of the Savoy, which was left a smoking ruin, or in the Tower of London, which was invaded by the rebels and was where their 14-year-old brother Henry was staying with their cousin King Richard. Robert Hales and Simon Sudbury were dragged out of the fortress and summarily beheaded on Tower Hill, and Henry of Lancaster, as the son and heir of the despised John of Gaunt, was, despite his youth, also in great danger. Thankfully, a man named John Ferrour saved his life, and Henry never forgot it.[6]

On 16 April 1382 at Rochford in Essex, Eleanor de Bohun, countess of Buckingham, gave birth to her first child, Humphrey of Gloucester (his father Thomas of Woodstock was to become duke of Gloucester in 1385). John of Gaunt and his son Henry of Lancaster, who had just turned 15 and was now safely reunited with his father after the trauma of the Uprising, heard the news of Humphrey's birth on 18 April, and John gave gifts of cash to little Humphrey's nurse and to his brother Thomas's squire, Westcombe, who brought him the news.[7] Although it is sometimes stated that it was Eleanor's younger sister Mary who gave birth in 1382 when she was little more than a child herself, this is a misunderstanding.[8] Mary was almost certainly born in or very soon before December 1370, as she and Henry of Lancaster were granted the lands of her inheritance from her late father on 22 December 1384, and as a married woman she came of age and was eligible to receive her lands at age 14.[9] It is physically impossible that she could have been Humphrey of Gloucester's mother as she was still only 11 years old at the time of his birth in April 1382 and only 10 when he was conceived, and Henry of Monmouth, the eldest of Henry of Lancaster and Mary de Bohun's six children, was born in September 1386 when his father was 19 and his mother probably 15 and 9 months.

Marie and Philippa de Coucy lost their mother when Isabella of Woodstock, countess of Bedford and Soissons, died in London on 5 October 1382 at the age of 50. She was buried in the church of the Greyfriars in London, where her aunt Joan of the Tower and her grandmother Isabella of France, queens of Scotland and England, had been buried in 1362 and 1358 respectively. John of Gaunt and Thomas of Woodstock, though apparently not Edmund of Langley who is not mentioned, were appointed as the supervisors of their late sister's will, and Isabella's executors requested their permission to sell a house of hers on Ludgate in London, called *Pembrokesyn* or 'Pembroke's Inn'. The money raised from the sale was intended to pay off the countess's large debts, to pay the outstanding wages due to her servants, and to distribute 'alms for her soul' under the royal brothers' supervision. It is often stated that Isabella died in 1379, but in fact the exact date of her death is given in an entry on the Close Roll dated 8 December 1382, which states 'from 5 October last, when the countess [of Bedford] died'. Other entries in the chancery rolls show that Isabella was alive in August 1379 and on 22 March and 25 June 1382.[10] Her death left her younger brothers John, Edmund and Thomas as the only surviving children of King Edward and Queen Philippa, and her widower Enguerrand de Coucy, from whom she had been living apart for about five years and was about 42 in 1382, married his second wife Isabelle of Lorraine in *c.* 1386 and had another daughter with her.

Shortly after Isabella of Woodstock's death, her nephew Richard II (or rather, the 15-year-old underage king's council, ruling for him) granted Philippa de Coucy and Robert de Vere the reversion of lands which Edward III had once granted to Philippa's father, 'in consideration of their not having land or other maintenance to support their estate'. Robert turned 21 in January 1383, proved his age that February, and finally received his late father Thomas's lands, minus the large dower in the hands of his mother Maud Ufford, dowager countess of Oxford.[11] Philippa turned 15 in November 1382, the month after her mother's death, and was probably now considered mature enough to live with Robert. Robert, however, might have had other interests; he was involved in some kind of intense relationship with Philippa's cousin King Richard, who was five years his junior and a few months older than Philippa herself. Chronicler Thomas Walsingham wrote that Richard and Robert had an 'obscene familiarity' and that Richard 'loved him [Robert de Vere] so much', while Jean Froissart said that Robert's hold over the king was so strong that if the earl claimed that black was white, Richard would not contradict him.[12] The two young men were extremely close, and it is certainly possible that they were lovers. Robert's influence over King Richard was generally considered malign by contemporaries.

Richard II, however, also had a very loving relationship with his wife. He married Anne of Bohemia (b. May 1366), daughter of the Holy Roman Emperor Karl IV (d. 1378) and his fourth wife, the Polish noblewoman Elżbieta of Pomerania, shortly after his fifteenth birthday in January 1382. The young couple became remarkably close and were rarely apart during the twelve and a half years of their marriage. In *c.* 1384/86, Anne sent a letter to her older half-brother the king of Germany and Bohemia expressing her sadness that she had not yet borne a child, and indeed she and Richard never would have children.[13] It seems highly likely that one of them was infertile, rather than living in a chaste marriage, as some modern writers have suggested. In November 1382 Richard talked of 'the king and queen and their children (when God gives them)', and in April 1383 asked three men in Warwick to 'celebrate divine service daily for the good estate of the king, the queen and their children'.[14] In the early years of his marriage, the king certainly expected that he and

Queen Anne would become parents. Philippa de Coucy and Robert de Vere had no children either, which possibly reveals that their personal relationship was not a happy or close one, or again, might simply mean that one of them was infertile. Neither Richard II nor Robert de Vere had any known illegitimate offspring either.

Chapter 10

Marie de Coucy and Henri de Bar

During a parliament held at Westminster in late February and early March 1383, Thomas of Woodstock, earl of Buckingham, and Hugh Stafford, earl of Stafford (b. *c*. mid-1340s) became involved in some kind of dispute.[1] The reason for their quarrel is not clear, but perhaps had something to do with John of Gaunt's wish to lead an expedition to the kingdom of Castile to claim his wife Costanza's throne, currently held by her cousin Juan I (son and successor of her illegitimate half-uncle Enrique of Trastámara, who had died in 1379), and parliament's reluctance in 1382/83 to give him the money to do so. Instead, funds were given to Henry Despenser, bishop of Norwich, to lead an expedition into Flanders, to the utter fury of Gaunt himself and, perhaps, of his youngest brother. Bishop Despenser's foray into Flanders proved an utter disaster which led to his impeachment.

Thomas of Woodstock's wife Eleanor de Bohun was pregnant at the time, and shortly before 6 May 1383 gave birth to her second child and first daughter, Anne of Gloucester.[2] Anne was just over a year younger than her brother Humphrey, later became countess of Stafford and Eu, and was an ancestor of the Stafford dukes of Buckingham and the Bourchier earls of Essex. Although she had an older brother and two younger sisters, she would be the only child of Eleanor de Bohun and Thomas of Woodstock who had children of her own, and was her parents' heir. The name Anne was fairly unusual at the time and it would have been rather more conventional to have named her after her paternal grandmother the late queen, Philippa of Hainault, so the little girl was perhaps the goddaughter of Anne of Bohemia, queen of England, or Anne Manny, dowager countess of Pembroke. One of Thomas's squires, name not stated, took the news of Anne's birth to John of Gaunt, and was rewarded with 40s. Gaunt subsequently rode to Pleshey to attend his little niece's baptism, and paid £46, 8s and 2d to Herman the goldsmith for a pair of gilded silver basins engraved with swans, motto of the de Bohun family, and the arms of 'our brother of Bukyngham, given to the daughter of our said brother on the day of her baptism at Pleshey'.

John also gave Anne a gilded silver ewer, a 'great tripod' and a silver cup with cover, for which he paid a total of £44, as further christening gifts. A payment of £8 went to 'a damsel of our sister of Bukyngham, the day of the baptism of Anne her daughter,' and £5 to another of Eleanor de Bohun's damsels assigned to be the *maistresse* of the little girl (i.e. the woman in charge of her household). Finally, John gave 20s to Eleanor's midwife, and 30s to Anne's *rokestare* or 'rocker', the girl or young woman who rocked her cradle. On the same day, John also bought a silver basin and ewer for the chamber of 'our daughter of Pembroke' from John Botesham, goldsmith of London.[3] This perhaps indicates that his second daughter Elizabeth of Lancaster went to the baptism of her much younger cousin Anne with him.

Thomas of Woodstock and Eleanor de Bohun had a second daughter, Joan, future Lady Talbot, who must have been born sometime in 1384 or 1385 though the date was not recorded, and their third daughter, Isabel, a nun who joined the convent of the Minoresses in London, was born on 23 April 1386.[4] Isabel of Gloucester was Edward III's youngest granddaughter, and was over thirty years younger than her eldest cousin, Philippa of Clarence. Some later writers gave Thomas of Woodstock and Eleanor de Bohun a fourth daughter, named Philippa. Primary source evidence that confirms her existence, however, is lacking, other than a confusing and ambiguous reference in a fifteenth-century manuscript, and she was not mentioned in any of the numerous de Bohun inquisitions post mortem in 1400 or in her mother's will of 1399. If there ever was a fourth Gloucester daughter named Philippa, she must have died young.

The very wealthy John of Gaunt, duke of Lancaster, was often very generous to his daughters. On 4 May 1381 at the Savoy, for example, Gaunt acknowledged receipt of the sum of £50 from Katherine Swynford, who had spent that amount on pearls for herself and the now 21-year-old Philippa of Lancaster. In September 1383, the duke sent valuable 'gold and silver vessels' to his 'beloved daughter Phelippe' and her stepmother Costanza, to whom Philippa was very close, and sent £50 to Lady Mohun for the household expenses of Philippa's half-sister Catalina.[5] In the early 1380s, Gaunt negotiated a possible future marriage for Philippa with Wilhelm, count of Ostrevant, son and heir of Gaunt's cousin Albrecht von Wittelsbach, duke of Bavaria. Wilhelm of Ostrevant was five years Philippa's junior. Duke Albrecht sent men to England to negotiate a dowry, but at the last minute decided against an English marriage for his son and arranged a match for him into the French royal family: Wilhelm married Marguerite of Burgundy, niece of Charles V of France, in April 1385. John of Gaunt, on hearing of this, became 'thoughtful and melancholic,' according to chronicler Jean Froissart, and sent a delegation to Duke Albrecht at his castle of Le Quesnoy to register his displeasure. However, a clearly annoyed Albrecht informed John that just as he would not presume to concern himself with the marriages of John's children, neither was it John's place to poke his nose into the marriages of Albrecht's children.[6] Another grand match was planned for Philippa of Lancaster in late 1383, to the young king of France, Charles VI. Born in December 1368, he was nearly nine years her junior. Sadly for Philippa, Charles's uncles were uncertain how they might proceed, given the endless state of war between France and England, and the idea came to nothing; Charles married the partly German, partly Italian Isabeau of Bavaria in 1385 instead.[7]

Marie de Coucy, Edward III's fourth eldest granddaughter, was also contracted to marry in 1383; she was betrothed to Henri de Bar on 26 November. Henri was the eldest son and heir of Robert, duke of Bar, and was a distant cousin of Marie and her sister Philippa, being descended from Edward I of England (r. 1272–1307) via Edward's eldest daughter Eleanor (1269–1298), countess of Bar.[8] The duchy, formerly county, of Bar lay in eastern France with its capital at Bar-le-Duc, 140 miles from Paris. Via his mother Marie de Valois, Marie de Coucy's husband Henri de Bar was a grandson of John II, king of France, and a great-grandson of John 'the Blind' (b. 1296), king of Bohemia, who was killed fighting against Marie's grandfather Edward III and uncle Edward of Woodstock at the battle of Crécy in 1346. Henri de Bar was about the same age as Marie de Coucy, and like her, was probably 17 or so when they wed; his parents were both born in 1344 and married on 5 October 1364.[9] Henri and Marie were both the grandchildren of kings and thus were well-matched by rank, and Henri's sister Yolande de Bar had become the queen-consort of Aragon in Spain in 1380 when she married King Joan I (d. 1396).

Marie's father Enguerrand de Coucy travelled to the duchy of Bar to discuss the matter of their children's marriage with Duke Robert in

1383, and promised a dowry of 5,000 francs per year for his daughter's marriage as well as the fortress of Châtillon-sur-Saône, now in the Vosges department of north-eastern France. Robert de Bar promised to look after and sustain the young couple, their retinues and any children they might have in his own household, though if it should happen that they wished to live separately from him, he would provide a suitable castle for them to reside in as well as lands to provide them with an income. Enguerrand also stated that his elder daughter would renounce any rights to the possessions that had once belonged to 'our dear consort Lady Coucy, her mother, without prejudice to the succession of the said mother in England'.[10]

Enguerrand intended to make his elder daughter a duchess, though ultimately this never came about as Henri de Bar died before his father. Henri and Marie did, however, have two sons, one named Robert after his paternal grandfather and one called Enguerrand after his other grandfather. The two were described as *biaux fils* or 'beautiful sons' by one of Henri de Bar's military associates, but Enguerrand de Bar died young in the late 1390s. Robert de Bar was still a minor, i.e. under 21, in 1408, and might have been as young as 5 or 6 years old when his father died in 1397.[11] As Marie de Coucy and Henri de Bar's first son was born in or around the early 1390s, a good few years after they married at the age of 17 in 1383, the couple might have had fertility issues.

Henri's maternal uncle Charles V of France died on 16 September 1380 and was succeeded by his son Charles VI, not yet 12 years old. Henri and his younger brother Philippe de Bar were knighted at the coronation of the young king, their cousin, in Rheims on 4 November. Before the knighting ceremony, both boys or young men were dressed as simple squires in tunics of grey cloth with no adornment, though for the ceremony itself they wore vermilion silk furred with miniver. Henri was perhaps delighted to marry Marie de Coucy three years later: the French writer Jean-Joseph Carlier declared in the nineteenth century that she was 'one of the most charming girls of the blood royal' in Europe at the time, and was the daughter of a dashing and widely-admired nobleman as well as the granddaughter of the late king of England.[12]

In 1383, John of Gaunt purchased two pack-horses for his daughter Elizabeth of Lancaster at a cost of £8 and £6, 7 shillings and 2 pence, which seems a curiously large amount of money to pay for pack-horses. Another £11 was spent on Elizabeth's expenses travelling from Hertford to Henley-on-Thames to visit her cousin the king for nine days. This visit is not dated, but Elizabeth of Lancaster was obviously in King Richard's presence on or a little before 24 September 1383 at Westminster, as on that date Richard granted a pardon to a Nicholas Parker of Brampt who had killed Thomas Dyke, at the request of 'the king's kinswoman, Elizabeth, countess of Pembroke.'[13] Elizabeth's twentieth birthday had passed in *c.* February 1383, and although in the summer of that year she had been married for three years, she had no immediate prospect of being able to live with her husband; John Hastings turned 11 in November 1383, and would not reach maturity for at least another three years and probably five.

Chapter 11

Madam of Ireland, and Elizabeth's Second Marriage

Richard II, his three uncles and much of the English nobility went on a military campaign to Scotland in the summer of 1385, during which the king quarrelled badly with his eldest uncle the duke of Lancaster but created his other two uncles duke of York (Edmund of Langley) and duke of Gloucester (Thomas of Woodstock). During the Scottish campaign, King Richard's half-brother Sir John Holland murdered Ralph Stafford, eldest of the five sons of Hugh, earl of Stafford, after a quarrel between members of their retinues. Ralph Stafford was a close friend of the king, and the furious Richard II seized his half-brother's lands, 'by reason of the contempt and rebellion of the said John', on 14 September 1385.[1] Holland fled into sanctuary at Beverley Minster for a while, and the grieving Hugh, earl of Stafford, died in September 1386, still only in his early forties, leaving his second son Thomas, born *c.* 25 March 1369, as his heir.[2] Richard II ignored the pleas of his and John Holland's mother Joan of Kent, dowager princess of Wales, to pardon Holland, but she died soon afterwards, and thereafter Richard did pardon Holland for the murder, albeit grudgingly. For a few months, he refused to acknowledge Holland as his brother as he did on every other occasion throughout his reign, and referred to him in February and March 1386 simply as a 'knight of the royal household'.[3] Later, after the king genuinely forgave him, John Holland became Richard's chamberlain and one of the staunchest of his allies. The two half-brothers were extremely close throughout the 1390s.

Richard II's relationship with his cousin Philippa de Coucy's husband Robert de Vere, earl of Oxford, continued, and on 1 December 1385 he made Robert marquess of Dublin, a brand-new title. On 13 October 1386, he, rather astonishingly, upgraded Robert's title to duke of Ireland, an unprecedented title which attracted much criticism.[4] Robert only held his controversial title for little more than a year, though Philippa de Coucy was addressed as 'duchess of Ireland' or 'Madam of Ireland' for the rest of her life, and is the only person in history to have held the title.

In the summer of 1386, John of Gaunt and Costanza of Castile finally departed from England and set sail for the Iberian Peninsula, where Gaunt attempted to realise his long-held dream of gaining control of Castile and Leon. Costanza's uncle Enrique of Trastámara had died in 1379 and his son Juan I (b. 1358) was now ruling the two kingdoms, while the unfortunate illegitimate sons of the late King Pedro, Duchess Costanza's half-brothers, remained in captivity. All three of John of Gaunt's legitimate daughters, Philippa, Elizabeth and Catalina of Lancaster, accompanied him and Costanza to Spain, though Gaunt's mistress Katherine Swynford and their four Beaufort children remained in England. Scandal struck the Lancaster family shortly before their departure: the six-year marriage of Elizabeth of Lancaster and John Hastings, who was still only 13, was annulled, and Elizabeth married the king's half-brother Sir John Holland instead. Holland was the second son of Joan of Kent (d. 1385), princess of Wales, and was the man who had killed Sir Ralph Stafford the previous year. In 1353, Elizabeth's uncle Edward of Woodstock, prince of Wales, gave an unnamed son of Sir Thomas Holland two silver basins which cost over £10, possibly as a christening gift. This might have been John, and if so, he was a decade older than Elizabeth (though it is possible that this was a reference to a Holland son who died in infancy, and that John was born some years after 1353).[5] Elizabeth and John were related; he was the great-grandson of Edward I from Edward's second marriage, while Elizabeth was Edward's great-great-granddaughter from his first marriage. As well as the necessary papal annulment of Elizabeth's previous unconsummated marriage to John Hastings, they therefore required a dispensation for consanguinity.

It is curiously difficult to discover exactly when Elizabeth's Hastings marriage was annulled or when her Holland marriage went ahead; there are no references to the matter in *Calendar of Papal Letters 1362–1404* or in *Petitions to the Pope 1342–1419*. One chronicler says that the Hastings marriage was annulled after the Lancastrian party left England, but according to another chronicle, the *Polychronicon*, John Holland fell deeply in love with Elizabeth and pressed his suit day and night, and that when the Lancastrian party departed from England Elizabeth was already pregnant.[6] It does, in fact, seem highly likely that Elizabeth was already pregnant by Holland when they married, as it would only have been possible for her to obtain an annulment of her Hastings marriage for the most pressing of reasons. Her personal unhappiness or her unwillingness to wait for an adolescent boy to grow up and become her husband in more than name only would under no circumstances have been considered adequate reasons. Her father, not to mention the pope, would only have permitted the annulment if Elizabeth's remaining in her Hastings marriage would have been an even greater scandal than ending it, and as John Hastings was still only 13 years old in June 1386 and in his grandmother the countess of Norfolk's custody, if Elizabeth was pregnant, the child could hardly have been passed off as his.

Elizabeth and John Holland's first child was almost certainly their daughter Constance ('Custance' or 'Custaunce' as it was then most often spelt) Holland, whose name must surely mean that Elizabeth's stepmother Costanza was the girl's godmother. This either implies Elizabeth's affection for Costanza, or reveals that she thought asking her stepmother to act as her child's godmother was a good way to assuage the duchess's sense of offended dignity over Elizabeth's behaviour. On 18 September 1391, Pope Boniface IX stated that Constance Holland was then in her fourth year, meaning that she was 3 years old. This would place her date of birth between September 1387 and September 1388. However, young Thomas Mowbray, the son and heir of the earl of Nottingham, whose future marriage to Constance was then being arranged, was said to be in his fifth year (i.e. 4 years old) in September 1391, when in fact he turned 6 that month. Constance Holland therefore may have been somewhat older than the pope's letter suggests, and was perhaps born in 1386 or the first few months of 1387.[7] Constance Holland was most probably born in Portugal or Castile. Her parents returned to England before 2 June 1388, when King Richard gave his half-brother, whom he had now completely forgiven for killing Ralph Stafford in 1385, the earldom of Huntingdon. Elizabeth and John's first son was called Richard Holland, and his name almost certainly means that Richard II was his godfather. This implies that he was born in the late 1380s or early 1390s after his parents' return to England.[8]

There is no doubt whatsoever that Sir John Holland was a violent and impetuous man, at least when he was young; as well as his murder of a young nobleman in 1385, he had a friar tortured to death in 1384 in an attempt to force him to reveal a supposed plot to kill King Richard, in which Elizabeth's father John of Gaunt was allegedly implicated. It might, in fact, have been Holland's propensity for fighting and his skills in the art of warfare which appealed to Elizabeth of Lancaster. In 1394, Holland went to fight against 'the Turks and other enemies of Christ', as Pope Boniface put it, and in 1397 would be appointed as captain-general of the pope's forces against the supporters of the 'anti-popes' in Avignon (see below for more information). Holland was also to win a prize as the best jouster during a famous tournament held in England in 1390. Elizabeth's third husband Sir John Cornwall, whom she married in 1400 within months of Holland's death, was also a champion jouster and a renowned soldier. Cornwall had, and still has, a reputation as the greatest, most honourable and most respected English warrior of the early fifteenth century.[9] Elizabeth's choice of John Cornwall as her third husband reveals something about her taste in men, and in 1386 she had no interest in waiting any longer for the adolescent John Hastings of Pembroke to grow up; she was 23 years old and she wanted a husband now, a husband who was an adult and a warrior.

From the late 1380s until the king's downfall in 1399, John Holland, earl of Huntingdon, was one of Richard II's staunchest supporters, and was well-rewarded for his loyalty: he was made an admiral, keeper of Carlisle, Tintagel and Conwy castles and the town and castle of Brest in Brittany, justice of Chester for life, chamberlain of England for life, and much else. At an unknown date, Holland negotiated with Duke John IV of Brittany regarding the marriage of the duke's son and heir to Holland and Elizabeth of Lancaster's 'young daughter' (*nostre joene fille*).[10] This presumably was not Constance, whose marriage to the earl of Nottingham's heir was arranged in 1391, but another of their daughters. Elizabeth of Lancaster probably spent time with Holland in the duchy of Brittany in the 1390s when he was captain of Brest and might have borne one of her children there, though her second son was born in Devon in March 1395. Given this birthdate, Elizabeth must also have accompanied her husband to Hungary on his long visit to Richard II's brother-in-law Sigismund, king of Hungary and Croatia, in 1394.[11]

At an unknown date, John Holland fathered an illegitimate son named William Huntingdon, who was ordained as a sub-deacon in December 1406 and who served as rector of the church of St James

Garlickhythe in London for almost half a century until his death in 1455. William's second name almost certainly means that he was born after John Holland received the earldom of Huntingdon in June 1388, and therefore that he was conceived and born during Holland's marriage to Elizabeth of Lancaster. Elizabeth and John's second son and ultimate heir, John Holland the younger, earl of Huntingdon, was to take after his father in at least some respects; he married three times and had five known illegitimate sons, at least two of whom also used the last name Huntingdon.[12]

Chapter 12

Queen Philippa and King João, and Agnes Launcecrona

Philippa of Lancaster married at last on St Valentine's Day, 14 February 1387, when she was almost 27 years old, and made a brilliant match to King João of Portugal. Born in 1357, he was the illegitimate son of Pedro I of Portugal (d. 1367), and was the half-brother of Fernando I (d. 1383). King Fernando left only one legitimate child, a daughter named Beatriz (b. 1373), and after his death in October 1383 there was an interregnum in Portugal for nearly two years. Beatriz had been betrothed to Edmund of Langley's son Edward of York when they were both children, but married the widowed Juan I of Castile instead, and died in obscurity in about 1420. Between 1383 and 1385, Juan I of Castile fought Beatriz's half-uncle João for the Portuguese throne, and João emerged victorious at the battle of Aljubarrota in August 1385 and was subsequently crowned king of Portugal.

Philippa and João's wedding took place in the cathedral of Porto (the city is also sometimes called Oporto) in northern Portugal; they had first been married by proxy twelve days earlier, before the necessary papal dispensation for the marriage arrived, with Dom João Rodrigues de Sá standing in for the king. The Portuguese chronicler Fernão Lopes, born around 1380, says that Philippa was accompanied to her wedding by her brother-in-law John Holland and her mother's first cousin Thomas Percy, the earl of Northumberland's younger brother, and that the English party was welcomed in Porto 'with great celebration and joy'. Philippa had the chance to meet her bridegroom before the wedding ceremony and they talked 'for some considerable time', with the bishop of Dax in south-west France acting as their chaperone (Lopes did not specify which language the couple used; presumably French, unless Philippa had been busily learning Portuguese). Afterwards, the two sent each other gifts of jewels: João's to Philippa was a brooch in the shape of a cockerel, studded with precious stones and mother-of-pearl, and hers to him was a pin 'studded with the costliest gems'. After the wedding ceremony, acrobats performed for the guests by tumbling, leaping over tables and balancing on tightropes, and everybody, including presumably the bridal couple, danced and sang. For fifteen days, feasts and jousting tournaments were held across Portugal.

John of Gaunt – who did not attend his daughter's wedding – and King João had agreed to take part in a joint military campaign against Castile, and sealed the deal with João's marriage to Gaunt's eldest child. In exchange for the Portuguese king's aid against King Juan of Castile, Gaunt stated that he would give his daughter and new son-in-law a narrow but long line of Castilian territory along the Portuguese border, once he was firmly ensconced as king of Castile and Leon in more than name only. The Anglo-Portuguese marriage that came about for the most unromantic of reasons resulted in six children who lived into adulthood, five sons and one daughter, who are known to Portuguese historians as the *Ínclita Geração*, the 'Illustrious Generation'. As the biographer of one of their sons once pointed out, from Philippa of Lancaster and King João's marriage stemmed a dynasty of 'brilliant monarchs and princes under whom Portugal rose from a small obscure power to the greatest maritime nation in the world'.[1]

Before his wedding, João had been the Grand Master of the Order of Saint Benedict of Aviz, a Portuguese monastic military order similar to the Knights Templar or the Knights Hospitaller, and was, and still is, often called João of Aviz as a result. He had taken binding religious vows of chastity and obedience as a member of the order, though had believed himself absolved of such vows after he became king of Portugal. Pope Boniface IX informed João and Philippa in early 1391, however, that at the time of their wedding in February 1387, the necessary dispensation had not yet been properly made out. He absolved João of the threat of excommunication for breaking his vows, and, no doubt to Philippa's great relief, declared their marriage lawful and their existing and future children legitimate.[2]

After her wedding, Queen Philippa travelled the 140 miles from Porto to Bragança (or Braganza) to bid farewell to her father, stepmother, sister Elizabeth and half-sister Catalina. Accompanied by the archbishop of Braga, Lourenço Vicente, she then made her way to Coímbra, where her household was established; her officials included Lopo Dias de Souza, her steward, Lourenço Eanes Fogaça, in charge of her finances, Gonçalo Vasques Coutinho, her head butler, and Beatriz de Castro, a niece of Juana and Inês de Castro, one of her ladies-in-waiting. Philippa became pregnant very soon after marrying, but miscarried in July 1387 while visiting João in Curval, where he lay seriously ill.[3] She became pregnant again quickly, and on 23 July 1388 gave birth to a daughter whom she called Branca in honour of her late mother Blanche of Lancaster. The little girl died young, and Philippa's eldest son Afonso, born two years later in July 1390, died in 1400. She gave some of her other children names that existed in her own family: Duarte for her paternal grandfather Edward III; Henrique for her younger brother and her maternal grandfather Duke Henry of Lancaster; Isabel for her maternal grandmother Isabella de Beaumont, duchess of Lancaster, and her sister Elizabeth of Lancaster; and João both for her husband and her father.[4]

Philippa of Lancaster is and always has been more famous in Portugal than in her native England, and praise for her piety, grace, charity and good government was unanimous among Portuguese writers, even long after the deaths of Philippa herself and her many children. She was famed as a devoted wife and mother, a very generous giver of alms and a woman who cared deeply for those less fortunate than herself, and as the very model of a queen. In this regard, Philippa stood in stark contrast to her predecessor as queen-consort, João's sister-in-law Leonor Teles de Meneses, wife of King Fernando. Leonor was believed in her own lifetime to have committed adultery with Juan Fernández de Andeiro, count of Ourém, and was widely disliked in Portugal.

Philippa's daughter Isabel's modern biographer considers that although King João was perhaps not the brightest of men, he was courageous and charismatic, a dreamer as much as a warrior. Though a romantic figure, he still managed to keep a tight hold over his kingdom for many years – he ruled over Portugal for close to half a century – with Philippa of Lancaster at his side. The chronicler Fernão Lopes commented on the great success of the Anglo-Portuguese royal marriage, and stated that God had granted Philippa a husband very much to her taste. Although João – despite his religious vow of chastity in the Order of Saint Benedict of Aviz – fathered three illegitimate children before he wed Philippa, of whom a son and a daughter lived into adulthood, he was, as far as is known, faithful to her throughout their long and fruitful marriage. Proud of his queen and her royal English ancestry, João often made grants *juntamente com minha molher*, 'jointly with my wife', or *ensembra com a Rainha dona Filipa*, 'together with the queen, Lady Philippa', and referred to her as *filha do muj nobre dom Joham ducque al Alancastre*, 'daughter of the most noble Lord John, duke of Lancaster'. Philippa soon became accustomed to living in her new country and appears to have found great happiness there. She became fluent in Portuguese after her marriage, and was taught about Portuguese customs and attitudes by another of her ladies-in-waiting, Beatriz Gonçalves de Moura. No breath of scandal ever attached to her, and she made herself widely loved and admired among her husband's subjects, to the point where Fernão Lopes talked of 'the perfect manner in which she lived' and stated that 'nothing she did was done out of rancour or hatred ... her way of speaking was sweet, gracious and most pleasing to all who heard her'.[5]

Back in England, it is possible that Robert de Vere, earl of Oxford, had his marriage to Philippa de Coucy annulled in or soon after 1387 in order to marry Agnes Lancecrona or Launcekrona, a lady-in-waiting of Queen Anne. Several contemporary chroniclers state that he did so, and a curious entry on the Patent Roll, dated 5 March 1389, stated that de Vere had abducted Agnes 'Lanchecron'.[6] Thomas Walsingham claimed that Agnes was the daughter of a saddler, but given her role as the queen's companion it seems far more likely that she was of noble birth, presumably of Czech or German background; Queen Anne was born in Prague and several of her brothers were born in Nuremberg, and they grew up bilingual in Czech and German. Various English chroniclers state that Agnes Launcecrona was 'Bohemian'.

According to the Westminster chronicler, Robert de Vere and Philippa de Coucy's marriage was annulled by papal bull in October 1389, and the *Polychronicon* says that de Vere sent a clerk called John Ripon to the papal court to seek the annulment on his behalf.[7] There is no official confirmation of the story that it was annulled in the papal registers or in extant petitions, though the fact that sometime before 24 July 1389, Philippa's father Enguerrand de Coucy, 'desiring to hear and know good news' of her, sent one of his knights, Sir Jehan de Chastelmurant, to England to 'talk with her about certain matters' on Enguerrand's behalf, may be significant.[8] It is not quite clear how de Vere might have persuaded the pope to annul his marriage merely because he had fallen in love or lust with someone else and because he 'grew to detest' Philippa de Coucy, in the words of the Westminster chronicler, though the *Polychronicon* claims that de Vere's clerk John Ripon presented false testimony to the pope in order to secure the annulment. The Westminster chronicler also says that Robert's mother Maud Ufford, dowager countess of Oxford, invited Philippa to live with her at her manor of Great Bentley in Essex, and ascribes Maud's action to her great affection for her daughter-in-law.[9]

By October 1389, the date given by the Westminster chronicler for the annulment of the marriage, de Vere had been living in exile on the Continent for almost two years, so the date does not fit the statements by other chroniclers that the marriage was annulled before he fled from England in late 1387. It does seem likely that the earl made Agnes Launcecrona his mistress, and the fact that one of his servants was imprisoned in chains in or before March 1389 for aiding him in the abduction of her strongly suggests that their relationship was not voluntary on Agnes's side. Whatever the truth of the matter, and if the statement that Robert de Vere 'detested' Philippa de Coucy is in any way accurate, Philippa was perhaps not too sad that her marriage came to an end, either because Robert succeeded in having it annulled or because he preferred to live with another woman. As Robert and Philippa had no children, the heir to his earldom was his father Thomas's younger brother Aubrey de Vere, while Philippa's heir was King Richard himself, as the son of her mother's eldest brother (Philippa's only full sibling, Marie, as a landowner in the hostile kingdom of France, was not eligible to inherit her lands in England).

Chapter 13

Catalina of Lancaster and Enrique of Castile

While John of Gaunt, the most powerful man in England, was absent in Castile and Portugal between 1386 and 1389, the political situation in Richard II's kingdom deteriorated. Five men formed themselves into a group called the Lords Appellant, as they wished to appeal the king's chief supporters and allies for treason. The five were Richard II's uncle Thomas of Woodstock, duke of Gloucester; Richard Fitzalan or Arundel, earl of Arundel; Thomas Beauchamp, earl of Warwick; John of Gaunt's son and heir Henry of Lancaster, earl of Derby; and Thomas Mowbray, earl of Nottingham. Mowbray's inclusion is perhaps surprising as he had previously always been a supporter, ally and friend of Richard, but he had married the earl of Arundel's daughter in *c.* 1384, and his nose had perhaps been put out of joint by Richard II's devotion to Robert de Vere.

Matters came to a head in December 1387 when Henry of Lancaster defeated Robert de Vere at Radcot Bridge in Oxfordshire, and almost captured him. De Vere marched an army from Cheshire towards London, intending to join the king, but Henry of Lancaster was waiting for him at Radcot Bridge with his own force. Robert managed to escape and fled from England; he would never return, and as far as is known, Philippa de Coucy, who was still only 20 years old, never saw her husband (or former husband, if de Vere did manage to end their marriage) again. Even if their marriage was not officially annulled, given that Philippa preferred to remain in England rather than accompany her husband overseas, their marriage would not appear to have been a happy one. On 25 March 1388, Richard II, or someone else acting in his name, confirmed a grant of lands to Philippa originally made to her and Robert in October 1382, 'in consideration of her being of the royal stock'.[1] A few weeks after Robert de Vere's flight, the Lords Appellant held a long and vengeful parliament in London known as the Merciless Parliament, and numerous other supporters of King Richard, including Michael de la Pole, earl of Suffolk, and Sir James Berners, were either executed or exiled. The king's uncle and Constance of York's father Edmund of Langley, a moderate politician and on good terms with Richard II throughout his reign – a not insignificant achievement – tried but failed to protect the men. Richard, shocked and grieving, was unable to protect his friends either, and vowed revenge on the Appellants or at least on the oldest three of them, Gloucester, Arundel and Warwick. It would take him close to a decade, but he finally managed to do so in the autumn of 1397.

Elizabeth of Lancaster and her husband Sir John Holland returned to England from Iberia in 1388, leaving her father, stepmother, sister and half-sister behind, and John was made earl of Huntingdon by his half-brother. Richard II gave John a 'certain inn in Lumbardestrete', i.e. Lombard Street in London, which had belonged to the exiled Michael de la Pole, earl of Suffolk, on 7 April 1388.[2] Elizabeth's former husband John Hastings, earl of Pembroke, still only 17 years old, was killed jousting during the Christmas festivities of 1389. He had married Philippa Mortimer, the younger daughter of Elizabeth's late cousin Philippa of Clarence, countess of March and Ulster, but she was only 14 when John died, and they had no children. Elizabeth's feelings about the sudden death of the young husband she had rejected were not recorded.

Elizabeth's father John of Gaunt, stepmother Costanza of Castile and half-sister Catalina of Lancaster were in Bordeaux in early 1388, where they watched five members of Gaunt's household jousting against five men of Charles VI of France's allegiance, who were members of the marshal of France's household, over three days in the square in front of the cathedral.[3] After this event, Froissart says, Duchess Costanza began preparing to travel to Castile to arrange and attend Catalina's wedding, which the couple had been planning all winter, to Catalina's second cousin Enrique of Castile, King Juan's son from his first marriage to Leonor of Aragon.

On 12 June 1387, John of Gaunt and King Juan of Castile had come to a preliminary agreement in Trancoso in Portugal, which was finally ratified in the Gascon city of Bayonne in July 1388 and is therefore generally known as the Treaty of Bayonne. The treaty stipulated that in exchange for renouncing all his and Costanza's claims to the kingdom of Castile, Gaunt would receive a one-off payment of £100,000 plus a pension of £6,600 every year for life. The money was to be transported to England on the backs of forty-seven mules. Both John of Gaunt and Duchess Costanza swore on the Gospels in 1387/88 that Catalina would marry Juan's son Enrique, and Juan in turn promised that the wedding would go ahead within two months of Catalina being handed over into his custody. The king also promised that Catalina would be looked after 'in seemly and secure conditions', at his own expense, by people whom her father would appoint, until Enrique was old enough for the marriage to be consummated. If anything happened to young Enrique before he married Catalina, she would marry his younger brother Don Fernando (born in November 1380, a future king of Aragon and Majorca) instead. Finally, if Catalina and Enrique failed to have children together, the kingdom of Castile would fall to Edward of York (b. 1373/74), as the first son of Costanza's sister Isabel of Castile and Gaunt's brother Edmund of Langley. It is unfortunate that Duchess Costanza's reaction to the treaty and to her daughter's marriage is not recorded; in his will of 1362, her father Pedro ordered her, Isabel and their older sister Beatriz never to marry into the family of Enrique of Trastámara, or the families of Enrique's younger brothers Tello and Sancho. If they did so, they would risk being cursed by God and by Pedro himself. He had not specifically said that his daughters should not arrange the marriages of their children into the illegitimate Trastámara branch of the family, but perhaps Costanza's conscience still troubled her.

The fifth article of the Treaty of Bayonne was an important one, stating that when young Enrique was acknowledged as rightful king of Castile after his father Juan's death, Catalina of Lancaster would be 'received and recognised' as queen. As it turned out, Enrique died in his twenties leaving his and Catalina's infant son Juan II as king, and Catalina thereafter ruled Castile as joint regent with her brother-in-law Don Fernando. On 5 August 1388, Catalina declared herself bound by the treaty and stated that she would freely enter into her Castilian marriage, and on 26 August, King Juan delivered sixty hostages to Gaunt. That same month, the king of Aragon addressed a letter to young Enrique of Castile as prince of Asturias, duke of Soria and lord of Molina, titles which, as his wife, Catalina of Lancaster would share. After her marriage, therefore, Catalina became known as the *princesa de Asturias*.[4] John of Gaunt's daughter and son-in-law would rule one day in Castile and Leon and would unite the rival branches of the Castilian royal family, but the duke of Lancaster's own long-term dream of becoming the ruler of two Spanish kingdoms by right of his wife was over.

Gaunt, Costanza and Catalina travelled from Bordeaux to Bayonne after watching the three-day jousting event in front of the cathedral, then Costanza and Catalina went on to Dax, while Gaunt returned to Bordeaux. Mother and daughter spent two days at Dax, then travelled through the Basque country, over the Pyrenees via the pass at Roncesvalles and on to Pamplona, where the king and queen of Navarre 'received them grandly and honourably' because Queen Leonor of Navarre was the sister of the king of Castile, and Costanza's first cousin.[5] Costanza and Catalina stayed for over a month in the kingdom of Navarre with the king and queen, and finally crossed the border into Castile. All the important people of Castile, Galicia, Seville, Cordoba and Toledo came to see them enter the kingdom, in order to see the young half-Castilian, half-English girl, Catalina of Lancaster, who would marry their king's son and would one day become their queen, while King Juan himself met them at Burgos.

Duchess Costanza then went to Montiel, where her father Pedro had been defeated in battle by her uncle Enrique of Trastámara in 1369. Pedro was buried in Montiel after Trastámara stabbed him to death in the aftermath of the battle, and Jean Froissart states, possibly incorrectly, that Costanza exhumed his remains and took his body to Seville where she had him 'richly and honourably' reinterred in the great cathedral there. King Juan attended the funeral of the man his father had killed, as did his son Enrique and his soon-to-be daughter-in-law Catalina, King Pedro's granddaughter and heir. Afterwards, Costanza went to Medina del Campo (or 'Medine-de-Camp' as chronicler Jean Froissart calls it, a 'beautiful and large city of which she was lady') thirty miles from Valladolid, and stayed there for a while with her retinue.

Froissart, unfortunately, gives no details of the subsequent wedding of young Enrique of Castile and Catalina of Lancaster, though no doubt it was a magnificent and well-attended state occasion, held in the cathedral of San Antolín in Palencia on 17 September 1388. A Spanish chronicler states that there were many jousts, feasts and 'very big celebrations', and that King Juan gave gifts of jewels to the English knights who were present. John of Gaunt remained in Bordeaux and did not attend his daughter's wedding in person, though sent King Juan *una corona de oro muy fermosa*, 'a very beautiful gold crown', with which the duke had once hoped to be crowned king of Castile and Leon himself. The bridegroom Enrique was born in October 1379 a few months after his grandfather Enrique of Trastámara died and his father acceded to the throne, and was not yet 9 years old when he married, while Catalina, born sometime between early June 1372 and the end of March 1373, was 15 or 16 (though the Spanish chronicler who wrote about her wedding thought that she was 14). Despite the age difference between them of at least six and a half years and perhaps more than seven, Enrique was to address his wife a few years later as 'the one I love as well as my own heart', *como aquella que amo como a mi coraçón.*[6] It seems highly likely that Catalina had been taught her mother's native Castilian while growing up in England, and communication with her new husband and her Spanish relatives was surely not a problem.

Another Spanish chronicler who stated, as noted above, that in adulthood Catalina was 'tall and very heavyset, fair, rosy and blonde', also said that she was 'very modest and carefully guarded herself and her reputation. She was liberal and generous, but highly influenced and easily swayed by her favourites ... not very well disciplined in her personal habits.' The same chronicler said of Enrique that when he grew to manhood,

> [h]e was of medium height and of quite a pleasant disposition. He was fair and blond and had a somewhat turned-up nose. But when he reached 17 or 18 years of age, he suffered several bouts of serious illness that weakened his body ... As a result, he lost the good looks that he at one time had. His illness was even the cause of great changes in his personality ... he became sad and irritable. He was unpleasant to look at and very hard to talk to.

Catalina and Enrique's son King Juan II (born in March 1405 sixteen and a half years after their wedding) took after his parents: he was described as 'tall and handsome, fair-skinned and slightly ruddy' with hair 'the colour of a very mature hazelnut, the nose a little snub, the eyes between green and blue ... very graceful legs and feet and hands'. Juan was an excellent musician and dancer, sang and composed poems, and enjoyed riding and hunting.[7]

Although Catalina's mother Costanza and her aunt Isabel, duchess of York, had lived in England since they were teenagers, Catalina did have other relatives in Castile: her mother's half-siblings. The Treaty of Bayonne provided for the release from prison of Duchess Costanza's half-brothers Juan and Diego, illegitimate sons of King Pedro, who had been incarcerated by their uncle King Enrique of Trastámara. A third illegitimate half-brother, Sancho, the elder son of Pedro's mistress Isabel de Sandoval and the full brother of Diego, had died in captivity in 1371 at the age of 8. In 1409 almost forty years after his death, Sancho's niece Catalina, then the dowager queen-consort of Castile, wrote to the prioress of Santo Domingo el Real in Toledo, Teresa de Ayala (who, following in the footsteps of her and King Pedro's illegitimate daughter María, had joined the priory in 1396). Catalina asked Teresa to take charge of reburying the remains of 'Don Sancho, my uncle' in her priory, from his original resting place in Toro.[8]

Unfortunately for Catalina's other uncles Juan and Diego, they were not released from prison in the late 1380s as they should have been, and Catalina's son Juan II finally set his great-uncle Diego free in 1424 after he had spent decades in captivity. Several letters from Diego to his half-sister María de Ayala in 1420 reveals that the long-dead Pedro the Cruel's illegitimate children enjoyed very close and affectionate relations, and that they kept in touch for many years. Diego referred to himself as *Yo don Diego fijo de my señor el rrey don Pedro que dios dé santo parayso*, 'I, Don Diego, son of my lord the king Don Pedro, may God grant him holy paradise', and addressed María as *hermana señora* or 'lady sister' and as 'the one I love in my heart'.[9] As for their half-brother Juan, a descendant of the kings of Castile via both his parents and a nephew of the famous Inês de Castro, the assassinated mistress or perhaps wife of King Pedro I of Portugal, he died still in captivity in Soria Castle in 1405 at the age of 50. In the meantime, he had married his warder Beltrán de Eril's daughter Elvira and fathered two children who lived into adulthood: Pedro (d. 1461), bishop of Osma and Palencia, and Costanza (d. 1478), another prioress of Santo Domingo el Real in Toledo, whom Juan and Elvira might have named in honour of Juan's half-sister who was only six months his senior, the duchess of Lancaster. While she was queen-consort and dowager queen-consort of Castile, Catalina of Lancaster did everything she could to support her cousins Pedro and Costanza forge successful careers in the Church, where she placed them for their own safety and protection; as legitimately-born grandchildren of King Pedro the Cruel, their Trastámara kinsmen might eventually come to view them as a threat to their position.[10]

Chapter 14

Two Queens and A Poet

Around 1390 or 1391, Thomas of Woodstock's eldest daughter Anne of Gloucester married Thomas Stafford, earl of Stafford, perhaps as a means of ending the feud between their fathers which had begun in 1383. Anne, born in early May 1383, was only about 7 or 8 years old when she married, and Thomas was fourteen years her senior. The marriage did not last long and was never consummated. Also around 1390 or a little later, Anne's cousin Marie de Coucy gave birth in France to one of her sons, Robert or Enguerrand de Bar (it is not entirely clear which of her two sons was the elder).[1]

Some of Queen Philippa of Portugal's letters still exist and reveal that she kept herself well informed of events in England, and took a keen interest in them and in her relatives there. She exchanged correspondence with the nobly-born bishop of Norwich, Henry Despenser (born *c.* 1341/42), who was a descendant of Edward I and thus Philippa's kinsman. Several of their amicable letters in French to each other survive, and reveal that Philippa addressed Henry as 'Reverend father in God, my dearest and most entirely beloved cousin' and that he addressed her as 'Very excellent and very dread, very gracious, and my sovereign lady'. Henry sent Philippa expensive cloth on two occasions for which she thanked him, and at another time told her that he had been 'a little ill' (*un poy malade*) but that God's mercy and Philippa's lovely letters containing good news of herself and her family had 'cured him completely'.[2]

Philippa's close association with Bishop Henry, given her father John of Gaunt's furious disgust that parliament gave Henry money to lead a campaign to Flanders in 1382/83 in preference to funding Gaunt's campaign in Iberia, is perhaps surprising. Bishop Henry might have been the person responsible for sending a manuscript of a poem by the English writer John Gower (*c.* 1330–1408) to Queen Philippa in Portugal. Philippa certainly owned a manuscript of Gower's poem *Confessio Amantis* ('The

Lover's Confession'), which was translated from Middle English into Portuguese by Robert Payn, an English-born canon of Lisbon Cathedral who was named as a member of Queen Philippa's household in the early 1400s. She might also have sent a copy of the Castilian translation of the poem to her half-sister Queen Catalina.[3] Unlike his near-contemporary Geoffrey Chaucer (*c.* 1342–1400), who wrote exclusively in English and specifically in the London dialect, John Gower composed his works in English, French and Latin, a fact perhaps appreciated by the trilingual Catalina of Lancaster. As well as the *Confessio Amantis*, which, despite its Latin title, was composed in English, Gower wrote the *Vox Clamantis* ('The Voice of One Crying') in Latin and the *Mirour de l'Omme* ('The Mirror of Mankind') in medieval French.

The prince and princess of Asturias succeeded as king and queen of Castile just after Enrique's eleventh birthday, after King Juan died on 9 October 1390 at only 32 years old, following a fall from his horse. Catalina, who was 17 or 18, became regent for her young husband, because unlike in England, there were many precedents in Castile for a female regent. One of them was Sancho IV's widow María de Molina (d. 1321), who ruled for her underage son Fernando IV in and after 1295 and again for her infant grandson Alfonso XI in and after 1312. Another was the great Queen Berenguela (1180–1246), eldest child of Alfonso VIII, who surrendered her rights to the throne of Castile to her 16-year-old son Fernando III in 1217 and who acted as his regent and chief adviser for many years. Catalina of Lancaster was descended from Queen Berenguela via both her parents, and must have been well aware of her illustrious predecessor. Over the next few years, Catalina and her half-sister Queen Philippa of Portugal pursued pro-English policies, promoted Portuguese and Castilian alliances with England, and kept in frequent touch with their English relatives.[4] The young King Enrique was, however, to assume power in his own right in August 1393 at not yet 14 years old , so Catalina's first regency in Castile – her second was for her underage son – proved rather short. The young king suffered from ill health and was, and still is, known as *Enrique el Doliente*, 'Henry the Sufferer'. As a result of his bad health, he was unable to lead armies, though is well-known for his jealous preservation of royal power. One modern writer has called Enrique 'a tenacious ruler' who 'tamed the nobility' of his kingdom.[5]

Thomas Mowbray, earl of Nottingham, sent a letter on 27 June 1391 to John Holland, earl of Huntingdon, regarding a marriage between his son and heir the younger Thomas (b. September 1385) and John and Elizabeth of Lancaster's daughter Constance Holland. The earl of Nottingham was the grandson and, since the death of his cousin, Elizabeth's first husband John Hastings of Pembroke, the sole heir of Margaret, countess of Norfolk. On 15 February 1392, Mowbray and Holland were still discussing the future marriage of their children, and the wedding went ahead before 12 September 1392. Richard II paid £200 for the festivities.[6] Young Thomas Mowbray was aged 7 or almost at the time of his wedding, and Constance was a year or so younger.

Philippa de Coucy, the duchess of Ireland and countess of Oxford, was in Richard II's company or just before 20 December 1391, when he pardoned a man for murder at her request.[7] A couple of months later on 27 February 1392, Philippa was 'about to go to France to the lord of Coucy, her father, there to stay for a time and to return to England'. According to Jean Froissart, who refers to her as 'a young lady who was called Madam of Ireland', while overseas Philippa took part in talks regarding a truce between France and England at Amiens, and travelled to her father's homeland in the company of her uncles John of Gaunt and Edmund of Langley. Froissart states that she had a 'very ardent desire' to see her father Enguerrand, who was also present, and indeed, it does seem that father and daughter had an affectionate and close relationship, for all that they had lived in different (and usually mutually hostile) countries since Philippa was 9 years old. Philippa, and the attendants she took to France with her, lodged with her father throughout her stay.[8] Perhaps she took the time to visit her sister Marie as well during her visit to her father's homeland, though there is little evidence that the two de Coucy sisters got on well. In the summer of 1392, Philippa's estranged and exiled husband Robert de Vere died, and it may be, according to one chronicler, that he was killed while hunting wild boar in Louvain in modern-day Belgium.[9] His body was returned for burial to his birthplace, Earls Colne Priory in Essex, three years later on 22 November 1395, and King Richard attended the funeral. Perhaps Philippa was there too, for her mother-in-law Maud Ufford's sake, if nothing else. Maud had gone to visit her son in exile: Richard II pardoned her in May 1391 'for crossing the sea without licence to

Brabant to confer with her son Robert de Veer, late earl of Oxford, and for relieving him with certain gifts'.[10]

Philippa spent more time at court with her cousin the king over the next few years. She and Thomas Mowbray, earl of Nottingham, worked together in April 1394 to secure a royal pardon for one Thomas Bilderston, convicted of murder, and Philippa was with Richard II again on 19 May 1396, 23 July 1396, 18 April 1397 and 19 May 1399.[11] On 21 August 1395, Richard II, and perhaps Philippa herself, considered the possibility that she might marry again: he granted her an income of 300 marks (£200) a year 'to cease during such time as she resides in the king's household or when she is married by the king'.[12] In fact, Philippa never did marry again, and had perhaps had little or no joy whatsoever from marriage to de Vere: he was involved in some kind of intense and perhaps sexual relationship with King Richard, and whether he truly did annul their marriage to wed Agnes Launcekrona instead, it seems almost certain that Agnes was his mistress.

Chapter 15

A Young Widow and a Visit to Hungary

Probably in March 1392, John of Gaunt supervised the wedding of his and Katherine Swynford's teenage daughter Joan Beaufort to the young nobleman Robert Ferrers. In Jean Froissart's detailed account of a jousting tournament held at St Inglevert near Calais in northern France two years earlier, from 20 March until 24 April 1390, four men are grouped together as the knights who took part in the jousts on 20 April, near the end of this famous tournament. They were Gaunt's heir Henry of Lancaster, earl of Derby (*le conte d'Erby*); Henry's half-brother, Gaunt's eldest illegitimate son Sir John Beaufort, 'bastard of Lancaster' (*Monseigneur Jehan de Biaufort, bastart de Lanclastre*); a man Froissart names as 'Sir Thomas Subincorde', which presumably is a garbled rendering of the name Swynford, identifying this man as Thomas Swynford, son of John of Gaunt's mistress Katherine and her late husband Sir Hugh Swynford, who, like Henry of Lancaster, was the Beaufort siblings' older half-brother; and Sir Robert Ferrers, whose inclusion in this family group strongly implies that his marriage to Joan Beaufort was already under discussion some two years before it took place. Another family member who competed in the St Inglevert jousts was Elizabeth of Lancaster's husband Sir John Holland (*Monseigneur Jehan de Holande*).[1] John was not, however, grouped together with the other four knights, and it may be that his controversial marriage to Elizabeth in the summer of 1386, and her possible pregnancy by him while she was still married to the adolescent earl of Pembroke, had created some tensions or conflict between Holland and Elizabeth's brother Henry and half-brother John Beaufort.

Robert Ferrers was born around 1371 or 1373 so was some years older than Joan Beaufort, and his father Robert the elder, first Lord Ferrers of Wem (d. 1381), was the younger brother of John, Lord Ferrers of Chartley, who was killed fighting alongside Gaunt, his brother Edward of Woodstock and King Pedro the Cruel at the battle of Nájera in 1367. An entry in Gaunt's register in February 1382 indicates that the younger Robert Ferrers was in Gaunt's wardship after his father died, so it makes sense that the duke would have arranged his young ward's marriage to his daughter.[2] Joan's new husband was heir to his late father and was also heir to the much larger inheritance of his mother Elizabeth Botiller or Boteler, though in the end Elizabeth outlived her son by many years, and he never held any of the lands which she kept in her own hands. Robert Ferrers of Wem the elder and Elizabeth Botiller were landowners in Warwickshire, Shropshire, Staffordshire and Leicestershire.[3]

Joan Ferrers née Beaufort gave birth to two Ferrers daughters: Elizabeth, named after Joan's mother-in-law, and Mary, perhaps named in honour of the Virgin Mary or after a godmother (although this is only speculation, perhaps her godmother was Joan's sister-in-law Mary de Bohun, countess of Derby, who certainly kept in frequent touch with her husband Henry of Lancaster's Beaufort half-kin). Between 24 August and 3 September 1411, the two Ferrers sisters were named as the heirs of their paternal grandmother Elizabeth Botiller when her inquisition post mortem was taken in various counties, and were said to be 18 and 17 years old at the time. These ages would place the elder daughter Elizabeth's birth sometime between August 1392 and August 1393, and the younger daughter Mary's sometime between August 1393 and August 1394.[4] Assuming Joan Beaufort and Robert Ferrers did marry in March 1392, the earliest possible birthdate for their first daughter is December 1392, so it is likely that Elizabeth Ferrers was born sometime between then and the following August. She was the first grandchild of John of Gaunt and Katherine Swynford.[5]

On 20 May 1392, Thomas of Woodstock betrothed his and Eleanor de Bohun's second daughter Joan of Gloucester to Gilbert, son and heir of Richard, Lord Talbot (d. September 1396) and Ankaret Lestrange. The couple married at an unknown date before 1400, though had no children together.[6] Gilbert Talbot was born after September 1383, probably not too long after, and was about 8 years old when he was betrothed in May 1392. Joan, born sometime between her older sister Anne in May 1383 and her younger sister Isabel in April 1386, was a little younger than he.[7] Just a few weeks later on 4 July 1392, Anne of Gloucester was left a widow at only 9 years old when Thomas, earl of Stafford, died in his early twenties. His heir was his brother William, third son of the late earl, Hugh (d. 1386). William, born on 22 September 1377, himself died on 6 April 1395 several years before he would have come of age at 21, leaving his brother Edmund Stafford, fourth of Hugh's five sons, as his heir. Edmund was said to be 17 in November 1395.[8] Anne was entitled by law to hold a third of her late husband's large inheritance, despite her youth and despite the fact that the marriage cannot have been consummated, and on 8 February 1393 she received a generous endowment of lands, including a third of the castle of Tonbridge in Kent. Custody of the other two-thirds of the Stafford inheritance was given to her father the duke of Gloucester on 24 July 1392, for him to hold until Thomas's brother and heir William Stafford came of age (though in fact he never did). Although Anne's parents were alive, three 'guardians' were appointed to look after her legal interests: John Burton and Thomas Ferriby, clerks, and William Nafferton.[9]

Anne's much older cousin Philippa of Lancaster, queen of Portugal, bore three sons between October 1391 and March 1394, and afterwards had a well-deserved break from childbearing for three years. On 31 October 1391, she gave birth to a son she named Duarte after her grandfather Edward III of England; Duarte was Philippa's second son, but after his older brother Afonso died in 1400, he became his father's heir and ultimately succeeded him as king of Portugal. Dom Pedro, later duke of Coímbra, was born on 9 December 1392, and Dom Henrique 'the Navigator', later duke of Viseu and a famous early European explorer, on 4 March 1394, perhaps in Porto, where he was baptised (a building there called the *Casa do Infante* or 'Prince's House' is traditionally said to be Henrique's birthplace). Queen Philippa, who continued to take a deep interest in the affairs of her homeland, remained in fairly frequent touch with her cousin Richard II, and in early 1393 he pardoned a man for murder 'at the request of the queen of Portugal'. The man was Simon Godard, 'servant in the Tolboth of Lenn', i.e. the tollbooth in the Norfolk port of King's Lynn, who some years earlier had killed one William Keche in the port. It may be that Simon Godard was a supporter of Philippa's friend and kinsman Henry Despenser, bishop of Norwich, who enjoyed considerable influence in the county of Norfolk, and that Despenser had asked the queen to intercede with her cousin on Godard's behalf.[10]

Constance of York lost her Spanish mother on 23 December 1392 when Isabel of Castile, duchess of York, died at the age of only 37 and was buried in Langley Priory, Hertfordshire, a few weeks later. In her will, Isabel left 'my beloved daughter Constance la Despenser' seven frets with pearls, i.e. head-coverings made of interlaced wire and jewels, her best fillet, i.e. a headband also made of interlaced wire and jewels, and various vessels of silver. She also left items to John Holland, earl of Huntingdon, and he was the only person left bequests who was not a close member of her family or a servant. This perhaps adds fuel to the fire of the allegations that Isabel and John had an affair, or at least that they had enjoyed some kind of close association. It is also surely revealing that Isabel did not mention her sister Costanza, duchess of Lancaster, at all in her will. She did leave a 'tablet of jasper' to Costanza's husband John of Gaunt, which Levon, king of Armenian Cilicia, had given to her during a visit to England a few years earlier, and a crown to her elder son Edward, with strict instructions never to sell it or give it away but to keep it within the family. This was perhaps the 'French crown' which her father had bequeathed to her in 1362 and which had once belonged to Pedro's mistreated wife Blanche de Bourbon, assuming that Isabel ever received the items left to her in Pedro's will. Her youngest child Richard of Conisbrough, earl of Cambridge (b. 1385), had a 'crown of Spain' in his possession in 1415, though this appears to have been more of a helmet than a crown likely to have been worn by a woman, and was most probably not the same one.[11]

The widowed Edmund of Langley married his second wife within a year of Duchess Isabel's death: Joan Holland, second of the five daughters of Thomas Holland, earl of Kent (d. 1397), and niece of John Holland, earl of Huntingdon. Joan was about thirty-five or forty years younger than her husband, and probably a little younger than Constance of York, her new stepdaughter. Constance and her husband Thomas Despenser must have consummated their marriage sometime in the early 1390s, depending when Constance reached maturity, and King Richard allowed Thomas possession of his large inheritance in Wales and England in March 1394, six months before he came of age at 21.[12]

In Castile, King Enrique III took personal control of his kingdom in August 1393, though he was still only 13 (he turned 14 that October). Catalina of Lancaster was now 20 or 21, and surely cannot have consummated her marriage until her husband was at least 14 and perhaps

16. As far as the record shows, she did not become pregnant until 1400 when Enrique was 20, though it is possible that she had miscarriages or stillbirths before that. Enrique's minority was not without incident: in 1391, a series of horrible anti-Jewish riots and pogroms had taken place across Castile. Catalina's grandfather King Pedro 'the Cruel' had, for all his deservedly atrocious reputation, been friendly towards his Jewish and Muslim subjects and had protected them; his half-brother Enrique of Trastámara sneered at him as 'the son of a Jewish whore, calling himself king of Castile', affecting to believe that Pedro's mother was a Jewish servant, not Alfonso XI's queen Maria of Portugal, which would explain his cordial relations with his Jewish subjects. Trastámara also made much use of Pedro's presumed fondness for Muslim Castilians as a propaganda tool against him.[13] By stark contrast, Trastámara himself – perhaps, at least in part, to differentiate himself from the legitimate half-brother he loathed and whose religious tolerance he emphatically did not share – ordered the massacre of large numbers of Jewish people on three known occasions, in 1355, 1360 and 1366.[14] In the late 1370s near the end of Enrique's reign, a man named Ferrand Martinez, who was the archdeacon of the town of Écija and was also a canon of the cathedral in nearby Seville, emerged as a zealous anti-Semitic fanatic determined to throw fuel on the fire started by King Enrique's intolerance towards his Jewish subjects. Martinez furiously denounced the Jewish population of Castile on every possible occasion, denied them their legal rights wherever possible, and sent letters to the local authorities throughout the diocese of Seville ordering them to expel their Jewish populations.

In 1382 and 1383, Juan I ordered Martinez to desist these provocations, but to little effect, and throughout the 1380s the situation worsened. King Juan's death in 1390 and the accession of the child-king Enrique III, and the death in the same year of Barroso, archbishop of Toledo and primate of Spain, emboldened Ferrand Martinez to greater heights – or rather, depths – of anti-Semitism. He ordered the destruction of all the synagogues in Seville and elsewhere in Castile and the seizure of all Jewish holy books, and his fanatical rabble-rousing led to tragic consequences when in June 1391 the Judería, the Jewish quarter of Seville, was sacked and most of its 4,000 inhabitants massacred. Murderous intolerance towards the Jewish population spread like wildfire through Castile, and many thousands were killed or forcibly converted to Christianity (thus creating a large class of people known as *conversos*). On assuming his majority in 1393, the teenage Enrique III did his utmost to restore order to his kingdom and to put an end to the tragic and terrible years of murderous anti-Semitic prejudice.[15]

John Holland, earl of Huntingdon, received letters of protection in January 1394 to travel as an envoy to Sigismund, king of Hungary and Croatia, younger brother of his sister-in-law Anne of Bohemia, queen of England. King Richard asked John to travel to Paris to talk to Charles VI of France after returning from his mission to Hungary, and on 5 June that year, John was also, according to the pope, 'going with some persons in his company against the Turks and other enemies of Christ'. It was a very busy year for him.[16] Elizabeth of Lancaster gave birth on 29 March 1395, so John Holland must either have been in England in late June or early July 1394 to conceive this child, or, much more probably, Elizabeth went with him on his long sojourn in Hungary, France and elsewhere. A Hungarian writer, Attila Bárány, has provided evidence that Holland was in Hungary in May and June 1394, having passed through the county of Savoy on his way there in very early March 1394, and did not return to England until the very end of 1394 or beginning of 1395. Assuming that Holland met Sigismund before 20 June 1394, Bárány states that he might have accompanied the Hungarian king on a campaign in Bosnia and therefore did fight against 'the Turks and other enemies of Christ', as stated by Pope Boniface IX. Sigismund set off on this campaign at the end of June 1394, more or less exactly the time when a child born on 29 March 1395 would have been conceived.[17] Presumably, as John acknowledged the child as his, Elizabeth was with him in Hungary to conceive the infant, though her presence there was not mentioned.

King Richard must have grieved deeply for the loss of Robert de Vere in 1392, and another terrible loss came in June 1394 when his beloved wife and queen Anne of Bohemia died at the age of only 28. The cause of her death is unknown, though the year 1394 was a bad one for English royal and noble ladies: Costanza of Castile, duchess of Lancaster, died in March that year at the age of not quite 40, and in early July, Mary de Bohun, countess of Derby, the sister-in-law of Costanza's stepdaughters Elizabeth and Philippa of Lancaster, died as well.[18] She left six children, and, probably born in or a little before December 1370, was only 23 years old. Neither lady left a will, and the many valuable items which Duchess Costanza's father King Pedro left her in his own will of November 1362 were presumably sent to her daughter and heir Catalina in Castile (assuming, given the chaotic circumstances of Pedro's downfall and death, that Costanza had ever received them). The items he had bequeathed to her included 100,000 *doblas doro* or gold coins, a sizeable number of seed pearls, a gold cup, a crown which had once belonged to Costanza's grandfather Alfonso XI, another crown decorated with eagles which had once belonged to Pedro's aunt Leonor of Castile, queen of Aragon (whose assassination Pedro ordered in 1359 because she rebelled against him and encouraged her sons to do the same), and a third crown which Pedro had had made in Seville. This last crown was set with a large balas ruby which had once been in the possession of 'King Bermejo', the name given by Pedro and other Christians to Abu Abdullah Muhammad VI, emir of Granada. A chronicler says that in April 1362, Pedro invited Muhammad and thirty-six members of his entourage to Seville, where, after dining with them, he had them killed and stripped of their valuables.[19] If this tale is true, the valuables presumably included the large ruby which Pedro willed to Costanza seven months later. Pedro bequeathed more of his possessions to Costanza than to her sisters Beatriz and Isabel, perhaps indicating that she was his favourite child.

Chapter 16

A Scandalous Marriage

Elizabeth of Lancaster gave birth to her second son, John Holland the younger, in Dartington, Devon, on 29 March 1395. Thomas Cullyng, abbot of Tavistock, and John Shealdon, prior of Plympton, were the boy's godfathers, and Shealdon gave the infant a generous gift of £20. Local knights Sir John Pomeroy and Sir John Dinham attended the baptism, and twenty-four men were hired to carry twenty-four 'large unlit candles' to the church, which were lit 'immediately after John's name was given'. John Holland the elder, who apparently by now had returned to England from fighting the Turks and from accompanying King Richard on a visit to Ireland during the winter of 1394/95, hired a local woman named Isabel Hugh to act as his son's wet-nurse, and told her husband John Hugh not to have marital relations with his wife for the duration. Hugh took himself off to Guernsey in the Channel Islands and remained there for three years.[1] John Holland the younger, though born as a second son, became his father's heir when his elder brother Richard died in childhood, and in the early 1430s was to become duke of Exeter.

Elizabeth had sufficiently recovered from the birth of her child by 9 June 1395 to travel the 200 miles to London with her husband, presumably leaving their infant in Dartington with his wet-nurse Isabel Hugh and other attendants. On that date, Elizabeth and John made a generous grant to two men named Martin Ferrers and Warin Waldegrave: the house in Lombard Street in London given to them by King Richard in 1388, and all their tenements in Lombard Street and Cornhill. The mayor of London, John Fresshe, and the two city sheriffs, William Brampton and Thomas Knolles, witnessed the grant.[2] Elizabeth and John were back at Dartington on 8 April 1396, when three men granted them the reversion of one manor and part of another manor. The list of witnesses included Edward Courtenay, earl of Devon (d. 1419), a descendant of

Edward I and thus a kinsman of both Elizabeth and Holland, and his uncle Sir Philip Courtenay (d. 1406), brother of William Courtenay, archbishop of Canterbury, who died later in 1396. The archbishop's successor was another nobleman, Thomas Arundel, younger brother of the earl of Arundel and the countesses of Hereford and Kent.[3] Arundel had been archbishop of York since 1388, when he was only in his mid-thirties, and was transferred to the see of Canterbury.

It seems that in the 1390s, as well as his journeys abroad to fight for the pope – he was to go again in 1397, as captain-general of the pope's army – John Holland, earl of Huntingdon, might have committed piracy in Denmark. At some point between 1388 and 1397, Holland's barge, the *Barge Seint Johan*, was seized and detained by the mayor and bailiffs of Kingston-on-Hull, because they believed the vessel 'was bound on a piratical expedition to Denmark'.[4] If he did, it would seem to fit quite well with what we know of his character, though John was apparently far more conventionally pious that one might expect of a man who committed torture and murder and who seduced married, royal women. A list of his possessions seized after his death included five breviaries (books containing the daily service for the divine office), a missal (books containing all the liturgical texts for the celebration of Mass throughout the year), and another dozen religious books worth a total of more than £45.[5] John's half-brother King Richard, meanwhile, attended the funeral of his cousin Philippa de Coucy's late husband Robert de Vere, earl of Oxford, in Essex in late 1395, and rather morbidly had the coffin opened so that he could gaze on the beloved earl's face. Most of the English nobility stayed away from the funeral, because they 'had not yet swallowed the hate they had conceived against Robert'.[6]

In February 1396 just under two years after Costanza of Castile's death, John of Gaunt caused a huge scandal when he married his long-term lover Katherine Swynford. It is almost impossible to overstate how incredibly unusual it was for an Englishman of royal birth to marry a knight's daughter who had been his lover for many years, but Gaunt deeply loved the remarkable Katherine and their children, and wished to make their four Beaufort children legitimate and to increase their fortunes. John's sister-in-law the duchess of Gloucester, Eleanor de Bohun, and his great-niece the countess of Pembroke and Arundel, Philippa Mortimer, publicly demonstrated their horror that a woman they considered of low birth now outranked them. Jean Froissart states that they refused to acknowledge the new duchess and declared that their 'hearts would burst with grief' if they had to give her precedence (Duchess Katherine became the first lady in England on marriage, as Queen Anne was dead and King Richard had not yet married his second wife).[7] A year later on 9 February 1397, Gaunt and Katherine's Beaufort children were legitimised, and John the eldest was made earl of Somerset.[8]

Joan Beaufort's husband Robert Ferrers of Wem might still have been alive on 7 July 1396, when an entry on the Patent Roll talks of 'trespasses' committed against him and does not explicitly state that he was then dead.[9] No inquisition post mortem exists for him, however, because his mother held all the lands of his inheritance and outlived him by a decade and a half, and therefore we do not know the date of his death. Joan, as the soon to be legitimate daughter of a royal duke who was the second man in the realm after his nephew the king, married her second husband Ralph Neville (b. *c.* 1364), one of the greatest noblemen in the north of England, before 29 November 1396 when they were first mentioned on the Patent Roll as a married couple.[10] Ralph's first wife Margaret Stafford had died on 9 June 1396, so both Joan and Ralph had been recently widowed when they married each other. Their marriage was to produce as many as thirteen or fourteen children, and their eldest child was probably Eleanor, Lady Despenser and countess of Northumberland, born perhaps in 1397. Their second daughter was Katherine, duchess of Norfolk, who was old enough to give birth in 1415, and their eldest son and heir was Richard, earl of Salisbury. As he had the same name as the king, it seems possible that Richard Neville was born before September 1399, when Joan Beaufort's half-brother Henry of Lancaster forced Richard II's abdication and became king of England.

Marie de Coucy's husband Henri de Bar and her father Enguerrand de Coucy both fought at the battle of Nicopolis on the River Danube in Bulgaria on 25 September 1396, and were, with numerous other French noblemen such as the counts of Nevers and Eu, both captured and held for ransom.[11] This battle was fought as part of the long Christian campaigns against the Muslim Ottomans, led by Sultan Bayezid; the overall Christian commander was Sigismund, king of Hungary and Croatia, younger brother of Richard II's late queen Anne of Bohemia. Sigismund, unlike Henri de Bar and his father-in-law Enguerrand, managed to flee from the battlefield after their heavy defeat. Marie de Coucy would never see her husband again; Henri died of plague while still held captive in Treviso near Venice in November 1397. His and Marie's young son Robert, born *c.* 1390 or 1392, should have become heir to his grandfather Duke Robert of Bar, who lived until 1411, though for some reason, the duke wished his third but eldest surviving son, Édouard de Bar, to succeed him rather than his grandson.[12] The year 1397 was a bad one for Marie de Coucy: she and her sister Philippa lost their father as well on 18 February 1397, when Enguerrand de Coucy died, also still held in captivity after the battle of Nicopolis, in Bursa, Anatolia. Marie, as the eldest of Enguerrand's three daughters – her half-sister Isabelle was still only a child – succeeded him as countess of Soissons and lady of Coucy. Enguerrand was also survived by his second wife, Isabelle of Lorraine, and Marie battled for years with her stepmother over possession of the de Coucy lands.

Richard II departed from England in October 1396 with a large retinue, and married his second wife Isabelle de Valois in early November. Isabelle was the eldest daughter of Charles VI of France and his Bavarian queen, Isabeau, and was painfully young; she turned 7 a few days after her wedding. The marriage was intended to cement a truce between the kingdoms of England and France set to last until 1426, though ultimately it did not. Richard, whose first wife Anne of Bohemia had been the daughter of an emperor, had insisted that he would marry no-one but a king's daughter, which necessarily limited the options severely; the only other plausible candidate to be found in the whole of western Europe was Yolande of Aragon (b. 1384), daughter of the king of Aragon, and later the queen-consort of Naples.

Edmund of Langley remained in England as regent while Richard II travelled to France, though his young second wife Joan Holland attended the royal wedding along with John of Gaunt, Katherine Swynford, Henry and Elizabeth of Lancaster, and numerous other English nobles. On 30 November 1396, Duke Edmund's daughter Constance of York gave birth to her only son, Richard Despenser, who became the Despenser heir from the moment of his birth.[13] Given his name, and given that Constance's husband Thomas was a close ally of Richard II, Richard Despenser was almost certainly the king's godson, though the newly-wed Richard II probably did not attend the baptism in person. The place of young Richard's birth is uncertain, though it was perhaps Cardiff: Thomas Despenser was there on 21 October 1396 and 16 February 1397, and Constance favoured their castle at Cardiff and gave birth to another child there in July 1400.[14]

Chapter 17

The Extermination of Schismatics

Far away in Portugal, Queen Philippa gave birth to her daughter Isabel of Portugal, future duchess of Burgundy, on 21 February 1397, after a three-year break from childbirth. Isabel was the sixth of the queen's eight children, and was the only royal Portuguese daughter who survived infancy. Queen Philippa sent a letter to Richard II on 1 October in either 1397, 1398 or 1399, calling herself *P. de Portugale*, 'P. of Portugal'.[1] If Philippa sent the letter in 1397, she was perhaps as yet unaware that Richard had had their uncle the duke of Gloucester murdered in Calais that September; if she sent it in 1399, her brother had in fact succeeded as king of England on 30 September that year, but she cannot yet have heard that news. Queen Philippa informed her cousin that she, her husband João and their four sons (Afonso, who was to die a year or two later, Duarte, Pedro, and Henrique) were in excellent health. She did not mention her daughter Isabel. Philippa sent her chancellor, Master Adam Davenport, who she said would bring Richard II more news from Portugal by word of mouth, to England with her letters, and she informed the English king that Adam wished to retire after serving her as chancellor for eight or nine years and to return to his native England. She asked Richard, therefore, to grant Adam a benefice 'in your very noble land of England' which would sustain him.

Elizabeth of Lancaster's brother-in-law Thomas Holland, earl of Kent, died on 25 April 1397. Thomas had made a will in English, in which he touchingly thanked *Alys my wyf* ('Alice my wife') for 'all the love and trust that hath been between us'.[2] Elizabeth's husband the earl of Huntingdon was perhaps not in England when his older brother died: in March 1397, he intended to 'come shortly to Italy and other parts for the extermination of schismatics and rebels and usurpers of cities and lands of the pope and the Roman church,' according to Pope Boniface IX. Boniface appointed Holland as *gonfalonier* (standard-bearer) of the Roman Church and captain-general of the papal forces in Italy.[3] Boniface was referring to a campaign against the supporters of Robert of Geneva or Pope Clement VII (d. 1394) and Pedro Martínez de Luna y Pérez de Gotor or Pope Benedict XIII (d. 1423), the popes who were based in Avignon rather than in Rome and who were later recognised by the Catholic Church as anti-popes. On the other hand, Holland was with King Richard on or soon before 16 June 1397, and was certainly in England that September, so might not have travelled south to 'exterminate' schismatics and rebels as planned.[4]

In the early autumn of 1397, Richard II took action against the three senior Lords Appellant who had presided over the Merciless Parliament in 1388 and had executed or exiled his friends: his uncle the duke of Gloucester, and the earls of Arundel and Warwick. John Holland, earl of Huntingdon, was his chief supporter in this venture, and according to the chronicler Thomas Walsingham, the plot was conceived at Holland's London house on the bank of the Thames, where Richard dined on 10 July 1397.[5] The king and his half-brother rode to Essex to arrest the duke of Gloucester at his castle of Pleshey, and Richard sent him to the port of Calais. Gloucester's three daughters Anne, Joan and Isabel, who were 14, 12 or 13 and 11, perhaps witnessed their father's arrest; one chronicle says that the duke of Gloucester was ill at the time of his arrest but that Richard deliberately disregarded the 'grief, tears and prayers' of his wife Eleanor de Bohun and the Gloucester household.[6]

During a parliament held in London in late September 1397, the elderly earl of Warwick, less noxious to the king than the two other senior Appellants, was exiled to the Isle of Man for life, and the earl of Arundel was beheaded on Tower Hill; he was accompanied to his execution by his nephew Thomas Holland, earl of Kent, and his son-in-law Thomas Mowbray, earl of Nottingham, both on horseback. Mowbray tied a blindfold around the eyes of the man who was his children's grandfather before an axe cleanly severed Arundel's neck.[7] Arundel's younger brother Thomas Arundel, formerly archbishop of York and now archbishop of Canterbury, was exiled from England by the vindictive King Richard. The earl of Arundel's son and heir Thomas Fitzalan or Arundel, born in October 1381, was not yet 16 when his father was beheaded, and the king placed him and his brother in the custody of John Holland, earl of Huntingdon, and Thomas Mowbray, earl of Nottingham. According to a chronicler, Holland abused the young nobleman in his

Top right and middle: The convent of the Minoresses in London, where Edward III's youngest granddaughter Isabel of Gloucester (1386–after 1424) served as abbess. (Public domain)

Below: Eltham Palace in Kent, the heavily restored medieval palace that was the birthplace of Edward III's eldest granddaughter Philippa of Clarence in 1355. (Duncan on Flickr and Wikimedia Commons)

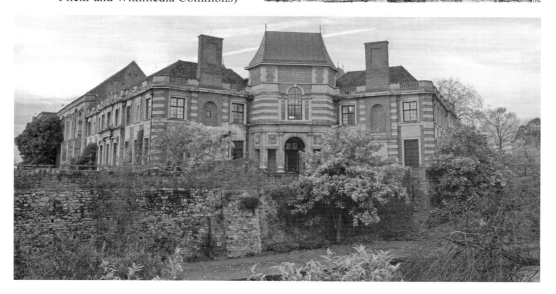

The cathedral of San Antolín in Palencia, where the teenage Catalina of Lancaster married Enrique of Castile, not yet 9, in September 1388. (Wikimedia Commons)

Toledo Cathedral, burial place of Catalina of Lancaster, queen of Castile and Leon, in 1418. (Wikimedia Commons)

Porto or Oporto Cathedral, where João of Aviz and Philippa of Lancaster married in February 1387. (Wikimedia Commons)

Above: Mosteiro de Batalha, Batalha Monastery, burial place of João of Aviz and Philippa of Lancaster, king and queen of Portugal. (Wikimedia Commons)

Right: The castle of Coucy in Picardy, northern France, chief seat of Marie and Philippa de Coucy's father Enguerrand, and inherited by Marie. (Public domain)

Castle of Coucy, near Laon, Aisne, France; 13th century. (This castle, a famous historic relic, but useless in modern warfare, was blown up by the Germans in March, 1917, during their retreat.)

a, fosse; *b*, gate; *c*, guard-rooms with sleeping-apartments; *d*, inner courtyard; *e*, covered buildings for defenders; *f*, apartments for family; *g*, grand staircase leading to them; *h*, great hall; *i*, donjon or keep; *k*, postern leading from donjon; *l, m, n, o,* chief towers flanking outer walls.

The castle of Castrojeriz in northern Spain, birthplace in 1354 of Catalina of Lancaster's mother Costanza of Castile. (Wikimedia Commons)

Above: The Alcázar in Seville, southern Spain, which Catalina would have known well, and where there were and are baths named after her grandmother María de Padilla. (Author's Collection)

Left: St Mary's Church in Burford, Shropshire, where Elizabeth of Lancaster, countess of Huntingdon, was buried. (Wikimedia Commons)

Right and below: Raby Castle, County Durham, the main seat of Joan Beaufort's second husband the earl of Westmorland and where she spent much of her married life. (Wikimedia Commons)

Lincoln Cathedral, burial place of Joan Beaufort, countess of Westmorland, and her mother Katherine Swynford, duchess of Lancaster. (Author's Collection)

Ludlow Castle, Shropshire, where Philippa of Clarence, countess of March, spent much of her married life and where she gave birth to two of her children. (Author's Collection)

Part of the ruins of Reading Abbey, where Constance of York, Lady Despenser, was buried in 1416. (Wikimedia Commons)

Pleshey Castle in Essex, main seat of Anne of Gloucester's father the duke of Gloucester, and her birthplace in early May 1383. (Wikimedia Commons)

The 'Casa do Infante' or Prince's House in Porto, Portugal, traditionally said to be the location where Philippa of Lancaster gave birth to her son Henrique the Navigator in 1394. (Public domain)

St Mary's church in Staindrop, County Durham, burial place of Joan Beaufort's second husband Ralph Neville and his first wife Margaret Stafford. (Wikimedia Commons)

Above: Llanthony Secunda Priory, Gloucester, burial place of Anne of Gloucester and her third husband William Bourchier. (Wikimedia Commons)

Left: An image of Catalina of Lancaster from a fifteenth-century manuscript. (Public domain)

care by entrusting him to the care of a knight called John Schevele, who treated the Arundel boy like a menial servant and forced him to wait on him.[8]

Elizabeth of Lancaster was certainly present at the September 1397 parliament, and one chronicler says that she won a prize as the best dancer during a celebration held to mark the end of parliament.[9] Richard II rewarded his supporters by promoting them to higher titles, and John Holland was made the first duke of Exeter; Elizabeth was now a duchess. Her brother Henry became duke of Hereford, the earldom once held by his father-in-law Humphrey de Bohun; her nephew-in-law Thomas Holland (b. 1372), earl of Kent, became duke of Surrey; her cousin Constance of York's husband Thomas Despenser became earl of Gloucester, a title once held by his ancestors (a gift of a diamond ring given to Richard II at an uncertain date in the 1390s by 'Madame de Gloucester' perhaps means Constance after Thomas's promotion to an earldom, though could also be a reference to Eleanor de Bohun); and Constance's brother Edward of York, earl of Rutland, became duke of Albemarle or Aumale.[10] Previously, the title of duke had been a rare one, borne only by Edward III's five sons who reached adulthood and by the royal cousin Henry of Grosmont, father-in-law of John of Gaunt from his first marriage to Blanche of Lancaster. Contemporaries sneered at the new *duketti*, 'little dukes', in the belief that Richard's numerous promotions rendered the title all but worthless. Despite his promotion to a dukedom, Henry of Lancaster was one of the two only remaining Lords Appellant of 1388, along with Thomas Mowbray, earl of Nottingham and now duke of Norfolk, and both young men must have wondered what, if anything, Richard would do with them now that he had destroyed their three former associates. They did not have to wait long to find out.

Chapter 18

Murder of a Royal Duke

The king's uncle Thomas of Woodstock, duke of Gloucester, was assassinated in Calais in September 1397, and the murder was arranged by Thomas Mowbray, earl of Nottingham and now also duke of Norfolk, acting on Richard II's orders in his capacity as keeper of the port of Calais. Duke Thomas's eldest child and only son, Humphrey of Gloucester, aged 15 in 1397, was his sole heir. Many of the jurors at the duke's inquisition post mortem were confused as to Thomas's date of death, and most stated that they did not know the correct date. The jurors who did give a precise date all seemed sure that Thomas died on a Saturday, either on 25 August, or 8 September, or 15 September, or 22 September. The writ to hold Thomas's inquisition post mortem was issued on 12 September and he was called 'Thomas, late duke of Gloucester' in the chancery rolls as early as 7 September 1397, though was officially summoned to appear before parliament on 21 September. In 1403, Thomas's nephew Henry of Lancaster, now king of England, stated that Thomas died on 'the feast of the Nativity of the Virgin', i.e. on 8 September, and it seems likely that he was smothered with a featherbed in the back room of a hostel in Calais during the night of 8 September.[1]

Duchess Eleanor wished to bury her husband in the chapel of St Edmund the King and St Thomas Becket in Westminster Abbey, and did so, though King Richard told her on 31 October that she must bury him in Bermondsey Priory. On 14 October, he had the duke's body delivered to his widow. Richard II had long held a loathing for his father's youngest brother, who had executed or exiled many of his friends in 1388, who had insulted him to his face, and with whom he had quarrelled on numerous occasions. In one conversation recorded by Jean Froissart, Gloucester had even complained to a retainer that his nephew's 'arse is too heavy to be shifted. All he ever wants to do is eat, drink and sleep, dance and caper about'.[2] Now Richard II, with the aid

80

of Thomas Mowbray, had committed murder; shockingly, the murder of a king's son and his own uncle.

Sometime before late June 1398, Thomas of Woodstock's eldest daughter Anne of Gloucester married her former brother-in-law Edmund Stafford, earl of Stafford, without royal permission. Edmund petitioned King Richard for a pardon for doing so, which was granted on 28 June 1398, and it is interesting to note that he referred to his wife in his petition as 'Anne, daughter of Alianore [Eleanor] de Bohun, duchess of Gloucester' rather than using the name of her recently-murdered and disgraced father.[3] Anne was now 15, and Edmund was not a great deal older. He was said to be 17 at his brother William's inquisition post mortem in November 1395, was still a 'minor in the king's wardship' on 22 November 1398, and was granted his full inheritance on 23 March 1399 even though 'Edmund is found not of full age', i.e. he was not yet 21 years old then.[4] His older brother William was born on 22 September 1377, so Edmund must have been born at least eleven or so months after that, so was born in or after August 1378. As Anne's marriage to Edmund's brother Thomas had never been consummated owing to her extreme youth, papal intervention was not necessary.

Philippa of Clarence's elder son Roger Mortimer, earl of March, was killed in a skirmish in Ireland in July 1398 at the age of only 24, leaving his 7-year-old son Edmund as his heir (and leaving a younger son also named Roger and a daughter, Anne, who according to an annalist was born on 27 December 1388 thirty-seven weeks after Roger's fourteenth birthday; the Mortimer men of the fourteenth century often became fathers at a very young age). Despite his descent from Edward III's second eldest surviving son and his closeness to the throne, Roger Mortimer had always been something of an outsider in English politics. Richard II had, according to the chronicler Adam of Usk, been planning to have Roger arrested by his own brother-in-law Thomas Holland the younger, earl of Kent and duke of Surrey, and to return him to England in disgrace.[5]

[1] It was still unclear exactly who the heir to the childless king's throne was, though in the late 1390s Richard began referring to his cousin Edward of York, the elder son of Edmund of Langley and Isabel of Castile, as his brother, which might indicate that he wished Edward to be his successor. John of Gaunt and his son Henry of Lancaster, however, had a better claim to the throne, as Gaunt was older than Langley. Richard

II had created Gaunt duke of Aquitaine in 1390, a title previously only held by the kings of England themselves or by their direct successors, which might indicate that, at least at this point, Richard considered his eldest living uncle to be his heir presumptive. A rebellion broke out in the duchy in 1394, however, when some of Gaunt's important vassals declared that they did not accept his authority as duke and only wished to be governed by the king or by his direct heir, so evidently they at least did not believe that John of Gaunt was likely to be King Richard's successor.

In these last years of his reign and especially after his destruction of the Lords Appellant in the autumn of 1397, Richard II allowed a dangerously factional atmosphere to take root at his court, and no man, no matter how close he appeared to be to the king, could consider himself safe. Three knights of comparatively low birth and obscure origins, Sir John Bushy, Sir William Bagot and Sir Henry Green(e), dominated politics and the king's favour in these peculiar end years both of the reign and of the century; two hundred years later, Shakespeare referred to the malign triumvirate as the 'caterpillars of the commonwealth'. On 3 March 1398, a royal clerk recorded that William Bagot had plotted to kill John of Gaunt, his wife Katherine and his children, and acknowledged that if the duke and his family 'shall in time to come be by him slain' and his guilt were proved, he could be put to death without due process.[6] That this was written down in the chancery rolls, as if plotting to kill the second man in the kingdom and his wife and children was normal government business, reveals much about the poisonous and dangerous atmosphere at Richard II's court in the late 1390s.

Another murderous plot came to light in 1398. The two surviving Lords Appellant of ten years earlier were Henry of Lancaster, duke of Hereford, and Thomas Mowbray, duke of Norfolk, and in late 1397 the two men encountered each other while riding between Brentford and London. As reported by Henry to the king shortly afterwards, Mowbray informed him that there had been a plan to seize and kill both Henry and his father when they went to Windsor after the Parliament of September 1397, but that he himself, Gaunt's nephew Edward of York (the new duke of Albemarle), Gaunt's son-in-law John Holland (the new duke of Exeter), and the duke of Lancaster's long-term associate the earl of Worcester (Thomas Percy) had prevented it because they had jointly sworn an oath that 'they would never assent to the ruin of any lord without just and reasonable cause'. Thomas Mowbray supposedly claimed to Henry of Lancaster that the duke of Surrey (Thomas Holland), the earl of Gloucester (Thomas Despenser), the earl of Salisbury (John Montacute) and the earl of Wiltshire (William Scrope) had sworn to destroy six lords: himself, John of Gaunt, Gaunt's sons Henry of Lancaster and John Beaufort, Edward of York, and John Holland. In the atmosphere of the late 1390s it is far from impossible that there was some truth to this, though why the duke of Surrey would have plotted to kill his own uncle the duke of Exeter is unclear.[7]

Richard II ordered Thomas Mowbray to be held captive in the royal wardrobe, a building near the Blackfriars' house in London, and later in Windsor Castle; the duke spent much of 1398 under arrest.[8] Henry of Lancaster, by contrast, was allowed to remain at liberty, and spent some of the year at court and much of the rest with his father. The king ordered his two kinsmen to settle their differences with a jousting duel, to be held near Coventry on 16 September 1398. Elizabeth of Lancaster surely supported her brother Henry in this endeavour, but perhaps the conflict gave her some anxious moments: her young daughter Constance Holland was married to Thomas Mowbray's namesake son and heir, who turned 13 in the autumn of 1398.

At the last moment, Richard rose from his seat and stopped the duel, and ordered the two men into exile. Mowbray was banished from England permanently and given permission to travel to 'Almain [Germany], Bohemia and Hungary, and to traverse the great sea on pilgrimage'. These were the territories ruled by Richard's brothers-in-law Wenzel and Sigismund, the late Queen Anne's brothers. Henry of Lancaster was exiled for ten years, though the king might have reduced the sentence to six; chronicler Jean Froissart claimed that he did.[9] Henry at first intended to travel to the Iberian peninsula to spend time with his older sister Queen Philippa and his younger half-sister Queen Catalina, though in the end he departed for Paris on the advice of his father Gaunt and was received with great honour there by the French court. Thomas Mowbray, meanwhile, travelled to Italy.[10]

Philippa de Coucy was possibly with Richard II two days after the duel on 18 September 1398, when he granted her a manor in Northamptonshire forfeited by Thomas Mowbray. At an unknown date in the 1390s, she gave her cousin the king three valuable gifts worth almost £50: a mirror set with large and small pearls, a tabernacle with an image of the Virgin Mary behind crystal, and a tablet also with an image of the Virgin Mary, in mother-of-pearl.[11] One wonders how Philippa got on with her cousin in the late 1390s, and how she perceived his murderously factional court. Richard II might have been severely lonely after losing both his beloved wife Queen Anne and his dear friend or lover Robert de Vere, Philippa's husband. Little Queen Isabelle was a mere child and could not be the king's companion in any more than name only, though he treated her with respect and affection as though she were his little sister, and Richard's cousin Edward of York and the three 'caterpillars', John Bushy, William Bagot and Henry Greene, though very influential at court, never reached the heights achieved by de Vere a few years earlier; Richard was not nearly so devoted to them as he had been to Philippa de Coucy's husband.

Chapter 19

Two Deaths

John of Gaunt, duke of Lancaster, died at his castle of Leicester on 3 February 1399, a month before his fifty-ninth birthday. In his very long will dictated on the day he died, John left bequests to his four living sons and four living daughters, as well as to his wife Katherine, his only surviving sibling Edmund of Langley, duke of York, and his nephew the king. 'Phylypp, queen of Portugal' received her father's second best gold drinking-horn and a goblet covered with gold, Queen Catalina ('Katerin, queen of Castile and Leon') received a golden goblet, Duchess Elizabeth received 'my white silk bed worked with blue eagles with outstretched wings, the curtains of matching decorated white taffeta and fourteen tapestries, and 'my best brooch that I have after those that have already been bequeathed', and Countess Joan ('my dearest daughter, countess of Westmorland and Lady Nevyll') received 'a bed of silk and a golden goblet, uncovered, with a ewer'.[1] For all his loyalty to his wayward nephew King Richard for many years, the duke was unable to prevent the exile of his beloved son and heir Henry, and died after a few weeks of illness probably brought on or exacerbated by his distress and rage over Henry's enforced exile. Soon after John's death, King Richard confiscated the entire Lancastrian inheritance, and made Henry's banishment from his homeland permanent.

Eleanor de Bohun, calling herself 'Alianore, duchess of Gloucester, countess of Essex', made her own will at Pleshey Castle in Essex on 9 August 1399, and requested burial in the chapel of St Edmund the King and St Thomas Becket in Westminster Abbey next to her late husband (though one chronicler claims that in fact she was buried in the convent of the Minoresses near the Tower of London). She dictated the will in French, though requested that her executors should have 1,000 masses sung for her and her husband's souls as soon as possible after her death, and asked that the priest should speak certain words in English on this occasion: *For the soule of Thomas sum tyme duc of Gloucestre and Alianore his wyf, and all cristeyn* [Christian] *soles*. To her eldest child and only son, Humphrey of Gloucester, Eleanor bequeathed a sizeable number of items, including a bed of black damask, a bed of blue silk, an illuminated psalter or book of psalms, a 'chronicle of France in French' which had been given to her by the duke of Burgundy (probably at Richard II and Isabelle de Valois's wedding in 1396), a 'book of vices and virtues', and a poem called 'The History of the Knight and the Swan', all in French. The swan was the heraldic emblem of Eleanor's natal family the de Bohuns.

To her eldest daughter Anne, countess of Stafford, Duchess Eleanor left an illuminated book about the lives of the saints called *Legenda Aurea* or 'Golden Legend', her best palfrey horse, and a pair of gold paternosters with four jet beads which had belonged to Anne's father Thomas. Her second daughter Joan ('Johanne') received Eleanor's best bed of black silk; a bed of cloth of gold from Cyprus with its canopy, embroidered with swans and the letter Y; a 'small bed for a closet' of white *tertaryn* (rich silk cloth) embroidered with lions and swans and with its canopy; numerous linen cloths and blankets; numerous silver pots, plates, jugs and cups; and 'a book with the psalter, primer and other devotions' which had two gold clasps. The youngest Gloucester daughter, Isabel, who already lived at the Minoresses' convent in London and had been there since infancy, received a large number of religious works, all in French, including a two-volume bible with gold clasps, a book of decretals, the *Lives of the Fathers*, an old psalter, and St Gregory's *Pastoral Rule*. Eleanor also gave her youngest daughter £40 in money, a bed of cloth of gold from Cyprus, and a black leather belt with a buckle and a chain of twelve pieces of gold which had belonged to Isabel's father. She also left a 'cask of good wine' and 10 marks in cash to the Minoresses of London, and bequeathed a pair of coral paternosters to her mother Joan, countess of Hereford, which were to be given to the Minoresses as well, if Joan died before her (in fact Joan outlived her daughter by two decades). The large number of books in Duchess Eleanor's will reveals her deep interest in reading and learning, and her late husband and her father Humphrey de Bohun (d. 1373) both loved books as well. Humphrey employed two *luminours* (i.e. manuscript illuminators), and no fewer than 123 manuscripts in Duke Thomas's possession were confiscated and inventoried after his murder, including the *Roman de la Rose*, a number of Arthurian tales, and 'a new book of the Gospels, glossed into English'. Thomas and Eleanor also owned a bible in English which they had commissioned, and which cost them 40 shillings.[2]

Clearly Eleanor was ill to the point where she thought she might die that August, and sadly, her son Humphrey died on 2 September 1399, aged 17. The cause of the young man's death is not known, and although the chronicler Adam of Usk repeated a rumour that Constance of York's husband Thomas Despenser, earl of Gloucester, had had him poisoned in Ireland and that Humphrey died on the island of Anglesey after the royal party's return to Wales, this is certainly untrue. Another chronicler states that he died of the 'pestilence'.[3] Humphrey's death appears to have been very sudden; on or just before 1 September, a day or so before he died, he was one of Richard II's two noble captors when the king was taken to the Tower of London to be imprisoned there (the teenaged Thomas Fitzalan, Eleanor de Bohun's cousin and the heir to his executed father Richard's earldom of Arundel, was the other).[4]

Humphrey's mother outlived him by a month and died on 3 October 1399, still only 33 years old herself. The chronicle which states, apparently incorrectly, that Duchess Eleanor was buried in the Minoresses' convent also states that she died of an illness which she contracted as a result of her 'exceedingly severe grief' (*nimis gravi tristitia*). After experiencing the murder of her husband and the death of her teenage son in rapid succession, this would hardly be surprising, though evidently Eleanor was already ill enough to dictate her will a few weeks before Humphrey died. Eleanor did not update the will after her son's death, and as Humphrey could not receive the items his mother had left him, they either passed instead to Anne as Eleanor's eldest daughter or were shared out equally among the three Gloucester sisters. Humphrey had been his parents' sole heir, but now, Anne and Joan, the two secular daughters, could expect to share Thomas of Woodstock's lands and a third of the large de Bohun inheritance (Isabel, as a soon-to-be nun, could receive gifts but was not allowed to own lands). Ultimately Anne and Joan of Gloucester were set to share a half of the de Bohun estate when their maternal grandmother Joan, the dowager countess of Hereford, died, with the other half passing to their cousin Henry of Monmouth (b. 1386), the late Mary de Bohun's eldest son.

When they lost their mother and their only brother, Anne was 16, Joan was 14 or 15 and Isabel was 13, and they had already endured the trauma of their royal father's murder on the orders of their cousin two years before. Even more drama was soon to come, although this time, the king himself bore the brunt of it. After the death of his uncle John of Gaunt, Richard had made the dramatic decision to exile John's son and heir Henry permanently and to confiscate his massive inheritance: all the Lancastrian lands including the duchy of Lancaster and the earldoms of Lincoln, Leicester and Derby, plus the third of the de Bohun lands which Henry held by right of his late wife Mary and the 'courtesy of England'. The king, with what appears, at least with hindsight, to be arrant, blind foolishness, then made the decision to travel again to Ireland, as he had done in 1394/95. His chief supporters were in his company: Edward of York, John Holland and his nephew Thomas Holland, Thomas Despenser, and John Montacute, earl of Salisbury (who had succeeded his elderly uncle William, born in 1328, in 1397). Edmund of Langley remained in England as regent. While Richard was away from his kingdom, Henry of Lancaster landed on the Yorkshire coast, supposedly only to claim his rightful inheritance but perhaps already intending to make a bid for his cousin's throne. Countless thousands of men flocked to his banner. Richard sailed back from Ireland to Wales to find that most of his support had simply evaporated, and he spent several weeks wandering helplessly around Wales with his few remaining important supporters before he was captured at Flint Castle on or about 20 August 1399 and sent in chains to the Tower of London, accompanied by Humphrey of Gloucester and Thomas Fitzalan as his captors. John Holland was arrested, and sent south with the king. The French author of the *Chronicque de la Traison et Mort de Richart Deux Roy Dengleterre* states that Holland told Henry of Lancaster 'My lord, it is but reasonable that I should show you respect, for your father was the king's son, and moreover my wife is your sister, wherefore I am bound to do so.'[5]

John Holland, however, in contrast to the king, was not held in captivity for long. On 24 September 1399, just days before his half-brother's deposition, John was in London and retained a squire named Thomas Prodefote ('Proudfoot') for life.[6] This probably implies that Elizabeth of Lancaster was also in London during the dramatic events that made her brother the king of England. The last day of Richard II's reign was 28 September 1399, and he was removed from the Tower of London and sent to imprisonment at Pontefract Castle in Yorkshire, a safe distance from London and from Richard's allies. Meanwhile, Thomas Mowbray, the exiled duke of Norfolk, had died in Venice on 22 September 1399, unaware of the momentous events in England and that the king who had banished him from his homeland was now in captivity and no longer occupied the throne.

Elizabeth of Lancaster almost certainly attended her brother's coronation as King Henry IV of England in Westminster Abbey on 13 October 1399, the feast day of Edward the Confessor (d. 1066), a very popular saint and former king of England whom the medieval royal family revered. She was perhaps delighted at the turn of events; her husband, although he helped to arrange Henry IV's coronation and attended it, emphatically was not, and began plotting with other men to bring down his brother-in-law and restore his half-brother to his lost throne. The higher titles which Richard II had bestowed on his followers, including John Holland, two years earlier were taken away, with two exceptions. One was Thomas Percy, the younger brother of the earl of Northumberland, who kept his earldom of Worcester thanks to his, his brother's and his nephew Henry Hotspur's support of the new king after his arrival in England. Another of Henry's chief supporters in 1399 was his brother-in-law, Joan Beaufort's second husband Ralph Neville, who was also allowed to keep the earldom of Westmorland granted to him by King Richard two years previously. By contrast, Elizabeth of Lancaster was once more only countess of Huntingdon and not duchess of Exeter, and another of their cousins, Constance of York, was no longer countess of Gloucester but merely Lady Despenser and lady of Glamorgan. Constance's brother Edward of York was also deprived of his dukedom, and once more was simply known as earl of Rutland, his previous title (though he remained the heir to his father Edmund's dukedom of York).

Another staunch supporter of King Richard was Henry Despenser, bishop of Norwich, the uncle-in-law of Constance of York, and a friend of Queen Philippa of Portugal. Sometime between early February and late September 1399, Philippa wrote to Thomas Arundel, archbishop of Canterbury, asking him to intercede with her brother Henry of Lancaster – he had not yet become king of England when she dictated the letter – on Bishop Despenser's behalf. Philippa wrote that her brother was displeased with Despenser because the latter had wronged him in some way, and asked Archbishop Arundel to ensure both that Henry forgave Despenser and that he did his best to be a good lord and friend to him. Queen Catalina also sent messengers to her half-brother in 1399, probably to congratulate him on his accession to the throne.[7]

Chapter 20

The Epiphany Rising

Two of Edward III's granddaughters, Elizabeth of Lancaster and Constance of York, were widowed in January 1400 when their husbands tried, and failed, to bring down King Henry IV and restore Richard II to the throne. The plot is known as the Epiphany Rising; the feast of the Epiphany on 6 January is the twelfth and last day of Christmas, and in 1400 was the former king's thirty-third birthday.

Richard's chief supporters were his half-brother John Holland; John's nephew Thomas, earl of Kent and formerly duke of Surrey; John Montacute, earl of Salisbury; Thomas Despenser, lord of Glamorgan; Thomas Merk, bishop of Carlisle; Thomas Colchester, abbot of Westminster; and Ralph, Lord Lumley, Sir Bernard Brocas, Sir Thomas Blount, and Roger Walden, formerly archbishop of Canterbury (Walden was displaced by Thomas Arundel, the exiled former incumbent now returned from exile in France). According to the Westminster chronicle, John Holland bitterly reproached his wife Elizabeth for her rejoicing at the accession of her brother and the overthrow of her cousin Richard, despite his own gloom over the whole affair.[1] John and his allies met on 17 December 1399 in a chamber of the abbot of Westminster's lodging, and hatched plans to enter Windsor Castle, where Henry IV was to spend the festive season of 1399/1400 with his six children, and capture the king. This, they hoped, would inspire popular uprisings across the country in Richard II's favour. It appears that Constance of York's brother Edward betrayed the plot to Henry IV on 3 January 1400, though one chronicle gives a very different story, claiming that a member of the king's household spent the night with a prostitute who had previously slept with a man in the retinue of one of Henry's enemies, and that she passed onto him details of the rebels' plans.[2]

Thomas Holland and John Montacute took a force of about 400 men to Windsor, but found that a forewarned Henry had already left and had sought refuge in the Tower of London, so they fled towards the west of England. For his part, John Holland failed to secure the city of London, and subsequently rode to Essex with a knight called Thomas Shelley. Thomas Despenser, on hearing of his allies' failure to capture London or to seize the king, boarded a ship in Cardiff in his lordship of Glamorgan, intending to flee abroad, but the crew were loyal to Henry IV and took Despenser instead to Bristol, where he was summarily beheaded by a mob. The king ordered his head to be sent to London for public display.[3] Whether Thomas ever knew it or not, his widow Constance of York was pregnant; she gave birth to his third child and second daughter, Isabelle Despenser, six and a half months after his death.

Elizabeth of Lancaster's nephew-in-law Thomas Holland, earl of Kent, was killed in Cirencester with John Montacute, earl of Salisbury, and the men's heads were sent to King Henry in a basket. As with Thomas Despenser, Henry sent the heads to London to be displayed in public. In Essex, John Holland, probably the last survivor of the earls taking part in the rebellion, sent greetings via a messenger to Henry Despenser, bishop of Norwich, who he surely knew was a close ally of his half-brother the former king. Despenser was staying at his manor of South Elmham in Suffolk, and insisted a little later that he had taken no part in the Epiphany Rising plot and knew nothing of it until 8 January, when Lord Scales told him. Despite his protestations, and despite his friend Queen Philippa doing her utmost to help him from distant Portugal, Henry IV remained frosty towards Despenser until at least July 1404. Henry Despenser did find time to send a comforting letter to the pregnant Constance of York, whom he addressed as his 'dearest and most entirely beloved with all my heart niece[-in-law]', not long after the Epiphany Rising and the sudden shocking demise of her husband of twenty years.[4]

John Holland and his companion Thomas Shelley tried to sail from the Essex coast in a small boat, intending to flee from England and seek sanctuary overseas, but they were blown back to the shore every time they set sail, 'until, in complete despair of help from Neptune, he gave up this plan'.[5] John sought refuge at Hadleigh Castle with the earl of Oxford, Robert de Vere's uncle and heir Aubrey de Vere, and later with a sympathiser of Richard II in Shoeburyness called John Prittlewell. He was discovered and arrested by a 'crowd of locals' while dining at the latter's house, and fell into the hands of the formidable Joan de Bohun, dowager countess of Hereford, Henry IV's mother-in-law and the grandmother of

Anne, Joan and Isabel of Gloucester. She had John beheaded at Pleshey Castle, supposedly on the spot where he and his half-brother Richard II had had her other son-in-law the duke of Gloucester arrested in the autumn of 1397. An inquisition of March 1405 gives 15 January 1400 as the date of John Holland's death, though it is also possible that he died on the 9th or 10th (the exact date of his nephew the earl of Kent's beheading in Cirencester is also not entirely clear).[6] Rather curiously, the indictment of the Epiphany Rising lords, including the two Hollands, that was read out in parliament a year later in January 1401 stated that as well as wishing to 'destroy our said lord the king and other great men of the realm', the men wished to 'populate the said realm [England] with people of another tongue'.[7]

As the men were deemed to have committed treason, all their goods were forfeit to the Crown. King Henry gave the rich and costly garments that Thomas Despenser was wearing when he was captured and executed in Bristol to two of his servants, though did allow Constance of York to take possession of some other items in Thomas's possession, which were worth £200: two dozen dishes, twelve silver saucers, four silver dishes, twelve silver spoons, four silver cups and four pots and basins.[8] Henry ordered £10 to be given to his sister Elizabeth in exchange for a 'black bed with its entire furniture' which had belonged to John Holland and was confiscated, while three other beds formerly in John's possession, two 'with their fittings and certain pillows called *quyssyns*' (i.e. cushions) and another one made of red *baudekyn* with curtains of red *sendal* (two different types of rich silk cloth), were given to Elizabeth's half-brother John Beaufort, earl of Somerset. Beaufort also received ten pillows of red cloth of gold, ten pillows of red velvet and twelve of white cloth of gold which had been seized by a royal official from one of John Holland and Elizabeth's residences in Devon. Other confiscated items in Holland's possession had once belonged to the earl of Arundel executed in 1397, including a number of religious books and a bed with a canopy embroidered with the arms of March and Pembroke, which probably belonged by right to Arundel's second wife Philippa Mortimer (1375–1400), daughter of Philippa of Clarence, countess of March and Ulster, and widow of the earl of Pembroke (d. 1389).[9]

Far away in Portugal on 13 January 1400, Elizabeth of Lancaster's sister Queen Philippa gave birth to her second youngest child, Dom João. He later became constable of Portugal, and is known as *O*

Infante Condestável or 'the Constable Prince'. João was to become the grandfather of both Queen Isabel la Católica of Castile and King Manuel I of Portugal, via his incestuous marriage to Isabel of Barcelos, daughter of his illegitimate half-brother Afonso, count of Barcelos and first duke of Braganza. The Lancaster sisters' cousin Philippa de Coucy was in London on 20 January 1400, a few days before the heads of John and Thomas Holland and Thomas Despenser were taken there for public display. On 22 November 1399, Henry had confirmed several grants previously made to Philippa by Richard II, including an annual income of 300 marks (£200) from the Exchequer.[10]

As for the former king, the failed plot to rescue him sealed his fate, and Sir Richard of Bordeaux died in Pontefract Castle on or around 14 February 1400, perhaps by being starved to death. Henry IV had him buried at Langley Priory in Hertfordshire, though Henry's son Henry V had the body moved to Westminster Abbey shortly after he became king in 1413, and Richard still lies there, next to his beloved first wife Anne of Bohemia. His child-widow Isabelle de Valois, born in November 1389 and still only 10 years old when she was left a widow, returned to her native France in 1401. She married her 11-year-old cousin Charles of Angoulême, future duke of Orléans, in 1406, and died after giving birth to her only child in 1409.

Chapter 21

Elizabeth's Third Marriage

Elizabeth of Lancaster had not long been a widow when she married her third husband, Sir John Cornwall (or Cornewaille or Cornewayll, as his name was usually spelt in his own lifetime). A chronicler states that the couple first met while John was participating in a jousting tournament in York in July 1400, but almost certainly they married before that.[1] Henry IV ordered John Cornwall to be arrested and imprisoned in the Tower of London on 6 April 1400. Although the reason for his arrest and incarceration was not given, it seems likely that he and Elizabeth had recently married without her brother's permission, and that the enraged king ordered John's imprisonment on hearing of it. If this was indeed the reason for John's arrest, Henry had evidently forgiven the couple by 12 December 1400, when he granted them a joint income of 1,000 marks annually from the 'petty custom in the port of London'.[2] Assuming that Elizabeth and Cornwall did marry before 6 April, this was less than three months after John Holland's summary execution in Essex.

Cornwall had been released from the Tower by 6 July 1400, when he and Janico Dartasso, a squire from Navarre with whom Cornwall had gone on crusade to North Africa in 1390, were told to 'prosecute certain feats of arms' against a French knight and squire in York (i.e. the jousting tournament where Cornwall supposedly first met Elizabeth of Lancaster).[3] Whatever Henry IV's personal feelings about John Cornwall and whether he had truly forgiven him for marrying Elizabeth without his permission by then or not, John was one of the greatest English warriors and jousters of the age and would certainly put up a good showing against the French – and indeed, he and his friend Dartasso duly defeated them. Cornwall's age is difficult to estimate, though as he lived until as late as 1443, he was probably a few years younger than Elizabeth of Lancaster, and might have been born in the late 1360s or early 1370s (probably no later than *c.* 1373, as he went on crusade in 1390). In *c.* late

94

1396, he became a knight of Richard II's household, and Richard paid him 100 marks a year.[4]

Sir John Cornwall had previously been rather briefly married to Philippa Sergeaux née Arundel (d. 13 September 1399), a granddaughter of the earls of Arundel and Salisbury, a descendant of King Edward I, and the widow of an influential landowner in the county of Cornwall named Sir Richard Sergeaux. Philippa gave birth to the first of her five children in 1367 or not long afterwards, so can hardly have been born later than the early 1350s, and became a grandmother in February 1393 when her eldest daughter Elizabeth Sergeaux gave birth to her son Thomas Marny. Philippa's first husband Richard died on 30 September 1393, and she married John Cornwall before 13 April 1398, probably not too long before. Philippa was many years older than John, perhaps fifteen or twenty years older, and had a 5-year-old grandson when they wed. He was about the same age as the eldest one or two of his five stepchildren.[5] John and Philippa did not have much chance to spend time together: John was said to be 'sailing to foreign parts' on 5 July 1398 and again on 21 February 1399. He travelled to Ireland with Richard II in the summer of 1399, though switched his allegiance to Henry IV later that year.[6]

As Sir John Cornwall persuaded two women who were both older, much richer and of much higher rank to marry him, he must have been attractive and desirable, and historian Juliet Barker has called him 'one of the most widely respected chivalric figures of the day'.[7] Whatever the late John Holland's many other faults and unpleasant characteristics, there is no doubt that Elizabeth's previous husband had also been a famed jouster and warrior, and clearly she found this an appealing trait in men. John Cornwall was of royal descent, albeit very distantly: his ancestor Sir Richard Cornwall (d. 1296/97) was an illegitimate son of Richard, earl of Cornwall and king of Germany (d. 1272), the younger son of King John of England (r. 1199–1216) and brother of Henry III (r. 1216–72). Supposedly, according to some modern writers, John Cornwall's mother was a niece of Duke John IV of Brittany (1339–1399), and he was born at sea off St Michael's Mount in Cornwall and baptised in the church of Marazion near Penzance.[8] The duke of Brittany, however, had only one known sister, Jeanne, Lady Basset, who died in England in 1402 and did not have children. Possibly, if the story is correct, the duke and Lady Basset had an illegitimate half-sibling whose daughter was John

Cornwall's mother, though as Duke John of Brittany was only about thirty years older than John Cornwall, the story does not seem terribly likely.

As the son of a third son of a second son, John could expect to inherit little in the way of lands, and was, to put it rather cynically, a man on the make. His marital record shows that he succeeded brilliantly; his stepchildren included the earl of Huntingdon, two countesses of Oxford and the countess of Norfolk, and he became the brother-in-law of the king of England and the queens of Portugal and Castile. In February 1399, John had been appointed as one of the keepers of the peace in the county of Cornwall alongside John Holland, duke of Exeter, a connection which may partly explain how he and Elizabeth of Lancaster became acquainted. John of Gaunt, duke of Lancaster, granted John Cornwall an annuity of 40 marks at an unknown date, and this connection to Elizabeth's father perhaps also explains how the couple came to know each other.[9] Sir John's first marriage to the widow of an influential and wealthy politician and landowner in the county of Cornwall, and his appointment as keeper of the peace in the county alongside John Holland, makes the story that he and Elizabeth first met at a jousting tournament in the summer of 1400 implausible. The late John Holland was a powerful figure in the west country in the 1380s and 1390s, and he and Elizabeth spent much of their time at their Devon manor of Dartington and operated in the same spheres of influence in the same region as John Cornwall. Elizabeth of Lancaster and John Cornwall certainly knew each other before 1400.

On 21 March 1400, Elizabeth's Holland children were living at Dartington when their uncle the king gave them and the servants living with them permission to travel anywhere in England, as often as they pleased.[10] Elizabeth had another two children with Sir John Cornwall who survived infancy, though neither of the Cornwall children had children of their own. Their daughter Constance Cornwall married John Arundel, earl of Arundel, who was born in February 1408, and died childless in or before 1427; her widower's son and heir from his second marriage was born in January 1429. Elizabeth might have named her youngest daughter in honour of her late stepmother Costanza of Castile, duchess of Lancaster. Perhaps, however, Elizabeth's cousin Constance of York, Lady Despenser, was the little girl's godmother – even though Lady Despenser was in disgrace with Elizabeth's brother the king in the early 1400s, both on her late husband Thomas's account and as a result of her own rebellion against Henry in 1405 (see below). Elizabeth and John Cornwall's son was named after his father, and his uncle Henry IV stood godfather to him on 15 February 1405.[11] Elizabeth turned 42 that year; it seems likely that John Cornwall the younger was her youngest child, and that John's sister Constance was older than he. Just months after Elizabeth of Lancaster married John Cornwall, on 3 September 1400, her eldest son Richard Holland died. Elizabeth's second son John Holland the younger, who turned 5 in March 1400, became the Holland heir, and she had a third Holland son as well, whose name was Edward. He had been knighted by April 1418, when Elizabeth's nephew Henry V called him 'the king's kinsman Edward Holland, knight'.[12]

Elizabeth was usually called, and called herself, 'Elizabeth Lancastre' throughout her marriage to John Cornwall, not 'Elizabeth de [of] Lancastre', as though Lancaster was her family name. In a petition of *c.* May 1403, for example, the couple called themselves 'John Cornewaill, *chivaler* [knight], and Elizabeth Lancastre, countess of Huntyngdon, his wife', and the response to the petition on the Patent Roll repeats this wording exactly.[13] Henry IV made numerous references over the years to 'the king's sister Elizabeth Lancastre, countess of Huntingdon', and had apparently entirely forgiven his brother-in-law for his unlicensed marriage to Elizabeth by the New Year of 1403, when he presented John, and three other people including his cousin Philippa de Coucy, with valuable devotional tablets.[14]

Chapter 22

The Coucy Sisters' Dispute

Constance of York gave birth to Thomas Despenser's posthumous daughter on 27 July 1400 in Cardiff, and called her Isabelle after her late Spanish mother the duchess of York. The child was baptised on the day of her birth in the church of St Mary, Cardiff, by Thomas, bishop of Llandaff.[1] It was possibly Constance who sent a letter in French to her 'dearest cousins', unidentified, telling them that she had borne 'a beautiful daughter' (*une belle fille*) and that she and the infant were in good health.[2] After the deaths of her brother Richard in 1413 and sister Elizabeth in or soon after 1405, Isabelle became sole heir to the large Despenser inheritance in South Wales and across the south of England. Her maternal grandfather Edmund of Langley, duke of York, was still alive when she was born, and passed away in 1402, the last survivor of Edward III and Philippa of Hainault's twelve children and the only one of them who lived past 1400. Constance's brother Edward was his heir.

As though the Gloucester family had not already suffered enough from the murder of their father Thomas of Woodstock in September 1397 and the early deaths of their brother Humphrey and mother Eleanor de Bohun in September and October 1399, the teenaged Joan of Gloucester, Lady Talbot, died as well on 16 August 1400.[3] She was 15 or 16 and her husband Gilbert 16 or 17; it is possible that she died in childbirth or during pregnancy, though this is not known for certain, and Joan left no surviving children. She was buried in Walden Abbey in Essex, the mausoleum of her mother's family the de Bohuns; the great Jacobean mansion Audley End House was built on the site 200 years later, after the Dissolution, and still stands there. Joan's widower Gilbert Talbot died in October 1418 leaving an infant daughter, Anchoret or Ankaret Talbot, named after his mother Ankaret Lestrange, from his second marriage.[4]

Isabel, the youngest Gloucester daughter, already lived at the London convent of the Minoresses – in April 1401, it was stated that she was placed there 'as an infant' – and was professed as a nun on 23 April 1402, her sixteenth birthday. Anne of Gloucester became the only member of her natal family still alive and in the secular world. She and her husband the earl of Stafford thus came to own all her parents' lands, as well as the Stafford lands that Edmund inherited from his father and older brothers. In less than three years, Anne lost both her parents, her brother and her sister, and her other sister chose to take lifelong vows as a nun. At least Anne still had her grandmother; Eleanor de Bohun's formidable mother Joan, dowager countess of Hereford, did not die until 1419. As for Isabel of Gloucester, almost nothing is known of the first twenty years or so of her life as a nun in the Minoresses' convent, except that on 28 June 1403, Henry IV granted a favour to one Richard Hendeman, a servant of the convent, 'at the supplication of the abbess of the Sisters Minoresses without Al[d]gate, London, and the king's kinswoman Isabel de Gloucestre'. The Minoresses' London house was a royal foundation, established in the early 1290s by Edmund of Lancaster (d. 1296), son of Henry III and younger brother of Edward I, and his second wife Blanche of Artois (d. 1302), niece of Louis IX of France and queen-consort of Navarre by her first marriage. The women who lived there were members of the Poor Clares, an order of Franciscan nuns established in 1212 by St Clare of Assisi and St Francis of Assisi, and in the Middle Ages the convent was usually called 'the abbey of St Clare without Aldgate' or 'the convent of Our Lady of the New Place without Aldgate'.

Edward I's granddaughter Elizabeth de Burgh née de Clare was buried in the London house of the Minoresses in 1360, and in 1399 John of Gaunt left the house £100 of silver to be shared out among all the sisters. Constance of York and Thomas Despenser, who owned a few properties in London, received permission sometime in the 1390s to create a doorway straight from their house into the Minoresses' church; after Thomas's death, the house came into the possession of a 'certain temporal lady of those parts' who annoyed and disturbed the nuns by using the doorway, so it was blocked up. Around 1400, its abbess was Margaret Holmystede, and another resident there in the late 1300s and early 1400s whom Isabel of Gloucester would have known was Marion Charteseye, daughter of a London draper. By the ninth year of her cousin Henry V's reign, which ran from March 1421 to March 1422, Isabel had become the abbess of the Minoresses, though little is known of her period of office, not even how long it lasted. She was still in office on

5 February 1424, when she successfully took legal action via her lawyer John Stafford regarding a building which the abbey part-owned in the London parish of All Hallows at the Hay.[5] The Minoresses' house was closed in 1539 during the Dissolution and the ruins were destroyed by fire at the end of the 1700s, though the street where it stood, near the Tower of London and Aldgate, is still called the Minories.

As was the case with the Gloucester sisters, their much older French cousin Marie de Coucy, countess of Soissons and lady of Coucy, Oisy and Marle, did not have a happy time in 1400. As a vulnerable widow, she was induced to sell much of her territory to Louis, duke of Orléans (b. 1372), brother of Charles VI and her late husband's cousin, at a great loss to herself and her heirs. This unfair deal took place on 15 November 1400, and although Marie herself was never able to have it overturned in her own lifetime, the duke of Orléans was assassinated in November 1407 leaving an underage son. In 1409, Marie's son and heir Robert de Bar was able to recover some of the lands, though his descendants and those of Orléans continued to dispute the lands.[6] The kingdom of France was in chaos in the late 1300s and early 1400s; Charles VI became insane in 1392 and for most of the remaining three decades of his life was incapable of ruling, and his brother Orléans and their uncle the duke of Burgundy, and later Burgundy's son and heir John the Fearless, battled for dominance.

Mere months after being induced to sell her lands to the duke of Orléans, Marie de Coucy became involved in a dispute with her English-born sister. Philippa de Coucy presented a petition to the parliament held at Westminster from 20 January to 10 March 1401 as 'Phelippe, formerly wife of Robert de Veer, duke of Ireland, whom God absolve' (an entirely conventional expression when referring to a deceased person, not an indication that Philippa believed Robert's soul was in need of absolution). She reminded the lords and the commons that King Henry's first parliament had declared that she should be able to enjoy her dowry from her marriage to Robert, despite the judgement against him at the Merciless Parliament of 1388, as she herself 'had not committed an offence of any kind'. She was of royal lineage, she pointed out, and had only a small income to maintain her rightful estate, and 'through forgetfulness and preoccupation with other burdensome matters' – a very tactful and clever way to put it – nothing had been done about her income. Robert de Vere's successor as earl of Oxford was his uncle

Aubrey, who died in 1400 leaving a son Richard, born in 1385. Henry IV declared that, while Richard was under age, Philippa should be able to hold her rightful lands, and that when Richard turned 21 he and Philippa could come to their own arrangement.[7]

Later in 1401, on 2 July, Henry IV issued a confirmation of certain 'letters of agreement between the king's kinswomen Philippa de Coucy, duchess of Ireland, and her sister Marie de Coucy, wife of the late Sir Henri de Bar'. Their much younger half-sister Isabelle de Coucy, born sometime after 1386, was also involved. The two Coucy sisters, though born near in age in 1366 and 1367, probably did not know each other well at all, having grown up in different countries, and were therefore perhaps not close. Philippa sued Marie in Paris, claiming that she had a right to half of the county of Soissons because their father Enguerrand had acquired it during his marriage to their mother Isabella of Woodstock. She also claimed a half of Origny, a fifth of Oisy, a sixth of Pinon and Baigneux, and so on, 'because by the custom of France, her mother's dower is the inheritance of the children born in marriage'. Philippa further claimed a third of her father's barony of Coucy, as one of his three daughters. Marie objected strenuously, pointing out, correctly as it happened, that by French custom the inheritance was indivisible and belonged by right to herself as Enguerrand's eldest daughter (in England, female heirs shared an inheritance equally in the absence of male heirs, but in France, it passed to the eldest daughter). Marie stated that Philippa owned all the lands in England which had belonged to their parents and were worth more than the French estates. Eventually, the sisters agreed to abide by the situation as it had already stood for decades: Marie would keep the French lands in their entirety and Philippa would keep the English lands in their entirety.[8] Henry IV referred to Philippa either as 'Madam of Ireland', 'Philippa, duchess of Ireland' or as 'Philippa de Coucy, duchess of Ireland and countess of Oxford', i.e. by her maiden name rather than by the family name of her late husband.[9] This was rather unconventional and therefore perhaps rather revealing.

Far away in Castile, Queen Catalina became pregnant around Christmas 1400 for the first time, or at least, experienced her first pregnancy that resulted in a living child. On 14 September 1401 in Segovia, she gave birth to her eldest child, Doña María of Castile; the infant was named after her 34-year-old godmother and great-aunt, María de Ayala, illegitimate daughter of King Pedro the Cruel. The queen was now in her late twenties, and King Enrique was 21 when his daughter was born. María of Castile was designated *princesa de Asturias*, and on 6 January 1402 at the *Cortes* of Toledo, King Enrique also named her as the *primogénita al trono*, the rightful, firstborn heir to his throne, a position María would hold until the birth of her younger brother some years later. Later in life, María, who became queen of Aragon and Sicily by marriage, sometimes referred to herself in letters as 'We the queen of Aragon and Sicily, firstborn [*primo génita*] of the kingdoms of Castile and Leon'.[10] In *c.* 1403, though the precise date is unfortunately not recorded, Queen Catalina gave birth to a second daughter, whom she named after herself.[11]

Anne of Gloucester and Edmund Stafford received full possession of all the lands that would have passed to her 16-year-old sister Isabel, recently professed as a Minoress in London, on 4 June 1402.[12] Edmund, presumably with Anne, was at Stafford Castle on 1 and 12 March and 15 May 1402, and Anne had become pregnant in late 1401.[13] On 15 August 1402, now aged 19, she gave birth to a son, and named him Humphrey after her late brother and her maternal grandfather (d. 1373), the earl of Hereford, Essex and Northampton. Humphrey Stafford, or Humfrai as the name was often spelt at the time, was born in Hereford, and his wet-nurse was Margaret Stevones.[14] Anne and Edmund also had a daughter whom Anne named after herself, whose date of birth is unknown; she might have been older than her brother.[15] Anne's much older cousin Queen Philippa of Portugal, now 42, gave birth to her ninth and youngest child, and the sixth who would live into adulthood, a few weeks later on 29 September 1402, in the town of Santarém. He was Infante Dom Fernando, later known as the Holy Prince or Saint Prince (*O Infante Santo*), and although he has never officially been canonised or beatified by the Catholic Church, he remains a popular unofficial saint in his native Portugal. Fernando's birth was a difficult one, which perhaps partly explains why Philippa had no more children, though her age was surely also a major factor.[16]

In the early 1400s, if not before, Queen Philippa became even more devout than ever, and took to spending almost all day in church or in her chapel. A Portuguese chronicler states 'As soon as it was morning, she immediately went to the church, where she stayed until noon, and as soon as she had eaten and taken a little rest, she subsequently returned to her prayers.' He adds that 'the greater part of her preoccupation was in praying', and that every day she prayed the canonical hours, the hours of Our Lady, the prayers of the dead, seven psalms, and 'many other devotions'.[17] This piety stood in stark contrast to Queen Philippa's maternal grandfather Duke Henry of Lancaster, who admitted in 1354 that he generally preferred to lie in bed in the mornings rather than get up to hear Mass, telling himself that he would hear it twice tomorrow instead.[18] Philippa's half-sister Joan Beaufort, countess of Westmorland, lost her mother on 10 May 1403, when the remarkable Katherine Swynford, dowager duchess of Lancaster, passed away and was buried in Lincoln Cathedral. Joan would be buried alongside her mother many years later.

Chapter 23

Queen Catalina's Son

Henry IV, widowed from Mary de Bohun in early July 1394, married his second wife in Winchester on 7 February 1403. She was the partly Spanish, partly French Juana of Navarre, daughter of Carlos II 'the Bad', king of Navarre (r. 1349–87) and the widow of John IV, duke of Brittany (d. 1399). Juana was the mother of the underage John V (b. 1389), now duke of Brittany, for whom she acted as regent until she moved to England to become its queen. Rather curiously, as Queen Juana had eight or nine children from her first marriage and was only in her early or mid-thirties in 1403, and Henry IV had six children with Mary de Bohun and an illegitimate son named Edmund Lebourde born at the start of the 1400s, the couple had no surviving offspring together in almost exactly a decade of marriage. Historian Gemma Hollman, however, citing a chronicle written in the north of England, states that Queen Juana might have given birth to stillborn twins at the end of 1403 (which, if true, suggests that she must have become pregnant almost immediately after her wedding).[1] If this was indeed the case, there is no other known record of these children. Henry and Juana's marriage seems to have been a love-match and they were a genuinely close and affectionate couple, and certainly Juana gave up her position as regent and ruler of Brittany to move to England to marry her second husband. Henry's biographer Ian Mortimer points out that the king was remarkably loyal to his friends and loved ones, and especially to both his wives, whom he loved dearly and to whom he was, as far as anyone can tell, faithful; his only known illegitimate child was born between his marriages.[2]

It was hardly the most propitious time for Juana, who was crowned queen in Westminster Abbey on 26 February 1403, to have arrived in England. The powerful Henry Percy, first earl of Northumberland, and his eldest son Henry 'Hotspur' Percy, had played a vital role in the downfall of Richard II and accession of Henry IV in 1399. The two Percys, however, along with the earl's younger brother Thomas Percy, earl of Worcester, grew disenchanted with the new king, and in 1403 Hotspur and his uncle Worcester rebelled against Henry. At the battle of Shrewsbury on 21 July 1403, Edmund, earl of Stafford, fought for the king against the Percys, and, although the royal side won victory, was killed there. Anne of Gloucester, still just 20, was now a widow for the second time, with a son less than a year old and a daughter as well. She received her dower in mid-November 1403 and took the customary oath not to marry again without the king's permission, an oath which she would in fact break a couple of years later. Anne now owned a considerable part of the Stafford lands as she still held her dower from her first husband Thomas, Edmund's older brother, and her annual income – from the Stafford estate, her own considerable share of the de Bohun lands, and her inheritance from her father Thomas of Woodstock – has been estimated at a large £2,200 net, making her one of the richest women in England. She held lands in eleven counties.

Henry 'Hotspur' Percy was killed during the battle of Shrewsbury, fighting on the opposite side to Edmund Stafford, and his uncle Thomas Percy, earl of Worcester, was executed shortly afterwards. Hotspur's father the earl of Northumberland was forced to submit to the king in York, where his son's head was spiked on one of the four gates leading into the city, but afterwards continued the Percy rebellion; he would be killed during the battle of Bramham Moor, the last battle of their rebellion, in February 1408. Joan Beaufort, meanwhile, received a grant of the marriage of John Clifford (b. late 1380s), heir of his late father Thomas, Lord Clifford (d. 1391), from her half-brother the king on 18 August 1403 a few weeks after the battle of Shrewsbury.[3] She and her husband Ralph Neville were high in the king's favour.

Elizabeth of Lancaster, dowager countess of Huntingdon, finally received her dower from her marriage to John Holland in June 1404 four and a half years after his death, after she and John of Cornwall (*monsire Johan Cornewaille*) presented a petition to the parliament held in Westminster in January 1404.[4] The lands lay mostly in Devon, including the castle of Barnstaple, with others in Somerset and Huntingdonshire. According to the *Oxford Dictionary of National Biography*, Elizabeth gave birth to her son John Cornwall the younger on 15 February 1405, which was most probably the month of her forty-second birthday.[5]

On 3 September 1404 at Segovia, Elizabeth's brother-in-law King Enrique III of Castile and Leon sent a letter to Queen Catalina which makes it apparent that he knew she was pregnant for the third time, though she was only about three months along:

> I, the king, send you warm greetings, as to the one I love
> as well as my own heart, and notify you that, considering
> the condition you are in at present, and so that you may
> have with you persons who will give you pleasure and free
> you of your cares, I have arranged to send for Doña Teresa
> de Ayala, prioress of the monastery of Santo Domingo el
> Real in Toledo. She, more than any other, is just the sort of
> person you will enjoy having with you.[6]

Decades earlier, the prioress Teresa de Ayala had been one of the many mistresses of Catalina's grandfather King Pedro 'the Cruel', and had a daughter with him in *c.* 1367, Doña María de Ayala, a half-sister of Catalina's late mother Costanza of Castile, duchess of Lancaster, and the godmother of Catalina and Enrique's eldest child. King Enrique referred to Doña María in both this letter to Catalina and another dated six days later on 9 September 1404 as *Donna María vuestra tya*, 'your aunt'. In extant letters of 1404 and 1410, Catalina herself addressed Teresa de Ayala as her 'dearest and much longed-for mother' (*muy cara e muy deseada madre*), and referred to María as 'our dearest and much honoured, and much longed-for, aunt, lady and mother, your daughter'.[7] By 1410, Catalina's mother Costanza of Castile had been dead for sixteen years and Catalina had not seen her for more than twenty years, and her letters to Teresa and María – who was only about five or six years older than the queen herself – are rather poignant and perhaps reveal that she missed Costanza deeply. In her letters to Teresa and María, Catalina referred to herself, as she always did in her correspondence, as *Yo la Reyna*, 'I, the queen'.

King Enrique's letters of September 1404 demonstrate his great affection for his wife and his concern for her wellbeing, and he sent another letter to Doña Teresa de Ayala and his marshal, Don Diego Fernández, 'as persons in whom I greatly trust' from Casa de la Rivera in Segovia on 26 February 1405, when Catalina's pregnancy was nearing term. This letter indicates that Teresa and Diego had been investigating twenty candidates as wet-nurses for the infant. Enrique carefully set out his conditions: the women chosen had to be between 20 and 30 years old; had to have 'clear skin, good colour and full figures'; must have given birth two to four months previously; must have infants who were well cared for and well developed; and must produce milk excellent in quantity, colour and quality. The suitable candidates also had to be 'of the best sort and condition of women', preferably noblewomen, and must not be the wives of foreigners. This was perhaps a rather curious condition for the king to impose, given that his own wife had been born in England and spent the first thirteen or fourteen years of her life there, from her birth in 1372 or 1373 until her family's departure for the Iberian peninsula in June 1386. Catalina spent part of her third pregnancy in Teresa de Ayala's company, as the king had wished; she wrote to her 'dearest and beloved mother' about Teresa's imminent arrival in Toro to see her on 12 December 1404, and on 29 December and again on 9 January 1405, King Enrique, in Madrid, wrote to Teresa thanking her for informing him that his wife was in good health.[8]

Catalina gave birth to her youngest child and only son, Infante Don Juan, named after both of his grandfathers (King Juan I of Castile and John of Gaunt, duke of Lancaster), in Segovia on 6 March 1405. Both she and Enrique must have been absolutely overjoyed to have a son, and the boy immediately displaced his 3-year-old sister María, *princesa de Asturias*, as heir to their father's throne. According to a chronicle called the *Gracia Dei*, Queen Catalina took advantage of her husband's joy at having a son to promote the entry of her cousin Pedro, son of Pedro the Cruel and Juana de Castro's son Juan (1355–1405) and his wife Elvira de Eril, into the priesthood. Pedro's sister Costanza probably joined the priory of Santo Domingo el Real in Toledo around the same time.[9] Catalina herself was so delighted to have a son that she overreached herself; Enrique III sent another letter to the prioress Teresa de Ayala and her daughter María de Ayala in Santo Domingo el Real on 13 March 1405, when Don Juan was only a week old:

> I have been led to understand that the queen has chosen and appointed several women around the infante, my son, as ladies-in-waiting, women to watch over him, and other such offices. I am greatly amazed at what she has done, since it is I who ought to make arrangements for all such officials.

Enrique told the two women to tell his wife 'not to meddle in any of these things. Leave her with no doubt that I am extremely annoyed by what she has done, and I will in no wise tolerate it'. He admitted that Catalina might have acted in the belief that she was doing something appropriate, but that she was wrong and it was certainly not fitting. She had 'done great injury and harm', thundered the king.[10] One hopes that he soon forgave his wife, given that she had produced a male heir for him and his kingdom and given his statement a few months earlier that he loved her as much as his own heart. His letter would seem to prove that the Spanish chronicler who stated that Enrique became 'sad and irritable' as a result of his mysterious recurring illness had a point. King Enrique had spent the festive season of 1404/05 in Madrid, which in the Middle Ages was merely a small town in central Spain and not the great city it was to become in the sixteenth century during the reign of Philip (or Felipe) II, Enrique and Catalina's great-great-great-grandson.[11] Enrique had the Palacio Real de El Pardo, the Royal Palace of El Pardo, built just outside Madrid around this time; it stood on the site of a former hunting-lodge.

Chapter 24

An Illegitimate Daughter and an Unlicensed Marriage

Philippa de Coucy, calling herself 'Philippe, duchess of Ireland and countess of Oxenford', presented a petition to her cousin the king in the early 1400s. She held half of the manor of Kendal (then in the county of Westmorland, now in Cumbria), and complained that a group of armed men had attacked some shops she owned there and had razed them to the ground (the petition was in French, but the word 'shops' was written in English, *shopes*). She asked the king to look into the matter, and Henry, who appears to have been very fond of Philippa and who doubtless appreciated her loyalty to him, did as she requested.[1]

Also sometime in the early 1400s, the widowed Constance of York had a relationship with the young earl of Kent, Edmund Holland. Edmund was born in early January 1382 or 1383, and was therefore a few years younger than Constance, who was most probably born in the mid-1370s and married Thomas Despenser as early as 1379, years before Edmund's birth.[2] He was the brother and heir of Thomas Holland, summarily executed during the Epiphany Rising in January 1400, as Constance's and Elizabeth of Lancaster's husbands had also been, and was a keen jouster and a famously excellent soldier. We would not know about this rather intriguing relationship except that Constance bore Edmund's illegitimate daughter, Alianore Holland, perhaps in or around 1405; Alianore's date of birth is not known, but Constance and Edmund might have named her after Edmund's eldest sister Alianore, dowager countess of March and Lady Charlton, who died on 23 October 1405. An entry on the Patent Roll dated 10 January 1405 records Henry IV's permission for Kent to 'marry whomsoever he will of the king's allegiance,' so perhaps his affair with Constance was over by then. On the other hand, that entry states that Kent was 'a minor in the king's custody', when in fact he had just turned 22 or 23 and was a year or two past his majority, so it might be dated incorrectly.[3]

Edmund Holland was killed fighting in Brittany on 15 September 1408, only in his mid-twenties; the heirs to the earldom of Kent were his four surviving sisters Joan, Margaret, Eleanor and Elizabeth, and the son of his late eldest sister, Alianore. His and Constance's daughter Alianore Holland launched an audacious, though unsuccessful, claim to be his legitimate daughter and heir in 1431, but the Kent heirs all worked against her and pointed out that Constance and Edmund had never married. Furthermore, they stated that Constance attended Edmund's wedding to the Italian noblewoman Lucia Visconti in January 1407 but did not speak up and state that Edmund was in fact already her husband. Were it not for Alianore Holland's bold though doomed claim to be her father's true-born and legitimate heir – Edmund and Lucia were to have no children during their brief twenty-month marriage – we would have no idea that a widowed noblewoman who was the granddaughter of two kings had an affair with a nobleman, and one who was a few years her junior to boot. One wonders how common such a situation might have been, and how many similar affairs happened which did not find their way onto written record.[4]

The chronicler of Tewkesbury Abbey in Gloucestershire, where Constance's husband Thomas Despenser and numerous ancestors of his were buried, believed wrongly that Constance married and had a child named Alianore with the earl of Arundel, Thomas Fitzalan, a first cousin of Edmund Holland. This is a rather interesting misunderstanding perhaps based on a betrothal between Constance and Thomas Fitzalan in the early 1400s, or at least on a discussion of one.[5] Born in 1381, Arundel was, like the earl of Kent, a few years younger than Constance, and married a Portuguese bride in 1405 (see below). He had no legitimate children either and his heir to his two earldoms and his lands was a cousin, and if he had indeed married Constance of York and had been the father of her daughter Alianore, Alianore would have been the Arundel heir.

In 1405, Constance took part in a plot to free the young sons of the late earl of March, Roger Mortimer (d. 1398). Edmund Mortimer, the elder brother, was born in 1391, and Roger the younger in 1393. As the senior male descendants of Edward III's third son Lionel of Antwerp, the boys, young though they were, posed a threat to Henry IV, who was the son of Edward III's fourth son John of Gaunt, and were held in captivity or at least under a kind of house arrest at Windsor Castle. Constance was, therefore, continuing her late husband's rebellion against her cousin, and, according to the Chronicle of London, committed treason against Henry IV by declaring the elder Mortimer boy, Edmund, to be the true king of England. Her lover the earl of Kent, though himself a half-nephew of the late Richard II and the brother and nephew of two of the other men executed in early 1400 during the Epiphany Rising, took no known part in Constance's rebellion – even though he was, thanks to the endlessly confusing and complicated marital tangles of the English noble elite in the late fourteenth and early fifteenth centuries, also the uncle of the two young Mortimer boys.[6] Constance's plan appears to have been to remove the Mortimers from Windsor Castle and to take them to Wales to Edmund Mortimer (b. 1376), Philippa of Clarence's youngest child and another of the Mortimer boys' uncles, and a man who would die in rebellion against Henry IV some years later. It is possible that Constance was pregnant at the time of her escapade, which failed in its aims, though the problem of the two male Mortimers and their claim to the throne rose its head again a decade later and was to bring about the death of Constance's younger brother Richard of Conisbrough. After she failed to spirit the boys away to Wales, her lands and goods were confiscated and given into the temporary custody of Queen Juana on 6 April 1405; Constance received her goods back on 19 January 1406 and her lands, finally, on 15 June 1407.[7]

Probably around the middle of October 1404, though the date is not entirely certain, Constance's cousin Marie de Coucy died while attending a wedding. Having spent a happy day in the company of other noble French ladies, Marie, now in her late thirties, was suddenly taken violently ill, and died during the night. There were rumours of poison, though the question of who might have wanted to poison the lady, and why, was left unexplained.[8] Marie left as her heir her only surviving son Robert de Bar, who was to spend several years battling against the Orléans family in regard to the unfair land deal they had forced on Marie some years before. Her sister Philippa de Coucy in England must have come to hear of her death; whether or to what extent she grieved for the loss of the sister with whom she had argued over lands, and whom she perhaps did not know very well, cannot be known.

The mother-in-law with whom Philippa was very close, Maud Ufford, dowager countess of Oxford, got into trouble with Henry IV in

1404. She distributed badges with Richard II's emblem of a white hart in Essex, to make it look as though the former king was still alive, and went so far as to join a conspiracy to depose King Henry. He imprisoned her in the Tower of London. An entry on the Close Roll dated 2 May 1404 talks of Henry IV's 'suspicion of the countess [of Oxford]', and states that one of Maud's damsels, Agnes Martyn, was ill in custody in London but that Maud herself had been taken from the Tower to Windsor Castle by then. Richard Botiller, another of Maud's servants, was also being held in custody in London at the time. Queen Juana pleaded with her husband to show clemency and to release the countess, who was now in her late fifties, and Maud was pardoned 'for all treasons, felonies, rebellions, misprisions, negligences and trespasses' on 5 December 1404 and restored to her lands and goods.[9]

Elizabeth of Lancaster's son-in-law Thomas Mowbray, earl of Norfolk, also became embroiled in a rebellion against his wife's uncle Henry IV, in the company of Richard Scrope, archbishop of York, and he and the archbishop were beheaded in a field outside York on 8 June 1405. Thomas, born in September 1385, was not yet 20 years old when he was executed, and his heir was his brother John, born in Calais in August 1390. Elizabeth's daughter Constance Holland was now a teenage widow.[10] Constance's sister Alice Holland, Elizabeth's second daughter, most probably married Richard de Vere (b. 1385), later earl of Oxford, at an uncertain date in the late 1300s, but she died before they had children. A petition presented to Henry IV in 1399 states that Richard de Vere *ad espose la file de vostre soere*, 'married the daughter of your sister', and it seems highly likely that one of Elizabeth's daughters was meant, and if so it must have been Alice Holland. After the failure of the Epiphany Rising in January 1400, John Holland, earl of Huntingdon, had sought refuge with Richard's father Aubrey de Vere, earl of Oxford (d. April 1400) in Hadleigh, Essex, perhaps because his daughter was already betrothed or married to Aubrey's son. Alice Holland died at an unknown date in or before 1407.[11]

Anne of Gloucester, dowager countess of Stafford, had married her second husband Edmund Stafford in 1398 without her cousin Richard II's permission, and she married her third husband without her cousin Henry IV's permission sometime before 20 November 1405, when Henry pardoned them for the unlicensed marriage.[12] He was William Bourchier or Bourgchier or Burghchier, who, despite his French-sounding last name, was an English knight whose great-grandfather John Bourchier (d. 1329) was a judge of the Court of Common Pleas. John's son Robert Bourchier, William's grandfather, was Chancellor of England, and died of the plague during the great pandemic of 1348/49. William's father William Bourchier the elder was Robert's second son and therefore was not the Bourchier heir; his elder brother John (d. 1400) left a son, Bartholomew, born around 1370, the first cousin of Anne of Gloucester's husband.[13] William's own date of birth is uncertain, but he was probably born in the mid-1370s or thereabouts and was therefore a few years Anne's senior. As he was not an heir and was not particularly wealthy or well-connected, her marriage to him must surely have been a love-match.

The first of Anne and William's children was a son named Henry Bourchier, a future count of Eu and earl of Essex. The *Complete Peerage* states, though without citing a primary source, that Henry was born before 28 May 1404.[14] As Anne's previous husband Edmund Stafford died on 21 July 1403 just ten months before this alleged date, she would have had to marry William Bourchier and become pregnant more or less immediately afterwards for this to be the case, and this seems unlikely. On the other hand, the Bourchier family were neighbours of Anne's late father the duke of Gloucester in Essex, and William probably spent time at Pleshey Castle in his youth. William certainly served in Duke Thomas's household as early as 1392, and in 1396 Thomas hired him as a member of his personal retinue and paid him a substantial £36 a year. Bourchier later joined the retinue of Henry of Monmouth, prince of Wales, and was trusted enough by Henry IV to be appointed as one of the men sent to Scandinavia to negotiate the marriage of Henry's younger daughter Philippa of Lancaster (b. 1394) to Erik of Pomerania, king of Norway, Denmark and Sweden.[15]

Anne of Gloucester and William Bourchier had already known each other for a very long time by *c.* 1403, and it may be that a previous attraction blossomed into love and a desire to marry not long after Earl Edmund's death. As well as Henry Bourchier, Anne and William had three younger sons and a daughter; their son Thomas Bourchier was archbishop of Canterbury from 1455 to 1486, and was elected as a cardinal in 1467. Anne's son Humphrey from her marriage to Edmund Stafford, meanwhile, was betrothed into the Neville family as early as 1408, when he was just 6 years old. Pope Gregory XII issued a dispensation for consanguinity in early August 1408 to enable Humphrey to marry Eleanor, eldest daughter of Ralph Neville and Joan Beaufort, earl and countess of Westmorland.[16] As it turned out, Eleanor married Constance of York's son Richard Despenser instead, and secondly the earl of Northumberland after she was widowed in her teens, while Humphrey Stafford married Anne Neville, one of Eleanor's many younger sisters.

Chapter 25

Queen Philippa and an Arundel Marriage

In 1405, Queen Philippa of Portugal took a deep interest in the marriage of her husband's illegitimate daughter Beatriz to the English earl of Arundel, Thomas Fitzalan. Born in March 1360, Philippa was old enough to be the mother of Earl Thomas, and she had departed from England in the summer of 1386 before he was even 5 years old, so she cannot have known him well, or indeed at all. He was, however, a double first cousin of Philippa's late sister-in-law Mary de Bohun, countess of Derby, and the queen must have heard plenty of positive things about Thomas for her to promote his and Beatriz's marriage to her husband. The young earl of Arundel was also a nephew of Thomas Arundel, archbishop of Canterbury, another fact surely in his favour, given how devout Queen Philippa was.[1] Beatriz was the daughter of King João and Inês Pires, a woman with whom João had a long-term relationship before he married Queen Philippa. Beatriz's full brother Afonso, first duke of Braganza and count of Barcelos – and a great-grandfather of the famous Isabel la Católica, queen of Castile and Aragon – was born in August 1377 and, rather remarkably, did not die until December 1461, and they had a sister, Branca, who died in infancy in *c*. 1378/79. Beatriz was born around 1380 or 1382, a few years before her father married Philippa.[2]

In Lisbon on 4 November 1405, Queen Philippa wrote to her brother on the matter in French, calling herself 'P. de P.' for 'Philippa of Portugal', and addressing Henry as her 'most exceeding best beloved brother' (he was in fact her only brother, not counting their three Beaufort half-brothers). King João also wrote to Henry, in his native Portuguese, calling himself *Dom Joham*, calling Beatriz *Dona Beatriz, minha filia* ('my daughter') and referring to the earl of Arundel as *nosso filho*, 'our son'. Earl Thomas was bound to pay Henry IV

115

2,000 marks for the royal permission granted to him in 1403 to choose his own bride, and the king and queen of Portugal both begged Henry to pardon this huge debt.[3] Beatriz of Portugal duly sailed to England and married Thomas Fitzalan at Lambeth on 26 November 1405; Thomas's uncle the archbishop of Canterbury performed the ceremony. Henry IV was present, as were his eldest son Henry of Monmouth, prince of Wales, the king's first cousin Edward, duke of York, Arundel's cousin Edmund Holland, earl of Kent, Richard Beauchamp, earl of Warwick, and Beatriz's brother Afonso, then count of Barcelos and later the first duke of Braganza.[4] Although Constance of York's lover, or perhaps her former lover, the earl of Kent attended his cousin of Arundel's wedding, Constance herself did not, being in disgrace with the king and probably still imprisoned after her attempt to free the Mortimer boys.

Earl Thomas of Arundel sent a letter to Henry IV from Arundel Castle in Surrey on 25 June 1406, seven months after he married Beatriz. Although the letter was written in French, Thomas, interestingly, referred to Beatriz as *ma muliere*, 'my wife', using the Portuguese word, rather than *ma compaigne* in French. (In modern Portuguese, *mulher* means 'woman', and 'wife' is *esposa*.) Although the earl had obviously learnt some words of Portuguese since his wedding, it is perhaps revealing that he did not use the words *ma treschere muliere*, 'my dearest wife', as would have been both conventional and affectionate; referring to Beatriz simply as 'my wife' comes across as rather abrupt and unamicable, and perhaps reveals that the early months of this Anglo-Portuguese marriage were not particularly happy ones (though in his will made in August 1415, Thomas referred to Beatriz far more conventionally as *nostre tresame compaigne*, 'our beloved wife'). Thomas apologised for not paying any of the money he owed to Henry, but because of the destruction of his lands in Wales and the great expenses of bringing *ma muliere* to England, he was unable to. Thomas referred to Philippa of Lancaster as 'the queen of Portugal, my very honoured lady, your sister', with reference to Henry obtaining a benefice in England for Queen Philippa's English-born chancellor, Adam Damport or Davenport.[5]

Far away in Castile, Henry IV and Queen Philippa's half-sister Queen Catalina was widowed on Christmas Day 1406 when Enrique III died at the age of just 27, during preparations for a military campaign against Granada. Most of the *Reconquista* or the 'Reconquest' of Spain, i.e. the centuries-long recapture of Spanish territory by the Christian kings from its Muslim rulers, was complete by the middle of the thirteenth century, and only the emirate of Granada remained. Granada would finally fall to King Fernando or Ferdinand of Aragon and Queen Isabel la Católica of Castile, a descendant of both Catalina and Philippa of Lancaster, in 1492. From the 1240s until 1492, the kings of Castile undertook frequent military campaigns against the emirate – though by the early 1400s, Castile and Granada had been at peace for decades – and Enrique died while the *Cortes* of Castile were gathered in Toledo to discuss the emirate's incursions into Castilian territory and what to do about it. Catalina, herself now 33 or 34, became co-regent for her infant son Juan II, who was well under two years old at the end of 1406. She ruled alongside her brother-in-law Fernando, who became known as Fernando of Antequera after he captured the Muslim-held stronghold of Antequera in Andalusia in 1410.

A close adviser, and indeed friend, of Queen Catalina during her regency was Leonor López de Córdoba, daughter of Martín López de Córdoba, once the *mayordomo mayor* or high steward of Catalina's uncle Don Sancho (1363–1371, one of King Pedro the Cruel's illegitimate children), and the master of the military orders of Calatrava and Alcántara. Leonor was ten years older than the queen, and is well-known in Spain for writing what is generally considered to be the first autobiography in Castilian, titled *Memorias*. She is also admired as Castile's first woman writer. The author of the *Chronicle of King Juan II* states that Catalina 'trusted [Leonor] so much, and loved her in such a manner, that nothing was ever done without her counsel', and chronicler Alvar García de Santa María wrote much the same thing. Another contemporary, however, failing to see in Leonor whatever Queen Catalina saw in her, described her as 'frivolous and wretched', and Catalina's brother-in-law Fernando of Antequera, alarmed at Leonor's influence over the queen, managed to have her banished from court in 1408 or 1409. Catalina continued to treat her friend with great affection, however.[6] Another contemporary chronicler stated that Catalina was 'very much governed' by her favourites, and a third that she was 'highly influenced and easily swayed by her favourites'.[7] To a certain extent this is surely true, though perhaps some of the chroniclers' tales of Catalina's presumed over-dependence on friends and advisors were rooted in their disbelief that a woman might rule successfully in her own right.

Another woman high in Catalina's favour, replacing Leonor in about 1414, was Inés de Torres. Some of the Castilian nobility, jealous of her influence over the regent, managed to engineer a sexual scandal and accused Inés of having an affair with Juan Alvarez de Osorio, lord of Villalobos and a knight of the Royal Guard (and formerly Catalina's steward), and forced her removal from court in 1416.[8] Despite her claimed over-dependence on favourites, however, Catalina proved a highly effective regent of Castile, especially after the death of her brother-in-law in 1416. For the next two years, Catalina was the sole regent of Castile, and worked to depose Benedict XIII at the council of Constance in 1416, made peace with the emirate of Granada in 1417, and smoothed relations with the Jewish population of Castile, which had been tense since the pogroms of 1391. Finally, she turned over power to her son Juan a few months before her death in 1418.[9] Throughout her regency, Catalina kept in close touch with her grandfather's former lover Teresa de Ayala at her priory in Toledo, continuing to address her as her beloved *madre* or 'mother'. In one letter of August 1409, the queen told Teresa that she, her son Juan and *las infantas* her daughters Doña María and Doña Catalina were all in good health, and added that it would please her greatly to hear good news of her beloved aunt María de Ayala. The queen's eldest child María of Castile also kept in close contact with the two de Ayala women and in one undated letter addressed them as 'those whom we much love and cherish', and Queen Catalina's son Juan II addressed María de Ayala as 'my aunt, whom I much love'.[10]

Joan Beaufort, countess of Westmorland, younger half-sister of the queens of Castile and Portugal, was another granddaughter of Edward III who was well versed in the art of wielding political influence, and sometimes used her relationship with her half-brother Henry IV to benefit her family, friends and adherents. One example is a petition she sent to Henry in 1407 concerning a squire named Christopher Standish, who had once worked in their father John of Gaunt's household and also served Henry in Wales. Christopher had married his wife Margaret 'purely for love', and Gaunt had, surely rather unfairly given that he married his third wife and Joan Beaufort's mother Katherine Swynford for similar reasons, dismissed him. Christopher and Margaret were destitute, and Joan therefore asked King Henry to appoint Margaret to a position in Queen Juana's household. The petition was written in medieval French by one of Joan's clerks, though a signature was added in what is believed to be her own handwriting: *Voster tres humble et obaisant serv[a]nt si vous plest J de W*, 'Your very humble and obedient servant, if it please you, J. of W.', meaning 'Joan of Westmorland'.[11]

Chapter 26

Queen Philippa's and Queen Catalina's Diplomacy

Philippa de Coucy, dowager duchess of Ireland and countess of Oxford, died on 24 September 1411 at the age of 43, and her inquisition post mortem was held in Essex, Middlesex, Yorkshire and Westmorland between October and December that year. Jurors determined that Henry IV was her heir, as he was the eldest son of her mother Isabella of Woodstock's brother John of Gaunt. Gaunt's eldest brother Edward of Woodstock's only legitimate son Richard II was dead without issue, and the next brother, Lionel of Antwerp, had no male issue. Philippa's only full sibling, Marie, was dead, Marie's son was French and not legally able to inherit lands in England, and King Henry was Philippa's closest living male and English relative. Henry IV had granted the reversion of Philippa's three Yorkshire manors and her lands in Westmorland to his and the late Mary de Bohun's third son John of Lancaster (b. 1389) on 24 January 1405, so John was named as Philippa's heir to them.[1] The heir to the dower lands Philippa had held from her marriage to the long-dead Robert de Vere was his much younger cousin Richard de Vere (b. 1385). Maud Ufford, the mother-in-law with whom Philippa had been so close, outlived her and died on 25 January 1413.[2] Marie and Philippa de Coucy's much younger half-sister Isabelle de Coucy also died in 1411 and her infant daughter died soon afterwards, leaving Marie's son Robert de Bar as the late Enguerrand de Coucy's only grandchild and heir.

The last few years of Henry IV's reign – he died in 1413 – proved to be a particularly fruitful period in Anglo-Portuguese relations, and this was due in large part to Henry's sister Philippa. The Treaty of Windsor, an agreement between England and Portugal to make and keep 'perpetual friendships, unions and alliances', sealed by Edward III and King Fernando in June 1373 and confirmed by Richard II and

King João in 1386, has never been broken and is the longest standing peace treaty in the world, and Queen Philippa's influence during the twenty-eight years of her marriage to João is often seen as instrumental in maintaining the treaty in those early decades. English relations with the kingdom of Castile were also warm and cordial in the first few years of the fifteenth century, especially while Henry's half-sister Catalina acted as regent for her son after 1406. Henry suggested to her in 1411 that they exchange sixty letters of safe-conduct to be used by Castilians and English people who wished to visit each other's countries, and in a treaty of 1408 between Castile and France, the French acknowledged their ally Castile's right to make truces with England.[3]

The Spanish historian César Olivera Serrano even considers that Catalina of Lancaster pursued policies that were more beneficial to her natal family than to her husband and children.[4] As well as their efforts to maintain close relationships with their brother in England, Queens Philippa and Catalina also did their best to promote excellent relations between Castile and Portugal. Fernão Lopes, the Portuguese chronicler, commented that after Enrique III's death in 1406, *Rainha dona Caterina*, Queen Catalina, 'worked hard so that she had good peace and friendship with Dom João, king of Portugal, married to her sister'. Both Lopes and another Portuguese chronicler, Gomes Eanes de Zurara, talk of the great efforts Catalina made to ensure peaceful and cordial relations with her brother-in-law's kingdom.[5] The great affection between the two Lancaster sisters is not in doubt, and it was shared by King João, who repeatedly addressed Catalina in his letters to her as his 'sister friend … whom we much love and cherish' (*irmaã amigua … que muito amamos e prezamos*).[6]

To further the two kingdoms' excellent relations, the Lancaster sisters made a double matrimonial alliance: Philippa's daughter Isabel of Portugal (b. 1397) would marry Catalina's son Juan II of Castile, who was eight years Isabel's junior, and Queen Catalina's second daughter Catalina of Castile (b. *c.* 1403) would marry Philippa's eldest surviving son Duarte (b. 1391), future king of Portugal. As it happened, neither marriage between these two sets of first cousins ultimately took place.[7] In 1414, King João and Queen Philippa of Portugal made an alternative suggestion: their then 17-year-old daughter Dona Isabel should marry another of her first cousins, Henry V of England. Although a papal dispensation for consanguinity was issued on 21 October 1414, this marriage did not come about either.[8] Isabel of Portugal finally married

Duke Philip the Good of Burgundy at the beginning of 1430 when she was almost 33, as his third wife.

Martí (b. 1356), king of Aragon, died on 31 May 1410, and left no surviving legitimate children. For the next two years, there was an interregnum in the kingdom of Aragon, and Queen Catalina of Castile mediated between several plausible candidates for the throne: Fadrique of Aragón, count of Luna, born *c.* 1401, an illegitimate grandson of King Martí; Catalina's brother-in-law Fernando of Antequera, grandson of Martí's's father King Pere IV (b. 1319, r. 1336–87) via his mother Leonor of Aragon, queen of Castile; Jaume, count of Urgell (b. 1380), great-grandson of Pere IV's father Alfonso IV (d. 1336) and married to Isabel, daughter of Pere IV and another sister of King Martí; Louis of Anjou (b. 1403), duke of Calabria and count of Provence, grandson of King Joan I (d. 1396, brother of Martí, Leonor and Isabel); the elderly Alfonso, duke of Gandia and count of Ribagorza, grandson of Jaume II (d. 1327) and cousin of Pere IV, who died in 1412 before the proceedings ended; and Catalina's own son Juan II of Castile, great-grandson of Pere IV and great-nephew of Martí. Catalina called a commission of experts to discuss and decide the matter, but Fernando of Antequera skilfully manipulated the proceedings and, by an act known as the Compromise of Caspe, became king of Aragon in 1412.[9] He was succeeded on his death in 1416 by his son Alfonso V, who by then had married his first cousin, Catalina of Lancaster's eldest child María of Castile.

Joan Beaufort and Ralph Neville's son Robert Neville, who was their second or third son after Richard and perhaps after William, joined the Church when he was very young. Robert, already called a 'cleric', was granted a papal dispensation just before Christmas 1410 'to hold, after attaining his eighteenth year, any benefice with cure, even of lay patronage'. He was said to be 'in or about his seventh year' at the time, placing his date of birth in about 1404.[10] Promoted and supported by his powerful uncle Bishop Henry Beaufort, Robert was elected bishop of Salisbury in 1426 when he was in his early twenties, though the election was disputed and Robert's consecration only went ahead a year later after a personal intervention by Henry Beaufort with Pope Martin V.[11] Joan and Henry's eldest brother John Beaufort, earl of Somerset, died in April 1410 leaving four sons and two daughters, one of whom was a future queen of Scotland, while his second son and ultimate heir John the younger was the grandfather of Henry VII.

Chapter 27

The Claiming of Castile

The brilliant reputation of Elizabeth of Lancaster's third husband Sir John Cornwall as a jouster and warrior continued in 1412. On 14 April that year, a 'Thenneguy de Chastell' was given a safe-conduct to travel to England and to fight against John Cornwall in Henry IV's presence. This means the Breton knight Tanneguy or Tanguy III du Châtel (1369–1449), who was given permission to bring 100 people to England in his retinue. The safe-conduct was valid for three months beginning on 1 May, and the combat took place in the lists at Smithfield.[1]

Elizabeth's brother Henry IV died on 20 March 1413 at not quite 46 years old, and was buried in Canterbury Cathedral. He had been ill for several years, and the prince of Wales, Henry of Monmouth, eldest of the king's four sons, had acted as virtual regent for some time, though father and son did not always get along. The coronation of Henry of Monmouth, now King Henry V, took place at Westminster Abbey on Passion Sunday, 9 April 1413. According to eyewitnesses, it was a snowy day. A number of young English noblemen were knighted the day before to mark the special occasion, including the long-dead Philippa of Clarence's grandsons Edmund and Roger Mortimer, Elizabeth of Lancaster's son John Holland, and Constance of York's only son, Richard Despenser.[2] Richard died not long afterwards, possibly in October 1413 and certainly before April 1414. One source states that he died on 11 October 1413 but is perhaps not reliable, though Richard was certainly dead by 16 April 1414 when he was called 'late Lord Despenser'.[3] Richard, whose seventeenth birthday fell at the end of November 1413, had married his second cousin Eleanor Neville, the eldest daughter and perhaps the eldest child of Ralph Neville and Joan Beaufort, earl and countess of Westmorland, in July 1411, but they had no children.[4] Constance and Thomas's daughter Elizabeth had died in or soon after 1405, and therefore the Despenser heir was Constance's daughter Isabelle, born in July 1400 six and a half months after her father's death and now Constance and Thomas's only living child. Isabelle Despenser was to marry twice, and both of her husbands were named Richard Beauchamp. She became countess of Worcester by her first marriage and countess of Warwick by her second.

According to the *Anales de la Corona de Aragón*, a history of the Spanish kingdom of Aragon written by the sixteenth-century historian and chronicler Jerónimo Zurita y Castro, Constance's brother Edward, duke of York, sent an emissary called Sir John de Monfort to his cousin Queen Catalina of Castile in 1413. The *Anales* state that Edward claimed the throne of Castile as the elder son and heir of the late Isabel of Castile, duchess of York. Although there was no doubt that Isabel was younger than her sister Costanza, Edward claimed a greater right to the Castilian throne by virtue of male descent, because Costanza only had a daughter, Catalina, whereas Edward was a son and therefore, he said, the rightful heir and successor of his and Catalina's mutual grandfather Pedro the Cruel. Furthermore, Edward proposed, via John de Monfort, a marriage between his nephew and heir Richard of York, born in 1411 as the son of Isabel of Castile's youngest child Richard, earl of Cambridge, and Leonor (b. 1402), Fernando of Antequera's youngest daughter and Catalina's niece.[5]

There is other evidence that Isabel of Castile, duchess of York, her husband Edmund of Langley, and their son Edward resented the fact that Isabel's sister Costanza and Edmund's brother John of Gaunt had supposedly set aside Isabel's rights to her late father's throne: sometime between August 1385 and December 1392, Edmund and Isabel issued a petition claiming that Gaunt had done so unjustly. The York couple argued that Pedro the Cruel had left his kingdom to his and María de Padilla's eldest daughter Beatriz (d. *c.* 1367/69) and her male heirs, then to Costanza and her male heirs, and finally to Isabel and her male heirs.[6] As Costanza had no male heirs, her only son John of Lancaster having died soon after birth in 1375 (according to chronicler Jean Froissart), Edmund and Isabel stated that Castile should fall to Isabel's male heirs instead, and their son made the same argument many years later. The Yorks were, in fact, mistaken. King Pedro's will of November 1362, which set out his planned succession to his throne, is cited in full in Pero López de Ayala's chronicle, and says that Beatriz was Pedro's primary heir. A legitimate son of Beatriz would be next in line, or failing a son, her legitimate daughter. Beatriz was followed by Costanza in the succession if Beatriz had no legitimate sons or daughters (as indeed she did not), followed by Isabel if neither Beatriz nor Costanza had legitimate sons or daughters. Pedro made a point of specifying that the sons, preferentially, or the daughters, failing the birth of sons, of his three daughters could inherit his kingdom.[7] Either Isabel, Edmund and Edward were unaware of this, or they knew it perfectly well but tried to claim the Castilian throne by right of male descent anyway.

Edward of York was the grandson of two kings, and many years previously in the early 1380s, his future marriage had been planned to King Fernando of Portugal's only child Beatriz, a marriage that under different circumstances might have made him king of Portugal. A few years later, he was put forward as a possible husband for one of the younger sisters of Isabelle de Valois, eldest daughter of Charles VI of France and the child-bride of Richard II, and in the early 1410s, he considered himself a possible king of Castile. In this context, Edward's marriage in the late 1390s to Philippa de Mohun, whose sister was the countess of Salisbury but who was otherwise a rather obscure English noblewoman, widowed from her two previous low-ranking husbands and much Edward of York's senior – perhaps past childbearing age when he wed her – is all the more remarkable.[8] For all his excellent royal connections, however, Edward of York made no headway in his claims to the throne of a country he had never set foot in, and the proposed marriage of his nephew and Catalina's niece did not take place either.

Chapter 28

Death of a Queen

In early May 1415, Joan Beaufort, countess of Westmorland, gave birth to the youngest of her many children: Cecily Neville, future duchess of York and the mother of two kings of England. Joan had borne two daughters in her first marriage to Robert Ferrers, and had another thirteen or fourteen children with Ralph Neville between *c*. 1397 and 1415, though several of them died young. Her eldest child, Elizabeth Ferrers, had wed John, Lord Greystoke as far back as October 1407, and her second child, Mary Ferrers, married her stepbrother, one of Ralph Neville's children from his first marriage.[1] Joan's close familial relationship to Henry IV and Henry V, and her and her husband's loyalty to them both, would enable their children to make excellent and highly advantageous marriages. Three of her Neville daughters became duchesses, of Norfolk, York and Buckingham, and another became a countess; her eldest son Richard married the heiress to the earldom of Salisbury, her second son became a bishop, and her three younger sons became Lords Fauconberg, Abergavenny, and Latimer.

In Valencia on 4 June 1415, Queen Catalina's eldest child Doña María, not yet 14, married her first cousin Alfonso of Aragon, who was born in 1396 as the eldest son of Fernando of Antequera (himself born in 1380; Fernando was only 15 or 16 at the birth of his son). Pope Benedict XIII personally presided over the festivities and had provided the necessary dispensation for the two cousins to wed, and it was a grand occasion with bonfires, fireworks, jousting, and public dancing in which the young couple took part.[2]

According to Gomes Eanes de Zurara, a Portuguese chronicler who wrote the text *Crónica da Tomada de Ceuta por el Rei D. João* (*Chronicle of the Taking of Ceuta by the King Dom João*), Doña María of Castile's aunt Queen Philippa of Portugal fell ill with the plague while staying at the monastery of Odivelas near Lisbon during the summer of 1415, and died there on 18 July, aged 55. Zurara, as impressed as everyone else with the English queen of Portugal, commented that Philippa embodied the four classical cardinal virtues, which are usually justice, prudence, fortitude and temperance, though he named them as justice, prudence, hope and fortitude (*justiça, prudemçia, esperamça, fortelleza*).[3] Before she passed away, Philippa called her five sons to her bedside and blessed them, and gave each of them a fragment of the True Cross and jewel-encrusted swords.[4] Her sons were knighted the day after her death and two of them, the second and third eldest, were given the title of duke for the first time in Portuguese history: Pedro became duke of Coímbra, and Henrique duke of Viseu.

Philippa's youngest child, Dom Fernando, later known as the *Infante Santo* or Holy Prince, was not yet 13 when he lost his mother. The queen's only daughter, 18-year-old Dona Isabel, was particularly devastated at her mother's death, as the two had always enjoyed a very close and affectionate relationship. Isabel's biographer believes that Isabel did everything she could to model herself on her mother throughout her long life; she lived until 1471 when she was 74, and was the last survivor of Philippa and João's children. In the period following the queen's death, the sorrowful Isabel retreated from the world for a while and sought refuge in needlework, books and music. As the only surviving royal daughter, however, once her period of mourning was over, Isabel took her place at the head of the queen's household. Philippa's chief lady-in-waiting and confidante, Beatriz Gonçalves de Moura, outlived the queen by three years, and accompanied and guided Isabel in her new role. Infante Pedro, the new duke of Coímbra, suggested to his father that as there was no other queen in the realm, all of Philippa's goods should be given to Isabel as her only daughter, and his brothers Duarte and Henrique agreed. Isabel remained head of the royal household until her marriage in early 1430 at the advanced (by the royal standards of the time) age of almost 33.

Philippa's widower and their older sons captured the port of Ceuta, on the coast of North Africa, a few weeks after her death on 21 August 1415, a significant first step in the development of Portugal's colonial empire and of its becoming a great maritime power. King João and three of his and Philippa's sons, Duarte, Pedro and Henrique, were appointed Knights of the Garter by their English relatives over the decades, as numbers 102, 144, 149 and 160. The king of Portugal was the first foreign recipient of the honour.[5]

Queen Philippa was not buried until 15 October 1416, fifteen months after her death, when she was finally laid to rest in the southernmost apse of the conventual church of the Dominican friary in Batalha in central Portugal. King João outlived her by eighteen years – he had never married again after losing his beloved wife – and on 14 August 1434 a year after his death, his and Philippa's bodies were reinterred in a joint tomb in the Founder's Chapel. Their five sons, Duarte, Pedro, Henrique, João and Fernando, and King João's illegitimate son Afonso of Barcelos from his pre-marital relationship with Inês Pires, carried their coffins into the chapel. The six men were followed by a procession of the royal couple's grandchildren, other members of the royal family, and numerous Portuguese lords and ladies. Joint tombs of a married couple were reasonably common in northern Europe but were completely unknown in Portugal at the time, so João's and Philippa's tomb broke new ground. João, aware of this and aware that the tomb-builders might be somewhat baffled by the request, left a detailed account in his will of precisely how he and the queen would lie together in their own joint monument. It seems likely that the idea had been Philippa's in the first place, given that her father John of Gaunt had been buried next to her mother Blanche of Lancaster in St Paul's Cathedral in 1399, and given also that in 1413, her nephew Henry V had moved her cousin Richard II from his original resting place in Langley Priory to a joint tomb with his first wife Anne of Bohemia in Westminster Abbey. It was perhaps also Philippa who requested that her and her husband's right hands should be joined on their effigies.[6]

In about 1415, Anne of Gloucester's daughter Anne Stafford married Edmund Mortimer, earl of March and Ulster. Born in 1391, Edmund was a few years his wife's senior, and was a grandson of Philippa of Clarence (d. *c.* 1378), countess of March and Ulster. In early 1415, he had received a general dispensation from the pope to marry a woman to whom he was related in the third degree of kindred, i.e. second cousins, on the grounds that he 'desires to have children, but being related to diverse magnates cannot find a wife suitable to his rank whom he can marry without papal dispensation'.[7] Sadly for Edmund, he was to have no children as he wished, and his heir was his older sister Anne's son Richard of York (b. 1411), who was also heir to his other, half-Castilian uncle, Edward, duke of York. Edward was killed at the battle of Agincourt on 25 October 1415, Henry V's great victory over the French. Marie de Coucy's only

127

son Robert de Bar was also killed at Agincourt, fighting for the French, as were his uncles Sir Édouard of Bar and Sir Jean of Bar. Robert left a daughter, Jeanne de Marle, born in the year of his death, who was his, her grandmother Marie's, and her great-grandfather Enguerrand's heir. Edward of York was one of the very few English noblemen who fell at Agincourt, though others had been forced to return to England before the battle because of the dysentery spreading through the English ranks. One of them was Thomas, earl of Arundel, husband of the late Queen Philippa of Portugal's stepdaughter Beatriz, who died on his thirty-fourth birthday a few days before the battle. Anne of Gloucester's husband William Bourchier, meanwhile, in charge of 102 soldiers on the battlefield, was said to have displayed great courage during the battle.[8]

Chapter 29

Joan Beaufort and Margery Kempe

In 1416, Sigismund, king of Hungary, Croatia and Germany, future king of Italy and Bohemia and Holy Roman Emperor, brother of Richard II's late queen Anne, visited England. His journey was connected to the Council of Constance, a congregation of numerous important European leaders which was held between 1414 and 1418 and ended the Great Schism, in which two (and later three) rival popes existed at the same time. Sigismund arrived at the port of Dover on 1 May, and a large number of English nobles waited for him at Rochester to accompany him to Blackheath close to London, where Henry V waited for him. Among them were Elizabeth of Lancaster's husband Sir John Cornwall and her son John Holland, who had turned 21 a few weeks earlier and had thus reached his majority, though his proof of age was not held until August 1418.[1]

Constance of York, Lady Despenser, died on 28 November 1416, aged about 40 or a little less, and was buried in Reading Abbey (which probably means that she passed away at the nearby Despenser manor of Caversham). She left her legitimate daughter, 16-year-old Isabelle Beauchamp née Despenser, to whom all of Constance's dower lands from her marriage to Thomas Despenser passed, and her illegitimate daughter Alianore Holland, who later married the widowed James Audley, Lord Tuchet (b. 1397). Isabelle arranged the marriage of her younger half-sister, and it seems that the two women and their families were close: Isabelle's son and heir Henry Beauchamp chose his aunt Alianore as the godmother of his daughter Anne in 1444.[2]

In 1401, Henry IV, at the behest of Thomas Arundel, archbishop of Canterbury, had passed a law in parliament called *De Heretico Comburendo*, which permitted the burning of heretics at the stake. The statute was issued in response to a wave of religious nonconformity, led by John Wyclif or Wycliffe (d. 1384), whose followers were called Lollards and who were called 'perfidious and perverse people of a certain new sect' who held and preached 'wicked, heretical and erroneous opinions' in the statute. This appallingly repressive landmark in religious persecution remained on the statute books until 1677, and stated that the punishment of being burned alive was intended to strike fear into people's hearts and to set an example for other Christians who might be tempted to believe erroneous doctrine.[3] Wyclif himself, though condemned as a heretic in his own lifetime, had been protected by the powerful John of Gaunt, and although Gaunt's son Henry IV did not share his father's religious tolerance, Gaunt's daughter Joan Beaufort apparently did.

Margery Kempe, née Brunham, was born in *c.* 1373 in a fairly well-off merchant family of King's Lynn in Norfolk, and was a devout Christian and mystic who had numerous religious visions and hallucinations. Her account of her experiences, *The Book of Margery Kempe*, composed in the 1420s, is considered the first autobiography in English. In 1417 or 1418, Margery was examined for orthodoxy by Henry Bowet, archbishop of York (d. 1423), and it was alleged that the previous Easter, she had visited the 'Lady of Westmorland', i.e. Joan Beaufort. Margery's own account of her interrogation – in her work, she always refers to herself as 'this creature' – reveals that the archbishop told her that Joan was 'well pleased with you, and liked your talk'. Margery was accused of advising Joan's eldest daughter Elizabeth née Ferrers, Lady Greystoke, to leave her husband, and offered to obtain a testimonial from Joan that she had done no such thing. Her visit to Joan Beaufort would appear to date to 1413, before Margery went on pilgrimage to Jerusalem probably in 1414, and she stated later that she told the countess the tale of a lady who was damned because she refused to love her enemies while a bailiff, widely regarded as evil, was saved because he did love his enemies.[4]

As well as evidently taking an interest in religious mysticism, Joan Beaufort was something of a bookworm. It ran in the family; her half-brother Henry IV's love of reading – he was, like their half-sister Queen Catalina, trilingual, and was able to read and write in English, French and Latin – is well known. While in exile in France in 1399, Henry attended and even commented on lectures at the University of Paris, as king of England in 1406, he spent several hours sitting in an abbey library reading, and owned so many books that he had a special study built at his palace of Eltham in Kent to accommodate them.[5] For her part, Joan lent a manuscript to her nephew Henry V, which he failed to return to her and which she had to petition his executors to get back after his death: 'a book containing the Chronicles of Jerusalem and the journey of Godfray Boylion'. Godfrey Bouillon, a French nobleman, was one of the leaders of the First Crusade to the Holy Land in the late 1090s, and evidently Joan's book about him was written in French; it might have been a translation of the Latin work *Historia Rerum in Partibus Transmarinis Gestarum* or 'History of Deeds Done Beyond the Sea' by William of Tyre (d. 1186). When Joan's brother Thomas Beaufort, duke of Exeter, died in 1426, he left her a book called *Tristram*, i.e. the ever-popular story of the tragic love triangle between Tristan, Isolde or Iseult and King Mark of Cornwall, and in 1431 a Yorkshire squire named John Morton left Joan 'a book in English, called Gower' (*unum librum de Anglico, vocatum Gower*).[6] Almost certainly this means John Gower's *Confessio Amantis*, the long poem translated from Middle English into Portuguese by a member of Philippa of Lancaster's household, and which we know was also owned in Castilian by Catalina of Lancaster. The poem was, therefore, known to and read by at least three of Edward III's granddaughters, and Henry IV also owned a copy of it in the original English, which was dedicated to him personally by Gower.[7] Joan Beaufort mentioned several other books in her will, which she bequeathed in succession to four of her five Neville sons who outlived her: psalters which had belonged to her mother Katherine Swynford, and, rather intriguingly, a 'great book about *Fisica*' (see Chapter 31 below). Another court poet, Thomas Hoccleve (*c.* 1368/69–1426), dedicated a volume of his poems to Joan probably in or around 1422, and in 1413 had dedicated a work named *De Regimine Principum* to her nephew Henry V on his accession to the throne.

Joan Beaufort's sibling Queen Catalina died in Valladolid on 2 June 1418 at the age of 45, and her 13-year-old son Juan II, just a few miles away in Simancas, hastened to her deathbed as soon as he heard the news that she was dying.[8] Lope de Barrientos (1382–1469), a long-lived Castilian chronicler, Dominican friar, professor of theology, confessor of Catalina's son Juan, and tutor of several of her grandchildren, commented some decades later on the deep instability that occurred in Castile as a result of the queen's death, and stated that her death damaged the kingdom greatly.[9] The queen's eldest child Doña María was in Aragon with her husband Alfonso, and, owing to a serious illness, was not able to travel to her homeland and attend Catalina's funeral.[10] The queen's illegitimate aunt María de Ayala, and María's mother Teresa, outlived her; both women died in August 1424, just fifteen days apart.[11] Catalina's uncle Diego, the last survivor of Pedro the Cruel's illegitimate offspring, also outlived her, and is thought to have died in or not long before 1440.

Catalina was buried in the same location as her husband, the *Capilla de los Reyes Nuevos* or 'Chapel of the New Kings' in Toledo Cathedral, where her effigy still exists. Her husband's grandparents King Enrique of Trastámara and Queen Juana Manuel, and his parents Juan I and Leonor of Aragon, were, and are, also buried in the chapel. An inscription on Catalina's tomb named her as 'the granddaughter of the righteous kings, King Edward of England [*el rey Duarte de Ynglaterra*] and King Don Pedro of Castile', though wrongly stated that Catalina's father John of Gaunt, 'the most noble prince Don Juan, duke of Alencastre', was the eldest son of Edward III.[12] Like her older half-sister Queen Philippa of Portugal, Queen Catalina made an enormous and lasting impact on the kingdom where she married and which was her mother's homeland, and these two remarkable daughters of John of Gaunt are still remembered in Portugal and Spain.

Catalina did not live long enough to see any of her grandchildren, though Juan II was a young father: his and his wife María of Aragon's eldest child, whom they named Catalina in the late queen's honour, was born on 5 October 1422 when Juan was 17 (the little girl died a few weeks before her second birthday in 1424). On 3 September 1422 a month before young Catalina was born, King Juan wrote to Doña María de Ayala, 'my aunt', to inform her that his wife was about to give birth.[13] Juan and Queen María's second child, Leonor, died in 1425 also a few weeks before her second birthday, and their son and Juan's successor, the ill-fated and weak Enrique IV 'the Impotent', was born at the beginning of 1425.[14]

Joan de Bohun née Fitzalan, dowager countess of Hereford, Essex and Northampton, died on 7 April 1419 at the age of about 73. The dower lands she had held since she was widowed from Humphrey de Bohun in 1373 passed to two of her grandchildren: Anne of Gloucester, countess of Stafford, as the only living secular child of Joan's elder daughter Eleanor, duchess of Gloucester; and Henry V, as the eldest son of Joan's younger daughter Mary, countess of Derby.[15] Because the de Bohun inheritance passed through the female line and because the system of primogeniture did not apply to women, the king had no advantage over his cousin Anne, despite being male, and they inherited equal parts of Joan's lands. In 1421, however, King Henry forced Anne to accept a re-division of the entire de Bohun inheritance which was unfavourable to her. Via his lawyers, he claimed that the original division made in 1380, when Eleanor de Bohun turned 14, had favoured Eleanor over her then underage sister Mary, and was therefore unfair.[16] Anne of Gloucester became a countess again on 10 June 1419, when Henry V created William Bourchier count of Eu in Normandy.[17] Neither Henry nor his late father, despite their undoubted respect and affection for William, allowed his marriage to Anne to disadvantage them in any way, and Anne's marriage to a man high in Henry V's favour did nothing to prevent the king from redistributing the de Bohun inheritance to benefit himself.

Chapter 30

The Infant King

William Bourchier did not have long to enjoy his new French title: he died in Troyes on 28 May 1420, having spent most or all of the previous few years campaigning in France on Henry V's behalf. His body was returned to England and buried at Llanthony Priory in Gloucestershire.[1] William's inquisition post mortem was held in Suffolk and Essex in October/November 1420 and his heir was his and Anne's eldest son Henry Bourchier, whom the jurors claimed to be 'sixteen and more', though whether this is accurate is unclear as no proof of age exists for him.[2]

Burying William at Llanthony was certainly Anne's decision, as John Wyche (d. 1436), prior of Llanthony, was a close friend of hers and one with whom she maintained a regular correspondence. Anne and John's letters reveal Anne's great interest in following the progress of her cousin Henry V's army in France, and show that she was intensely proud of her second husband and the 'valiant prowess, wisdom and good governance' which he displayed. A few years later, Anne would request burial next to William in her will, employed two priests at her manor of Little Easton to sing mass daily for his soul, and also had daily masses sung for him at Llanthony Priory.[3] Anne was still only 37 years old in 1420, but chose not to marry again, which is probably another indication that her marriage to William Bourchier had been a happy one. He was, of course, her third husband if one counts her first unconsummated marriage to Thomas Stafford in childhood, which might have been another reason for her unwillingness to marry yet again, though other English noblewomen of the era did wed four times: Elizabeth Arundel, duchess of Norfolk (d. 1425), and Joan Holland, duchess of York (d. 1434), each married four husbands.

On 2 June 1420 a few days after William Bourchier's death, also in Troyes, Henry V married Katherine de Valois, the youngest daughter of Charles VI of France and sister of Richard II's late queen Isabelle (d. 1409). Katherine's childhood, given that her father the king had endured increasingly frequent episodes of insanity since 1392 a few years before she was born, was probably a difficult one, though the extent of the cruel neglect to which she was supposedly subjected by her mother Queen Isabeau has been massively exaggerated by later writers. Katherine's Bavarian mother was in fact an involved and affectionate mother who took a keen interest in her children's education and often bought them books, toys, clothes, birthday presents and pets, including parrots and turtle doves. Isabeau bought a Book of Hours for her daughter Jeanne in 1398 and an alphabet psalter for her daughter Michelle in 1403. She came from a close-knit German family, and, far from allegations that she let her children go dirty, cold and hungry, and committed adultery with her own brother-in-law the duke of Orléans, did her best to recreate the warmth of her natal family ties with her own children, despite the immense difficulties caused by her husband's severe mental health issues.[4]

The battle of Baugé was fought on 22 March 1421 between French forces and the forces of Thomas, duke of Clarence, the brother closest in age to Henry V (they were almost certainly born merely eleven months apart). Elizabeth of Lancaster's son John Holland was captured and was held in captivity in France for several years, and the late Constance of York's son-in-law Richard Beauchamp, recently made earl of Worcester, was killed (his widow Isabelle Despenser married his cousin Richard Beauchamp, earl of Warwick, a few months later). John Holland's stepfather Sir John Cornwall fought in the battle though evaded capture, and afterwards he and Elizabeth of Lancaster had to raise huge sums for the ransom of her son.[5] If Elizabeth believed that the capture and imprisonment of one of her sons was bad enough, far worse was to come later in the awful year of 1421. Her 16-year-old son John Cornwall the younger was killed that December, while an English force was besieging the town of Meaux: the teenager was standing next to his father when a gun-stone took his head off. John Cornwall the father was wounded, and the shock of seeing his child die next to him supposedly made him vow never to wage war against Christians again. Indeed, after six years of fighting in France, after 1421 John did not return there for another fifteen years.[6] Elizabeth and John's daughter Constance Cornwall also died sometime in the next few years, leaving no children; John Cornwall the elder had no grandchildren from his marriage to Elizabeth. Another man killed during the siege of Meaux was John, Lord Clifford, whose marriage had been granted to Joan Beaufort in 1403.

Henry V did not live long to enjoy his marriage to Katherine de Valois: he died probably of dysentery, or of complications caused by dysentery, in Vincennes on 31 August 1422, aged not quite 36. Katherine had borne their son, inevitably also called Henry, at Windsor Castle the previous December, and the infant, not yet nine months old, now succeeded as king of England. The late king's brother John, duke of Bedford, was appointed as his regent of France – by the terms of the 1419 Treaty of Troyes, Henry V would succeed his father-in-law Charles VI as king of France on the latter's death – and his youngest brother Humphrey, duke of Gloucester, as regent of England. As it happened, King Charles outlived King Henry by less than two months, and his baby grandson in England duly became king of France as well, at least in name, disinheriting his uncle, the Dauphin Charles (b. 1403). Henry V made three wills; in the third one, he left bequests to his aunt Joan Beaufort, countess of Westmorland. His body was returned to England from France and buried in Westminster Abbey on 7 November 1422. Just four days later, the body of his father-in-law Charles VI was interred in the abbey of Saint-Denis in Paris, where almost all of the kings of France were laid to rest over the centuries.

On 13 December 1423, Joan Beaufort and Ralph Neville were given the wardship of Richard of York, the greatest young heir in the kingdom, and within a year he had married their youngest daughter Cecily; he was 13, born in September 1411, and she, born in May 1415, was just 9. Although the wardship cost the Nevilles a massive £2,000, their investment paid off when young Richard's maternal uncle Edmund Mortimer, earl of March and Ulster, died childless in early 1425 and left Richard as his heir.[7] Ralph Neville, earl of Westmorland, did not have too much longer to live, and bequeathed Richard of York's wardship to Joan after his death. He made his will on 18 October 1425, at his castle and main seat of Raby in County Durham, and died three days later, at the age of about 60 or a little more. Ralph named his wife Joan first among his executors, and left her one-third of his goods and moveable goods to maintain herself and their children, as well a his best cup of gold (*optimo cipho meo auri*) with six matching chargers, i.e. flat dishes, twenty-four silver dishes, a 'bed of Arras' cloth worked with gold thread, probably their marital bed, and 100 cows, 1,000 sheep, and 24 mares. To their eldest son Richard Neville, whom he appointed as another of his executors, Ralph left his four 'wildehorsez', the word written in English in the middle of the Latin text, and left to their son William a grey sheep, twenty-four cows and a bull, and a gilded cup.

Ralph also bequeathed possessions to his and Joan's other two secular sons, George and Edward Neville, and to their daughters: Katherine, whom Ralph named as 'Countess Marshal' because her husband John Mowbray was Earl Marshal of England; Anne, countess of Stafford, Anne of Gloucester's daughter-in-law; Eleanor, countess of Northumberland and dowager Lady Despenser; and Cecily, whom her father named as *Ciciliae Ducissae Eborum* or 'Cecily, duchess of York', even though she was only 10 years old. Perhaps not surprisingly given the fraught relations between himself and his sons from his second marriage to Joan on one side, and his sons with his first wife Margaret Stafford on the other, Ralph left nothing to the latter, though did give gilded cups to his and Margaret's daughters Maud, Lady Mauley, Alice, Lady Grey, Philippa, Lady Dacre, and Margaret, Lady Scrope. Two of the supervisors Ralph appointed were his brothers-in-law Henry Beaufort, bishop of Winchester, and Thomas Beaufort, duke of Exeter, who in fact outlived him by only fourteen months. Ralph's will reveals that he owned a house in the London parish of St Olave, in Farringdon ward, called *Neville Inne*, as well as a house also called *Nevilsin* on Westgate in Newcastle-upon-Tyne.[8]

Ralph Neville was buried in St Mary's Church in the village of Staindrop, a mile from Raby Castle. After his death, their son-in-law Richard of York remained in Countess Joan's custody as Ralph had wished, and she received 200 marks a year to look after him, raised to 300 marks on 20 May 1426 after he was knighted. A sizable number of young English noblemen, some of them extremely young, were knighted on the same day as Richard of York, including Joan Beaufort's grandsons John Mowbray (b. 1415), son of her daughter Katherine Neville, and Henry Percy (b. 1421), son of her daughter Eleanor Neville, during a parliament held in Leicester. By far the most important new knight, however, was the young king, Henry VI, who was barely 4 1/2 years old. He was knighted by his uncle John, duke of Bedford, then himself knighted all the others. Joan, her daughter Cecily and her son-in-law Richard lived at the child-king's court in the years after Ralph's death.[9]

Joan was granted her large dower, the customary one third of her late husband's estate, on 5 December 1425.[10] One property which came to her was the 'Erber' in Dowgate ward, London, 'with all lands, rents, houses, solars, cellars, and shops pertaining to it', which her half-brother Henry IV had given to Ralph Neville on 11 December 1399, only a few weeks after his accession to the throne. Ralph's inquisition post mortem states that the Erber was 244 feet wide (its length was also given, but unfortunately that part of the manuscript is damaged and unreadable), had two cellars and four shops, and was a 'garden and tenement' worth £10 annually.[11] This property famously belonged to Joan Beaufort and Ralph Neville's grandson Richard Neville, earl of Warwick (1428–1471), in later decades, though it has long since disappeared. Another resident of London, taking legal action in February 1424 regarding a property her convent owned in the parish of All Hallows at the Hay, was Joan's cousin Isabel of Gloucester, called the 'abbess of St Clare without Al[d]gate', i.e. the Minoresses.[12] It is very difficult to find Isabel again on record after this date, though as she was born in April 1386 and was not quite 38 years old in February 1424, she might have lived and served as the Minoresses' abbess for many more years.

Chapter 31

The Last Granddaughters

Elizabeth of Lancaster, countess of Huntingdon, the last living child of the long-dead Blanche, duchess of Lancaster, and the sister of two queens and a king, died on 24 November 1425, probably aged 62. She was buried in the church of St Mary in Burford, Shropshire, a rather obscure (albeit lovely) building for the daughter of a duke and the granddaughter of a king to select as a final resting place, and Elizabeth's choice surely related to the fact that a branch of her husband's Cornwall family were lords of Burford. Her remarkable effigy can still be seen in the church and is lavishly painted, or rather, repainted at some point in the last 600 years. Elizabeth left no will, but this was not unexpected as she was a married woman and would have needed her husband's permission to dispose of what were, legally, his possessions rather than merely hers. Her inquisition post mortem was held in six counties in December 1425 and January 1426, and the dower lands she held from her second husband John Holland passed to their son John Holland the younger.

Elizabeth's widower John Cornwall outlived her by many years. In 1431, he was an executor of the will of the long-lived Philippa de Mohun, dowager duchess of York, who was born in the 1360s at the latest, perhaps even in the 1350s. Another of the duchess's executors was Thomas Chaucer (b. c. 1367), son of the poet Geoffrey, father of Alice Chaucer (b. 1404), countess of Salisbury by her second marriage and duchess of Suffolk by her third, and nephew of Katherine Swynford, late duchess of Lancaster.[1] Duchess Philippa left John Cornwall £20 and two silver pots sprinkled with lilies. On the last day of the parliament held at Westminster between May and July 1432, Henry VI created John Baron Fanhope, and called him 'John Cornwall, knight, who was joined by the bonds of marriage to the dearest great-aunt of the lord king, to wit, Elizabeth, previously countess of Huntingdon'. The young king praised the 'fruitful and laudable labours, honours and services' performed by John during his many years of faithful service to Henry VI himself, his father and his grandfather.[2]

John Cornwall, Baron Fanhope, died on 10 or 11 December 1443, without an heir, as both of his legitimate children from his marriage to Elizabeth died before him. His will, made at his castle of Ampthill on 10 December 1443 shortly before his death, mentions two illegitimate sons (*bastardorum meorum*, 'my bastards'), John and Thomas. They were both underage, i.e. under 21, in 1443, which most probably means that the two were conceived and born after Elizabeth of Lancaster died, and that John took a lover after losing his wife of a quarter of a century. John left his son John, who was named first and was therefore almost certainly the elder of the two boys or young men, 50 marks, and his son Thomas 300 marks, and appointed guardians to look after them until they came of age. The discrepancy in the bequests suggests that John had also settled some lands on the elder of his two sons which would provide the younger John with a good income.[3] He requested burial not with Elizabeth in Burford, but in the Chapel of the Blessed Virgin he himself had founded in the churchyard of the Friars Preacher, i.e. the Dominican order, in London. John's manor and castle of Ampthill reverted to the Crown in the absence of heirs, and a few decades later Henry VIII often stayed there while on his hunting expeditions.[4]

Cornwall's stepson, Elizabeth's son John Holland, earl of Huntingdon and later duke of Exeter, married Beatriz of Portugal, dowager countess of Arundel and the stepdaughter of Elizabeth's sister Queen Philippa, as his second wife in the early 1430s (Anne of Gloucester's daughter Anne Stafford, however, was the mother of his children). Born around 1380/82, Beatriz was about a decade and a half older than John, and had been a widow for more than seventeen years when she married John. Holland's long will of 1447, in English, mentioned his first wife Anne Stafford, his third wife Anne Montacute, his 'suster Custaunce', i.e. his sister Constance Holland, his legitimate children and two of his illegitimate sons, but not, rather interestingly, his second, Portuguese wife Beatriz.[5]

By the mid-1430s, the ongoing quarrel between Joan Beaufort's sons and her late husband's grandsons from his first marriage had become very serious. Ralph Neville the younger was born in April 1406 as the son of John Neville (*c.* 1387–1420), Earl Ralph's eldest son from his first marriage to Margaret Stafford. Ralph the younger was named as his grandfather's heir when the earl died in October 1425, and became the second earl of Westmorland when he came of age at 21, but Earl Ralph strongly favoured his and Joan Beaufort's sons over his sons from his first marriage, and young Ralph saw most of his family's wealth pass to his half-uncle Richard Neville. According to his own account, his annual income fell from an expected £2,600 to a mere £400.[6]

This led to a long feud between the two branches of the Neville family: the Nevilles of Raby, the senior branch descended from Margaret Stafford, and the Nevilles of Middleham, the cadet though much wealthier and better connected branch, descended from Joan Beaufort. In the early 1400s, it appears that Ralph Neville, earl of Westmorland, did not intend to substantially disinherit his children from his first marriage, but over the next few years, he gradually entailed more and more of his lands on his children with Joan. Rather curiously, it appears that his eldest son from his first marriage, John, made little if any effort to prevent this and might even have acquiesced to it; he is known to have personally witnessed at least one of the transfers of land to his younger half-brothers.[7] Whatever the reason for this, although John's son inherited his grandfather's earldom of Westmorland, this branch of the family received only the castles and manors of Raby and Brancepeth in County Durham, while Joan Beaufort's eldest son Richard inherited the bulk of the sizeable Neville estate, and became the largest secular landowner and lord in Yorkshire. Historian Charles Ross once described the goings-on as 'an ambitious family fraud'.

In addition to his inheriting most of his wealthy father's estate, a favourable marriage for Richard Neville was arranged in 1420 with Alice Montacute (b. 1407), only child and heir of Thomas Montacute, earl of Salisbury (1388–1428). Richard duly became earl of Salisbury after his father-in-law's demise.[8] In 1435, Richard, earl of Salisbury and his brother William, Lord Fauconberg, were unable to leave England without the consent of their mother Joan, because in their absence their half-nephews Ralph, earl of Westmorland, and his younger brothers John and Thomas might make 'unlawful entries' into their properties. Some years earlier in August 1430, Joan Beaufort herself had had to make a recognisance that she would do 'no hurt or harm' to her late husband's grandson, and young Ralph did the same, on pain of paying a fine of £2,000.[9]

Anne of Gloucester, dowager countess of Stafford and Eu, died on 16 October 1438, the same day as she made her will in English: *I, Anne, countesse of Stafford, Bockingh[am], Her[e]ford and Northampton, and lady of Brecknoc* [Brecon, Wales], *of hool and avised mynde, ordeyne and make my testament in English tonge, for my most profit.* She requested burial in Llanthony Secunda Priory in Gloucester, where she had buried William Bourchier in 1420, and mentioned the 'college of Plecy' i.e. Pleshey in Essex, founded by her father. Otherwise, the will is not terribly interesting or illuminating except for the mention of *my welbelovid sone Humfrey erle of Stafford*, who, as Anne's eldest son, was her sole heir to all the lands she had inherited from her parents as well as the sole heir to the father who had died before Humphrey was even a year old, Edmund Stafford. Anne appointed her four Bourchier sons – Thomas, bishop of Worcester, Henry, count of Eu, William, and John – and six other men as her executors. Henry Bourchier often appears on record from the 1420s onwards as 'the brother of the earl of Stafford'.[10] Anne was a grandmother several times over when she died, as Humphrey Stafford and his wife Anne Neville, one of Joan Beaufort's many daughters, had produced several children by 1438.

Assuming that Anne's youngest sister Isabel of Gloucester, prioress of the Minoress convent in London, was already dead, Joan Beaufort was the only granddaughter of Edward III now still alive. Joan's son Robert Neville had been elected bishop of Durham earlier in 1438, and the Yorkshire manor of Howden, a few miles outside York, came into his possession. Joan lived there for the last years of her life, from 1438 to 1440.[11]

Joan, dowager countess of Westmorland, died at the manor of Howden on 13 November 1440. Both of her Ferrers daughters, Elizabeth and Mary, five of her Neville sons (Richard, Robert, William, George and Edward) and five of her Neville daughters (Eleanor, Katherine, Anne, Joan and Cecily) outlived her, and her heir was her eldest son, Richard Neville, earl of Salisbury. He was said in her inquisition post mortem, held between December 1440 and October 1441, to be aged either 40 and more, 30 and more, or 34 and more.[12] Joan had made a will in Latin half a year before her death on 10 May 1440, at Howden, and one of the executors whom she appointed was her daughter Katherine Mowbray, née Neville, dowager duchess of Norfolk (whose husband John Mowbray had died in 1432). Joan also appointed three of her sons as executors,

Robert, bishop of Durham, Richard, earl of Salisbury, and George, Lord Latimer, while the two supervisors of the will were her brother Cardinal Beaufort (d. 1447), the only one of John of Gaunt's many children who outlived Joan, and the cardinal-archbishop of York, John Kemp, to whom Joan gave a missal covered with black damask cloth. Joan's youngest son Edward, Lord Abergavenny, was present when Joan dictated her will; he was one of the six people named as having witnessed it.

Richard, earl of Salisbury, received a gold jewel called *le Trinitee*, and Joan left the psalters she owned and which had previously belonged to 'the illustrious lady, my mother, Lady Katherine, duchess of Lancaster' to her second or third son William Neville, Lord Fauconberg, to pass in succession to her other three secular sons, George, Lord Latimer, then Edward, Lord Abergavenny, and finally to Earl Richard, if William died without heirs. Joan mentioned a 'gold ring with a stone, with which I was consecrated to God, called the mother of jewels, highly valuable and precious', and 'a great book about *Fisica*', *librum magnum de Fisica*, most probably meaning medical advice relating to the physical human body, both of which she also bequeathed to her four secular sons in succession. To her daughter-in-law Alice Montacute, countess of Salisbury, Joan left a gold cup which had once been given to her by her sister-in-law Juana of Navarre, queen of England (who had died in June 1437 and was buried with Henry IV in Canterbury Cathedral). William, Lord Fauconberg received three pieces of arras cloth and a gold bowl, George, Lord Latimer was to have two beds with canopies and a silver cup, Robert, bishop of Durham received a gold cup studded with pearls, and Edward, Lord Abergavenny was bequeathed a silver pottle, i.e. a vessel which held half a gallon of liquid. Joan's granddaughter Joan Neville, daughter of William and his Fauconberg wife, was given £100 sterling for her dowry when she was old enough to marry, though only on condition that she was not one of her parents' heirs.

Finally, the countess's grandson Richard Neville (b. 1428), future earl of Warwick, eldest son and heir of his parents Richard the elder and Alice Montacute – and known to posterity as the 'Kingmaker' – was given a silver-gilt jug. Countess Joan did not leave anything else to any of her other grandchildren, and made no specific bequests to any of her seven living daughters either.[13] An effigy of Joan, lying next to Ralph Neville with his first wife Margaret Stafford on his other side, still exists in St Mary's Church in Staindrop. Joan herself, however, was not buried there; her tomb can still be seen in Lincoln Cathedral, where she was interred next to her mother Katherine Swynford, duchess of Lancaster, as she had requested in her will. For many years, both Ralph Neville and Joan appear to have believed that they would both be buried in Staindrop, and Joan left her best palfrey horse as a mortuary – a gift to a parish church from a deceased parishioner – to the church of St Mary.[14] She changed her mind, however, and on 28 November 1437 was granted a licence to 'found a perpetual chantry of two chaplains to celebrate divine service daily at the altar before which her mother Katherine, late duchess of Lancaster, is buried ... the said chantry to be called the Chantry of Katherine, late duchess of Lancaster'.[15] Joan decided to lie for eternity alongside her mother rather than with her either of her husbands or in a location more significant to the Neville family, a fact which reveals much about her great affection for Katherine Swynford, the comparatively lowborn long-term mistress of a duke, and about her own unconventionality.

And so, eighty-five years after Edward III and Philippa of Hainault's first granddaughter was born, the last one died, and this generation of eleven remarkable and fascinating women slipped into history.

Appendix

Descendants

Philippa of Lancaster's third son, Henrique (1394–1460), duke of Viseu, is known as 'Henry the Navigator', and was a famous and trailblazing early European explorer who initiated the Age of Discovery. Her second son, Pedro (1392–1449), duke of Coímbra, also travelled extensively, and is known as *Dom Pedro das Sete Partidas*, meaning 'of the seven parts' (of the world). Via her eldest son King Duarte of Portugal, Queen Philippa was the grandmother of Leonor of Portugal, Holy Roman Empress (d. 1467), who was the mother of Emperor Maximilian I (d. 1519), the great-grandmother of Emperor Charles V (d. 1558), and the great-great-grandmother of Philip II of Spain (d. 1598). Philippa was also the grandmother of a cardinal-archbishop of Lisbon, Dom Jaime; of Dom João, titular prince of Antioch and husband of the queen of Cyprus; and of Charles the Bold, duke of Burgundy. Via her second-youngest son João (1400–1442), constable of Portugal, Philippa was a great-grandmother of Manuel I (1469–1521), king of Portugal, and of Isabel la Católica (1451–1504), queen-regnant of Castile. Her younger half-sister Catalina was Isabel la Católica's grandmother.

Elizabeth of Lancaster was the grandmother of Edmund Grey, earl of Kent (1416–1490), and of Henry Holland, duke of Exeter (1430–1475), who married Edward IV and Richard III's eldest sister Anne of York. Her daughter Constance Holland and her son John Holland were her only children who had issue of their own.

Neither of Catalina of Lancaster's two daughters had children of their own, while her son Juan II had six children, of whom three daughters and a son died young. His only surviving child from his first marriage to María of Aragon was his successor, the ill-fated Enrique IV (r. 1454–74), and from his second marriage to Isabel of Portugal, he was the father of

145

Isabel la Católica, queen-regnant of Castile. Queen Isabel la Católica's youngest child Katherine of Aragon (1485–1536), Henry VIII's first wife, was named after her great-grandmother Catalina.

Joan Beaufort, countess of Westmorland, was the grandmother of two kings of England, Edward IV and his brother Richard III, via her youngest child Cecily Neville, duchess of York, and had dozens of grandchildren; it would probably be easier to specify which important English people of the fifteenth and sixteenth centuries were not descended from Joan rather than those who were. Among many others, she was an ancestor of the Mowbray dukes of Norfolk, the Stafford dukes of Buckingham, the Percy earls of Northumberland, and the Neville earls of Warwick. Four of her Neville daughters lived very long lives: Katherine, duchess of Norfolk, was still alive in 1483 when she attended her nephew Richard III's coronation, aged well over 80; Eleanor, countess of Northumberland, died in 1473 in her mid-seventies; Anne, duchess of Buckingham, died in 1480 also in her seventies; and Cecily, duchess of York, died in 1495 at age 80.

Philippa of Clarence, countess of March and Ulster, was also an ancestor of Edward IV and Richard III. Her second child, Roger Mortimer, fourth earl of March (1374–1398), became a father at just 14 when his daughter Anne was born in December 1388; if Philippa had still been alive then, she would have been a grandmother at just 33 years old. Anne Mortimer married Isabel of Castile's youngest child Richard of Conisbrough, earl of Cambridge, and was the mother of Richard, duke of York (1411–1460), father of Edward IV and Richard III. Philippa of Clarence's eldest child Elizabeth Mortimer, Lady Percy (1371–1417), was the mother of Henry Percy, second earl of Northumberland (1393–1455), and ancestor of the later Percys.

Via her daughter Isabelle Beauchamp née Despenser (1400–1439), countess of Worcester and Warwick, Constance of York was a great-grandmother of Richard III's queen Anne Neville (1456–1485) and her sister Isabel (1452–1478), duchess of Clarence, the wife of Richard III's older brother George. Margaret Pole, the elderly countess of Salisbury executed by Henry VIII in 1541, was Constance's great-great-granddaughter, and she also had and has numerous descendants via her granddaughter Elizabeth, Baroness Abergavenny (d. 1448), who married Edward Neville, the youngest of Joan Beaufort's sons. Constance's illegitimate daughter Alianore Holland, Lady Tuchet, was the mother of the long-lived Edmund Audley, bishop of Rochester, Hereford and Salisbury, who was old enough to graduate from university in the early 1460s and died in 1524, and she was the grandmother of John Grey, Baron Grey of Powys (d. 1497).

Via her son Robert de Bar and his daughter Jeanne de Bar (d. 1462), countess of Soissons and Marle, Marie de Coucy was an ancestor of Mary, Queen of Scots (r. 1542–67); Henri IV, the first Bourbon king of France (r. 1589–1610); and Henri's grandsons Charles II, king of England (r. 1660-85) and his younger brother James II (r. 1685–88)

Anne of Gloucester, countess of Stafford and Eu, was the great-grandmother of Henry Stafford, duke of Buckingham, executed by Richard III in 1483, and the great-great-grandmother of Edward Stafford, duke of Buckingham, executed by Henry VIII in 1521. Her son Thomas Bourchier (d. 1486) became archbishop of Canterbury in 1454, chancellor of England in 1455, and a cardinal in 1467, and her eldest Bourchier son, Henry, was made earl of Essex in 1462. Via her daughter Anne Bourchier, Anne of Gloucester was the grandmother of John Mowbray, duke of Norfolk (1444–1476), who was also a grandson of Joan Beaufort's daughter Katherine Neville.

Abbreviations

ANLP	Anglo-Norman Letters and Petitions, ed. Legge
C	Chancery (National Archives)
Collection	A Collection of All the Wills now Known to be Extant
CCR	Calendar of Close Rolls
CIPM	Calendar of Inquisitions Post Mortem
CFR	Calendar of Fine Rolls
CP	Complete Peerage
CPL	Calendar of Entries in the Papal Registers Relating to Great Britain and Ireland: Papal Letters
CPR	Calendar of Patent Rolls
DL	Duchy of Lancaster (National Archives)
E	Exchequer (National Archives)
ODNB	Oxford Dictionary of National Biography
PROME	The Parliament Rolls of Medieval England
SC	Special Collections (National Archives)
TNA	The National Archives
TV	Testamenta Vetusta, vol. 1

Notes

Introduction

1. Edward III was born in Windsor Castle on 13 November 1312, and, according to the chronicler Jean Froissart, Philippa of Hainault was almost 14 when she married Edward in early 1328. If he was correct on this point, she was probably born in *c.* February or March 1314. She was almost certainly not born on 24 June 1314, as often stated; the 24th of June was the birthdate of her eldest sister Margareta, Holy Roman Empress, in 1310, and the date has often been wrongly assigned to Philippa.

Chapter 1: The First Granddaughter

1. *Calendar of Inquisitions Post Mortem 1365–69*, no. 385.
2. *Calendar of Patent Rolls 1340–43*, p. 569; *CPR 1343–45*, p. 42; *Oeuvres de Froissart*, ed. Kervyn de Lettenhove, vol. 7, pp. 246-47; *The Brut or the Chronicles of England*, ed. F. W. D. Brie, part 2, pp. 306, 309.
3. The wedding date is given in *Calendar of Select Plea and Memoranda Rolls of the City of London*, vol. 1, 1323–1364, p. 153, and confirmed by the chronicler and royal clerk Adam Murimuth in *Adae Murimuth Continuatio Chronicarum*, ed. E.M. Thompson, p. 125.
4. *CIPM 1327–36*, no. 537, for Elizabeth's date of birth; her father William was murdered in June 1333 when he was not yet 21 and Elizabeth was 11 months. William's mother Elizabeth the elder was a granddaughter of King Edward I (r. 1272–1307) via her mother Joan of Acre, countess of Gloucester.
5. *Register of the Black Prince*, vol. 4, p. 251.

6. *CPR 1354–58*, p. 352. Maud, b. *c.* 1310/12, was the third of the six daughters of Henry of Lancaster, earl of Lancaster and Leicester (*c.* 1280–1345), grandson of King Henry III, nephew of Edward I, and great-uncle of Edward III. Maud's second husband Ralph Ufford, justiciar of Ireland and the earl of Suffolk's brother, was the father of her younger daughter Maud Ufford, later countess of Oxford, born in late 1345 or 1346.

7. Frederick Devon, *Issues of the Exchequer*, pp. 171-2; W. M. Ormrod, 'Edward III and his Family', *Journal of British Studies*, 26 (1987), p. 410 note 46, for the date of the two weddings. *CIPM 1370–73*, no. 293, is Edmund's proof of age. His godmother was his paternal grandmother Elizabeth de Bohun, née Badlesmere, formerly Mortimer, countess of Northampton, and one of his godfathers was his half-uncle Humphrey de Bohun, born in March 1342 and the future earl of Hereford, Essex and Northampton, Elizabeth's son from her second marriage.

8. *Calendar of Close Rolls 1354–60*, pp. 93-4. Alice later married Thomas Holland (b. *c.* 1351), earl of Kent. Edmund's great-grandmother Joan Geneville (b. 1286), dowager countess of March and widow of Roger Mortimer (d. 1330), was still alive at the time of his first betrothal, and died in 1356. Edmund's father Roger Mortimer the younger, second earl of March, died not long after Edmund married Philippa, still only at the beginning of his thirties.

9. *CPR 1358–61*, p. 456.

10. Bridget Wells-Furby, 'Marriage and Inheritance: The Element of Chance in the Development of Lay Estates in the Fourteenth Century', *Fourteenth Century England X*, ed. Gwilym Dodd (2018), p. 125; S.J. Payling, 'The Economics of Marriage in Late Medieval England: The Marriage of Heiresses', *Economic History Review*, 54 (2001), p. 422.

11. *CIPM 1327–36*, no. 387. *CIPM 1347–52*, no. 247, is Roger's proof of age. Roger's mother Elizabeth, Edmund's widow, later married William de Bohun, earl of Northampton.

12. *Complete Peerage*, vol. 8, p. 443; *CCR 1346–9*, pp. 101, 199.

Chapter 2: John and Blanche

1. *John of Gaunt's Register 1379–83*, no. 811 ('Phellipe'); The National Archives SC 1/43/81 is Maud's letter, also printed in the

original French in *Recueil de Lettres Anglo-Françaises, 1265–1399,* ed. F. J. Tanqueray (1916), no. 163, and in John of Gaunt's *Register 1371–75*, no. 1809.

2. Elisabeth was the daughter of Queen Philippa's older sister Johanna of Hainault, duchess of Jülich (*c.* 1312-74), and married Edward III's cousin John, earl of Kent (b. 1330) in 1348; he died childless in December 1352.

Chapter 3: Isabella and Enguerrand

1. Cited in Jessica Lutkin, 'Isabella de Coucy, Daughter of Edward III: The Exception Who Proves the Rule', pp. 137-8.
2. *CPR 1330–34*, p. 564.
3. *Calendar of Charter Rolls 1341–1417*, p. 193; Jean-Joseph Carlier, 'Henri d'Oisy, Fragment d'Études Historiques', *Mémoire de la Société Dunkerquoise pour l'Encouragement des Sciences, des Lettres et des Arts* (1858), pp. 104-5.
4. Lutkin, 'Isabella de Coucy', pp. 137-8.
5. *CPR 1364–7*, pp. 183, 190; *CPR 1396–9*, p. 583. Enguerrand, presumably with Isabella, was in Cosham near Portsmouth on 10 September 1365 and in London a month later: *CPR 1377–81*, p. 501; *CPR 1381–5*, p. 179.
6. Jean-Joseph Carlier, in 'Henri d'Oisy: Fragment d'Études Historiques', p. 109. Mary Anne Everett Green, *Lives of the Princesses*, vol. 3, p. 205, states that Marie was born at her father's castle of Coucy in France, which has often been repeated by later writers. Enguerrand de Coucy departed from England in January or February 1368, and returned by early April 1369: *CPR 1367–70*, pp. 75, 128, 228, 271, 295; *CPR 1377–81*, 267. He was in Prague in January 1369: *CPR 1370–74*, p. 17; *CPR 1377–81*, pp. 375-6. The payment of 100 marks to a messenger for announcing Marie's birth is cited in *Notes and Queries*, fifth series, vol. 2 (July-December 1874), p. 253, and Henry's birth is in Devon, *Issues of the Exchequer*, p. 191.
7. *CPR 1396–9*, p. 583, states that Philippa de Coucy was born at Eltham. Ormrod, *Edward III*, p. 486 note 70, citing TNA E 403/433, mentions a gift Edward III gave to his daughter Isabella's physician after she gave birth to Philippa, dated 18 November 1367. See also

Lutkin, 'Exception who Proves the Rule', p. 139; Green, *Lives of the Princesses*, vol. 3, pp. 206-7. Barbara Tuchman's *A Distant Mirror* states that Philippa was born before Easter (18 April) 1367, but does not cite a source.
8. Carlier, 'Henri d'Oisy', p. 109.

Chapter 4: Many Losses

1. *CPL 1362–1404*, p. 27; *TV*, pp. 70-71.
2. *CIPM 1365–69*, no. 332.
3. J.J.N. Palmer, 'The Historical Context of the "Book of the Duchess": A Revision', *The Chaucer Review*, vol. 8, No. 4 (1974), pp. 253-5.
4. *CIPM 1365–69*, no. 385.
5. *CCR 1369–74*, pp. 55-6.
6. *CCR 1369–74*, pp. 159, 418.
7. *Life-Records of Chaucer,* ed. Walford D. Selby, F.J. Furnivall, Edward A. Bond and R. E.G. Kirk (1900), no. 58, pp. 172-5.

Chapter 5: Doña María's Daughter and the Duke

1. *Complete Peerage*, vol. 8, p. 448. Usk was one of the lordships which had come to Philippa of Clarence from her great-grandmother Elizabeth de Burgh the elder; it had belonged to Elizabeth's brother Gilbert Clare, earl of Gloucester (1291–1314). Ludlow passed to the Mortimers in 1301 on the marriage of Roger Mortimer, later the first earl of March (d. 1330) to the heiress Joan Geneville (d. 1356).
2. *CIPM 1352–60*, no. 638 (the IPM of Thomas's father John, giving his age); *CPR 1370–74*, p. 137 (marriage rights).
3. *CIPM 1377–84*, no. 889, is Robert's proof of age in February 1383. It was the custom for boys to have two godfathers and a godmother, and for girls to have two godmothers and a godfather.
4. *CIPM 1370–73*, no. 125, is Thomas's IPM, with the date and place of death and Maud being 'feeble'. *TV*, p. 87, is Thomas's will, dated 1 August 1371. Maud Ufford's mother Maud of Lancaster (*c.* 1310/12–1377) married firstly William de Burgh, earl of Ulster (1312–1333) and secondly the earl of Suffolk's brother Sir Ralph Ufford (d. 1346).
5. *CPR 1370–74*, p. 463.

6. *CCR 1369–74*, pp. 272-3; *CPR 1399–1401*, pp. 414-15, 519.
7. *Oeuvres de Froissart*, ed. Lettenhove, vol. 8, pp. 43, 105-7.
8. *Crónicas de los Reyes de Castilla Don Pedro, Don Enrique II, Don Juan I, Don Enrique III por D. Pedro López de Ayala*, ed. Don Eugenio de Llaguno Amirola, vol. 1 (1779), pp. 83, 130-31, 194, 350, 366-7, 558-70; Francisco de Paula Cañas Gálvez, 'Don Sancho de Castilla (1363–1371): Apuntes Biográficos de un Hijo Ilegítimo de Pedro I', *Mundos Medievales, Espacios, Sociedares y Poder: Homenaje al Profesor José Ángel García de Cortazar y Ruiz de Aguirre* (2012), vol. 2, p. 1129; Ronald E. Surtz, *Writing Women in Late Medieval and Early Modern Spain* (2016), p. 41; Clara Estow, *Pedro the Cruel of Castile 1350-1369* (1996), p. 217. According to López de Ayala, King Pedro had yet another mistress as well, Doña Aldonza Coronel, daughter of Don Alfonso Ferrandez Coronel and wife of Don Alvar Pérez de Guzmán: *Crónicas de los Reyes de Castilla ... por D. Pedro López de Ayala*, ed. Amirola, vol. 1, pp. 234-6.
9. Pedro's will is cited in full in *Crónicas de los Reyes de Castilla ... por D. Pedro López de Ayala*, pp. 558-70; Estow, *Pedro the Cruel of Castile*, pp. 131-2, 139-40, 146-7, 211-12. Jean Froissart states (see Chapter 13 of this book) that Costanza re-buried her father in Seville in the late 1380s, though according to Estow (p. xxxiii, note 57) Pedro was re-buried in Madrid in 1446 and only moved to Seville in 1877. Estow (p. 211) discusses the possibility that Pedro had Blanche killed, and states that it is impossible to come to a firm conclusion based on the available evidence; some contemporary Castilian chronicles thought he was guilty of poisoning her, others believed she died naturally. Blanche's mother Isabelle de Valois, duchess of Bourbon, was a granddaughter of Philip III of France and a younger half-sister of Philip VI, and Blanche's older sister Jeanne married their cousin the future Charles V of France (r. 1364–80) in 1350. For Pedro's relationships and children, see Enrique Flórez, *Memorias de las Reynas Catholicas: Historia Genealogica de la Casa Real de Castilla y de León*, vol. 2 (1770), pp. 635ff (Costanza's and her siblings' dates of birth and birthplaces are given on pp. 654-5); Cañas Gálvez, 'Don Sancho de Castilla (1363–1371)', p. 1126, note 1; and Covadonga Valdaliso, 'Las Mujeres del Rey don Pedro de Castilla de J.B. Sitges desde una Perspectiva de Género', *Investigaciones Feministas*, 1 (2010), p. 215. María de Padilla's

youngest daughter Isabel, duchess of York, had three children, and the youngest, Richard, earl of Cambridge (executed in 1415), had a son, Richard, duke of York (1411–1460), who was the father of Edward IV (b. 1442) and Richard III (b. 1452). María's second daughter Costanza, duchess of Lancaster, had a daughter, Catalina of Lancaster, queen-consort of Castile, who was the mother of Juan II of Castile and the grandmother of Isabel la Católica.

10. *Crónicas de los Reyes de Castilla ... por D. Pedro López de Ayala*, p. 563 (*'la corona Francesa que fué de Doña Blanca fija del duc de Borbon'*). Pedro divided María de Padilla's goods and jewels into six parts, and left three to Beatriz, two to Costanza, and one to Isabel. All of his own silver vessels were to be divided into eight parts, three each for Beatriz and Costanza and one each for Isabel and their half-brother Juan.

Chapter 6: Spanish Weddings

1. *Gaunt's Register 1371–75*, nos. 215, 878.
2. *Gaunt's Register 1371–75*, nos. 940, 1241; TNA SC 8/163/8116; *CPR 1370–74*, p. 370. John and Thomas's father John died in 1368, and their mother Elizabeth Segrave, elder daughter and co-heir of the countess of Norfolk, was already dead.
3. *CPR 1374–77*, p. 347; *CPR 1377–81*, pp. 440-41; *CPR 1381–85*, p. 574.
4. The petition is TNA SC 8/103/5145, and see also Chapter 27 below; *The Anonimalle Chronicle 1333 to 1381*, ed. Vivian Hunter Galbraith, p. 69, for Costanza in London.
5. TNA SC 1/56/73 and 74.
6. *Gaunt's Register 1371–75*, nos. 1123-24.
7. Walsingham cited in the *Oxford Dictionary of National Biography*; the descriptions of María are from Robert Folger, *Generaciones Y Semblanzas: Memory and Genealogy in Medieval Iberian Historiography* (2003), p. 51 (*fermosa e pequeña de cuerpo*) and *Crónicas de los Reyes de Castilla ... por D. Pedro López de Ayala*, ed. Amirola, vol. 1, pp. 76-7, 332-3, 427 (*'una doncella muy fermosa'*); and *The Anonimalle Chronicle*, pp. 69, 153, for Costanza.
8. G.H. Cowling, 'Chaucer's Complaintes of Mars and of Venus', *The Review of English Studies*, 2 (1926), pp. 405-10; Isabel's will is TNA PROB 11/1/53, and see also Chapter 15 below.

9. *Gaunt's Register 1371–75*, nos. 983-84, 1728.
10. Devon, *Issues of the Exchequer*, p. 195.
11. *Oeuvres de Froissart*, ed. Lettenhove, vol. 8, pp. 466-7.
12. Fernán Pérez de Guzmán, *Pen Portraits of Illustrious Castilians* (2003), p. 12; Ana Echevarría Arsuaga, 'Catalina de Lancaster, the Castilian Monarchy, and Coexistence', *Medieval Spain: Culture, Conflict, and Coexistence: Studies in Honour of Angus McKay*, ed. Roger Collins and Anthony Goodman (2002), p. 102.
13. Clara Estow, 'Royal Madness in the Crónica del Rey Don Pedro', *Mediterranean Studies*, 6 (1996), p. 19; Estow, *Pedro the Cruel of Castile*, pp. 30, 134; John Pohl and Garry Embleton, *Armies of Castile and Aragon 1370-1516* (2015), p. 44; Margaretta Jolly, ed., *Encyclopedia of Life Writing: Autobiographical and Biographical Forms* (2013), p. 698; Folger, *Generaciones Y Semblanzas*, p. 187; Guzmán, *Pen Portraits of Illustrious Castilians*, pp. 8, 12.
14. See Theresa Earenfight, *The King's Other Body: María of Castile and the Crown of Aragon* (2010), p. 21, for Catalina's languages; *Oeuvres de Froissart*, ed. Lettenhove, vol. 13, p. 134.
15. *Gaunt's Register 1371–75*, nos. 670, 699, 718, 1171, 1456, 1458, 1597, 1611, 1727, 1737, 1781. Agnes Bonsergeant was Catalina's nurse and not Katherine Swynford's, as claimed by some modern writers (including Anthony Goodman, Alison Weir and Nathen Amin) who overlooked the word *fille*, 'daughter', in the entry in Gaunt's register referring to her.
16. *Gaunt's Register 1371–75*, no. 1343.
17. *Gaunt's Register 1371–75*, nos. 245, 1147, 1167, 1263. The letters about Philippa's marriage talk of the *aide a nous ottroiez pur nostre eisne fille marier*. The count of Foix in question presumably means one of the sons of Gaston Fébus (d. 1391), count of Foix, who were born in the early 1360s; one died young and the other died before his father.

Chapter 7: The Beauforts and the Yorks

1. *Foedera, Conventiones, Litterae et Cujuscunque Acta Publica,* ed. Thomas Rymer, *1373–97*, 490; *CIPM 1384–92*, nos. 847-50; *CIPM 1399–1405*, no. 313; *CPL 1362–1404*, pp. 96, 135-6, 146. Blanche of Lancaster inherited Beaufort and other French lordships from her

father and ultimately from her great-uncle John of Lancaster, who died childless in 1317. John, the obscure third and youngest son of Edmund of Lancaster (d. 1296) and Blanche of Artois (d. 1302), spent most of his life in his mother's native France and almost never appears on English record.

2. *ODNB*; *Complete Peerage*, vol. 12A, pp. 39-40. John Beaufort's Wikipedia page (accessed 10 November 2021) also gives *c.* 1371 as his year of birth. The *Complete Peerage* cites an entry on the Patent Roll which states that Beaufort was granted 100 marks a year to serve in the retinue of his cousin Richard II on 7 June 1392 (*CPR 1391–96*, p. 63). A later memorandum underneath this entry adds that the grant was cancelled because Richard II had granted Beaufort issues and profits from the royal castle and lordship of Wallingford instead, on '10 September in his twenty-first year.' This means the twenty-first year of Richard II's reign, which ran from 22 June 1397 to 21 June 1398, not the twenty-first year of John Beaufort's life as the *Complete Peerage* states, and does not mean that Beaufort was 21 years old or in his twenty-first year of age at the time of the original grant in June 1392. It is certainly not evidence that Beaufort was born in 1371, as has sometimes been assumed.

3. *Gaunt's Register 1371–75*, no. 1608.

4. Her two Ferrers daughters, Elizabeth and Mary, were said to be 18 and 17 years old in August/September 1411: *CIPM 1405–13*, nos. 821-4.

5. *Gaunt's Register 1379–83*, nos. 108-15, 1060. Anthony Goodman, in his *'My Most Illustrious Mother, the Lady Katherine': Katherine Swynford and her Daughter Joan*, p. 5, agrees that 1379 'appears a bit late' to be Joan's correct birth year, given that her first child was almost certainly born in 1393. In his *ODNB* article about Joan, Anthony Tuck states that she 'was probably born in 1379', based on 'the pattern of gifts from Gaunt and also from the mayor of Leicester to Katherine [Swynford]', though why these gifts mean that Joan was probably born in 1379 is not explained. Sometime between September 1377 and September 1379, an entry in the *Records of the Borough of Leicester* records the gift of a horse from the mayor of Leicester to Katherine, and another entry made sometime between September 1372 and September 1376 states that the mayor sent Katherine 16 shillings 'for wine'. None of the Beaufort children

are mentioned. *Records of the Borough of Leicester*, vol. 2, 1327–1509, ed. Mary Bateson (1901), pp. 154-5, 169-71. One very young medieval mother was Margaret Beaufort, granddaughter of John of Gaunt and Katherine Swynford's eldest son John Beaufort; Margaret was almost certainly born in May 1443 and gave birth to Henry Tudor, later Henry VII, in January 1457 at the age of 13 and 8 months. Margaret was, however, heir to her father the duke of Somerset (d. 1444) and to her wealthy great-uncle Henry, Cardinal Beaufort (d. 1447), and thanks to the 'courtesy of England', her husband Edmund Tudor had a strong incentive to produce a child with her as soon as possible. No such incentive attached itself to Margaret's great-aunt Joan Beaufort.

6. Ian Mortimer, 'Richard II and the Succession to the Crown' in his *Medieval Intrigue: Decoding Royal Conspiracies* (2010), pp. 259-78; Michael Bennett, 'Edward III's Entail and the Succession to the Crown, 1376–1471', *English Historical Review*, 113 (1998), pp. 580-609.

7. *Gaunt's Register 1371–75*, no. 1431; *CPR 1374–77*, p. 337.

8. Eleanor was said to be of age, i.e. 14 as she was already married, on 8 May 1380. *CPR 1377–81*, p. 502; *CCR 1377–81*, pp. 390-95; *CIPM 1377–84*, no. 201. Mary and Henry of Lancaster received her lands on 22 December 1384, suggesting Mary had recently turned 14 and thus had come of age: *CCR 1381–85*, pp. 511-16, 548.

Chapter 8: A Coronation and an Early Death

1. *CPR 1374–77*, p. 368, which states that Robert had 'taken [Philippa] to wife'. Maud Ufford was married to, or at least betrothed to, Thomas de Vere by 10 June 1350 when she was 4: *CPR 1348–50*, p. 511.

2. Tuchman, *A Distant Mirror*, pp. 609-10. Jeanne de Bourbon was the older sister of Blanche de Bourbon (d. 1361), King Pedro of Castile's repudiated and imprisoned wife.

3. *CPR 1374–77*, p. 477. In the early 1370s, Enguerrand acted as the 'captain of the forces of the Roman church in Lombardy', and fought alongside the famous English mercenary Sir John Hawkwood: *CPL 1362–1404*, pp. 120, 123, 128.

4. *CPR 1377–81*, pp. 174-5.

5. *Chronicon Angliae 1328–1388*, ed. Maunde Thompson, p. 154; *The Anonimalle Chronicle 1333–81*, ed. Galbraith, pp. 107-14; *CPR 1377–81*, pp. 2-5; *CCR 1377–81*, pp. 1-5.

6. *CPR 1374–77*, p. 432; *CPR 1377–81*, p. 412; *Notes and Queries*, fourth series, vol. 10 (July-December 1872), p. 259. The references to 'Philippa, countess of March' in 1378/79 almost certainly refer to Philippa of Clarence's mother-in-law Philippa Mortimer née Montacute. *CCR 1377–81*, pp. 230, 527; *CPR 1377–81*, pp. 261, 271, 608.

7. *Complete Peerage*, vol. 8, pp. 447-8, states correctly that Philippa of Clarence died before Edmund Mortimer, but cites her mother-in-law's will as though it is hers. Philippa of Clarence's Wikipedia page, accessed 20 January 2022, currently says both that she died on 5 January 1381 and that she died in 1382.

8. *CIPM 1377–84*, nos. 534-61 is Edmund's IPM, and nos. 562-66 is Philippa's. *CFR 1377–83*, p. 302, is the order of 8 January 1382 to take the lands of 'Philippa late the wife of Roger de Mortuo Mari, earl of March' into the king's hands; the same order for 'Edmund de Mortuo Mari, earl of March and Ulster' was issued on 10 January.

9. Philippa's full will in the original French is in *Collection*, pp. 98-103, and a much abridged English translation is in *TV*, p. 101. Philippa requested burial in Bisham Priory, which her father William Montacute, earl of Salisbury, had founded in 1335 and where he was buried in 1344.

10. *Collection*, pp. 104-17, is the entire will in French, and a much abridged translation is in *TV*, pp. 110-13. He prepared to go to Ireland in early May 1380: *CPR 1377–81*, pp. 460, 463.

11. *Complete Peerage*, vol. 9, p. 715. Elizabeth and Henry were betrothed or married by 6 March 1380: *CPR 1377–81*, p. 447. Philippa Mortimer (b. 1375) was to die childless in 1400 a few weeks before her twenty-fifth birthday, having married the earl of Pembroke, the earl of Arundel, and Lord Poynings. Her younger brother Edmund Mortimer starved to death in Harlech Castle in 1411, and their sister Elizabeth, Lady Percy and Camoys, died in 1417 at the age of 46, the last survivor of the four rather short-lived Mortimer children.

12. *John of Gaunt's Register 1379–83*, p. 50. Thomas Despenser's marriage had been granted to Edmund of Langley, 'for the purpose of marrying the said heir to his daughter', on 16 April 1379: *CPR*

1377–81, p. 186, incorrectly calling Thomas 'Edward', his father's name.

13. *CPR 1377–81*, p. 225; *CPR 1381–85*, p. 364.

Chapter 9: The Young Bridegroom

1. *Complete Peerage*, vol. 10, p. 395; *Knighton's Chronicle 1337-1396*, ed. Martin, vol. 2, p. 208; *Gaunt's Register 1379–83*, no. 463; *CPR 1374–77*, p. 340. John Hastings' father of the same name, born in August 1347, had married John of Gaunt's youngest sister Margaret of Windsor (b. July 1346) in 1359, but she died at the beginning of the 1360s before they had children, and he later married Anne Manny, a great-granddaughter of Edward I.

2. Margaret of Norfolk's younger daughter Anne Manny, John Hastings' mother, was to die in 1384; her elder daughter, John and Thomas Mowbray's mother Elizabeth Segrave, had died in 1367 or 1368. Elizabeth of Lancaster's future second husband Sir John Holland was one of her wedding guests, *Register 1379–83*, no. 463.

3. John was 'aged two on the feast of St Martin last' in May/July 1375 and 'aged eleven years on the feast of St Martin in the Winter last' in June 1384: *CIPM 1370–73*, no. 148; *CIPM 1384–92*, nos. 12, 13, 20 (the feast of St Martin is 11 November). He was knighted by Richard II on 15 August 1381: *Complete Peerage*, vol. 10, 395.

4. *Register 1379–83*, nos. 803, 890, 898 etc; *Register 1379–83*, nos. 971-72, for Elizabeth's servants.

5. *CPR 1381–85*, 437; TNA SC 8/125/6209-6211, SC 8/129/6440.

6. Ian Mortimer, *The Fears of Henry IV*, pp. 18, 208-9.

7. James Hamilton Wylie, *History of England Under Henry the Fourth*, vol. 4, p. 166; Mortimer, *Fears of Henry IV*, pp. 370-71.

8. See Mortimer, *Fears of Henry IV*, pp. 370-71. Alison Weir, *Katherine Swynford*, p. 186, claims that the infant was born at Rochford Hall in Essex on 24 April 1382, was named Edward, and lived for only four days. No sources are cited for any of these statements.

9. *CCR 1381–85*, pp. 511-16, 548.

10. *CCR 1381–85*, p. 186, gives the exact date of Isabella's death. See Lutkin, 'Exception who Proves the Rule', pp. 132-33, citing the *Westminster Chronicle*, pp. 28-29, which gives Isabella's places of death and burial (*obiit London ... que apud Fratres Minores London*

sepulta est) as well as the date. That Isabella was alive in August 1379 and March and June 1382 is in *CPR 1381–85*, pp. 105, 149, and *CCR 1377–81*, p. 265, and she was also obviously still alive at the end of March 1382 when she was named in the Yorkshire inquisition post mortem of Katherine de la Pole: *CIPM 1377–84*, nos. 577, 579. *CPR 1381–85*, p. 177, states on 25 October 1382 that Isabella was dead. For Isabella's executors, see TNA SC 8/249/12442, and *CPR 1381–85*, pp. 204-5.

11. *CPR 1381–85*, p. 177; *CIPM 1377–84*, no. 889.
12. *Historia Anglicana*, vol. 2, p. 148; the Froissart quotation is taken from Robert's entry in the *ODNB*.
13. Kristen L. Geaman, 'A Personal Letter Written by Anne of Bohemia', pp. 1089-94; and see Geaman, 'Anne of Bohemia and her Struggle to Conceive', pp. 1-21.
14. *CPR 1381–85*, pp. 192, 263.

Chapter 10: Marie de Coucy and Henri de Bar

1. The dispute is mentioned in TNA SC 8/20/990, which is a petition by the abbot of Notley, Buckinghamshire, dated *c.* 1384.
2. The date is given in *John of Gaunt's Register 1379–83*, no. 803.
3. All these details are in *Register 1379–83*, no. 803, pp. 258-9.
4. *CIPM 1399–1405*, nos. 123-204, are the IPMs of Thomas, Eleanor and their daughter Joan in 1400.
5. *Register 1379–83*, nos. 803, 943, 1141.
6. *Oeuvres de Froissart*, ed. Lettenhove, vol. 10, pp. 312-14, and Anthony Tuck, 'Richard II and the House of Luxemburg', *Richard II: The Art of Kingship*, ed. Anthony Goodman and James Gillespie (1999), p. 224. Duke Albrecht's mother Margaretha of Hainault (d. 1356), Holy Roman Empress, was the older sister of Gaunt's mother Queen Philippa, and Albrecht's older brother Wilhelm (1330-1388) had been married to Philippa's aunt Maud of Lancaster (1340–1362).
7. Joyce Coleman, 'The Flower, the Leaf, and Philippa of Lancaster', p. 42.
8. Eleanor had a son, Édouard I, count of Bar (*c.* 1294/95–1336), who had a son, Henri IV, count of Bar (1321–1344). Count Henri's second son Robert, who succeeded his elder brother Édouard II and

was the first duke (rather than merely count) of Bar, was Henri's father.

9. Carlier, 'Henri d'Oisy, Fragment d'Études Historiques', p. 4.
10. Augustin Calmet, *Histoire Ecclésiastique et Civile de Lorraine*, vol. 2 (1728), columns DCLXVI-DCLXVII.
11. Carlier, 'Henry d'Oisy', pp. 109-11.
12. Carlier, 'Henry d'Oisy', pp. 22-25, for this paragraph.
13. *Register 1379–83*, no. 803, pp. 259-60; *CPR 1381–85*, p. 336.

Chapter 11: Madam of Ireland and Elizabeth's Second Marriage

1. *CFR 1383–91*, pp. 120-21, 123.
2. *CIPM 1384–92*, nos. 432-54, 938-9. Thomas proved his age not long before 20 October 1390, *CCR 1389–92*, pp. 231-2, 256. The earl of Stafford came to an agreement with John Holland that the latter should establish a chantry of three chaplains to sing for Ralph's soul. *CPR 1385–89*, pp. 114, 386; TNA SC 8/254/12673.
3. *CPR 1385–89*, pp. 99, 122.
4. *CChR 1341–1417*, pp. 301, 307.
5. *Register of the Black Prince*, vol. 4, p. 87. John's older brother Thomas Holland, who became earl of Kent and Lord Wake in 1385 as their mother's eldest son and heir, was probably born in 1350 or 1351; he was said to be either 9 or 10 years old in early 1361. *CIPM 1352–60*, no. 657.
6. *Polychronicon Ranulphi Higden*, vol. 9, pp. 96-7, and see *Complete Peerage*, vol. 10, p. 396. Elizabeth and John Hastings were still married on 16 June 1384 not long after the death of his mother Anne: TNA SC 8/224/11176, printed in William Rees, ed., *Calendar of Ancient Petitions Relating to Wales* (1975), pp. 375-6. This petition by John and his grandmother the countess of Norfolk, unfortunately not dated, states that Elizabeth 'has disagreed to the marriage, and is [now] married elsewhere'. According to an entry on the Patent Roll in 1401, John Holland was at Berkhamsted on 1 August 1386 ('1 August, 10 Richard II'), but this might be dated incorrectly: *CPR 1399–1401*, pp. 405-6. The National Archives website (https://discovery.nationalarchives.gov.uk/details/r/c36349b9-701c-4cb2-94b3-96329c78ebed, accessed 28 November 2021) states that

Elizabeth's Hastings marriage was dissolved on 24 February 1383, but does not cite a source.

7. *CPL 1362–1404*, p. 396. *CIPM 1399–1405*, nos. 264, 269-70, says that young Thomas Mowbray was 'fourteen on 17 September last' in January 1400, so he was born on 17 September 1385. TNA E 41/202 is the arrangement between the earls of Huntingdon and Nottingham for their children to marry, dated 27 June 1391.

8. *CChR 1341–1417*, p. 309; *CIPM 1413–18*, no. 597. John Holland was at Berkhamsted Castle, presumably with Elizabeth, on 11 June 1388. King Richard granted him custody of the castle for life in January 1391, but perhaps he was already unofficially acting as its keeper. *CPR 1389–92*, pp. 369, 372; *CPR 1399–1401*, p. 261.

9. Juliet Barker, in her *Agincourt: The King, the Campaign, the Battle* (2006), pp. 158, 161, calls John Cornwall 'one of the most widely respected chivalric figures of the day' who demonstrated 'military prowess', and gives details of his many fascinating exploits.

10. *Anglo-Norman Letters and Petitions*, ed. Legge, no. 268, p. 328. Duke John IV of Brittany (d. 1399) was the widower of Holland's sister Joan Holland (d. 1384) and of Edward III's fourth daughter Mary of Waltham (d. 1361/62); his children were all born to his third wife, Juana of Navarre, who married Elizabeth of Lancaster's brother Henry as her second husband in 1403.

11. Holland was in London on 30 January 1392 and in Brittany in May that year: *CPR 1391–6*, pp. 60, 208.

12. The illegitimate William is mentioned in Christian Steer, "For Quicke and Deade Memory Masses': Merchant Piety in Late Medieval London', *Medieval Merchants and Money: Essays in Honour of James L. Bolton*, ed. Martin Allen and Matthew Davies (2016), pp. 85-7. I am grateful to Sandra Heath Wilson for bringing this article to my attention. John Holland the younger named two illegitimate sons of his own in his will of 1447, William and Thomas, and had three others named Robert, John and William (another one): *Collection of All the Wills*, pp. 285, 287, 'my ii bastards sones William and Thomas'; Douglas Richardson, *Plantagenet Ancestry: A Study in Medieval and Colonial Families* (second edition, 2011), pp. 26-7. John and the second William were both at Cambridge University in 1440-42, and used the last name Huntyngdon: P.N.R. Zutshi, ed., *Medieval Cambridge: Essays on the Pre-Reformation University* (1993), pp. 56-7.

Chapter 12: Queen Philippa and King João, and Agnes Launcecrona

1. The translation of Fernão Lopes' chronicle is in *Medieval Iberia: Readings from Christian, Muslim, and Jewish Sources*, ed. Olivia Remie Constable and Damian Zurro, pp. 442-6. Ernle Bradford, *A Wind From the North: The Life of Henry the Navigator* (1960), p. 13, for the 'brilliant monarchs' quotation. Manuela Santos Silva, 'The Portuguese Household of an English Queen: Sources, Purposes, Social Meaning (1387-1415)', *Royal and Elite Households in Medieval and Early Modern Europe, More Than Just a Castle*, ed. Theresa Earenfight, p. 272, for Gaunt and João's arrangement. João of Aviz was the illegitimate son of King Pedro I of Portugal (1320–1367) from his relationship with a mistress named Teresa Lourenço, a commoner from Lisbon. King Pedro, father of Fernando I from his marriage to Costanza Manuel of Villena, also had a long relationship with, and claimed to be married to, Inês de Castro (murdered in early 1355), whose sister Doña Juana was the mistress and also allegedly the wife of Pedro's maternal nephew Pedro 'the Cruel' of Castile.
2. *CPL 1362–1404*, p. 367.
3. *Medieval Iberia: Readings from Christian, Muslim, and Jewish Sources*, pp. 446-7; Manuela Santos Silva, 'Felipa de Lancáster, la Dama Inglesa que fue Modelo de Reginalidad en Portugal (1387–1415)', *Anuario de Estudios Medievales*, 46 (2016), p. 209; Anthony Goodman, *John of Gaunt: The Exercise of Princely Power in Fourteenth-Century Europe*, p. 130.
4. See Ana Rodrigues Oliveira's article 'Philippa of Lancaster: The Memory of a Model Queen', *Queenship in the Mediterranean: Negotiating the Role of the Queen in the Medieval and Early Modern Eras*.
5. *Medieval Iberia: Readings*, pp. 447-8; Coleman, 'The Flower, the Leaf', pp. 47-8; Aline S. Taylor, *Isabel of Burgundy: The Duchess Who Played Politics in the Age of Joan of Arc, 1397–1471* (2001), pp. 28-9; Santos Silva, 'Felipa de Lancáster, la Dama Inglesa', p. 211; Santos Silva, 'The Portuguese Household of an English Queen', p. 281.
6. *CPR 1389–92*, p. 20.

7. Cited in Robert's entry in the *ODNB*, and see also *Complete Peerage*, vol. 10, pp. 231-2.
8. *Foedera*, vol. 7, 1373–97, p. 636. Richard II granted Jehan de Chastelmurant a safe-conduct on 24 July 1389.
9. *The Westminster Chronicle 1381–1394*, ed. L.C. Hector and B.F. Harvey (1982), pp. 190, 404.

Chapter 13: Catalina of Lancaster and Enrique of Castile

1. *CPR 1385–89*, pp. 423-4.
2. *CFR 1383–91*, p. 224.
3. Goodman, *John of Gaunt*, p. 360; *Froissart*, ed. Lettenhove, vol. 13, pp. 301-2.
4. For the last two paragraphs, see *Chronica Maiora of Thomas Walsingham, 1376–1422*, ed. Richard Barber, translated David Preest, p. 276; McHardy, *Reign of Richard II*, pp. 172-4; Given-Wilson, *Henry IV*, pp. 61, 71, 76; Goodman, *John of Gaunt*, pp. 128, 131, 345; Earenfight, *María of Castile and the Crown of Aragon,* pp. 21-22. The relevant section in Pedro the Cruel's will is in *Crónicas de los Reyes de Castilla ... por D. Pedro López de Ayala*, ed. Amirola, vol. 1, p. 560.
5. Leonor of Castile, daughter of Enrique of Trastámara and sister of Juan I, was married to Carlos III of Navarre, son of King Carlos II 'the Bad' (d. 1387) and brother of Juana of Navarre, duchess of Brittany and later queen of England.
6. *Froissart*, ed. Lettenhove, vol. 13, pp. 301-4; *Crónicas de los Reyes de Castilla desde Don Alfonso el Sabio hasta los Católicos Don Fernando y Doña Isabel*, ed. Cayetano Rosell, vol. 2 (1877), pp. 120-21; Ana Echevarría Arsuaga, *Catalina de Lancaster: Reina Regente de Castilla, 1372–1418* (2002), pp. 48-9; Ana Echevarría, 'Catalina de Lancaster, the Castilian Monarchy, and Coexistence', p. 106; García Rey, 'La Famosa Priora Doña Teresa de Ayala (su Correspondencia Íntima con los Monarcas de su Tiempo)', *Boletín de la Real Academia de la Historia*, 96 (1930), p. 739. In the late 1380s, Duchess Costanza acquired the lordships of Medina del Campo, Olmedo and Guadalajara: *Crónicas de los Reyes de Castilla desde Don Alfonso el Sabio*, p. 120; Luis Suárez Fernández, *Historia del Reinado de Juan I de Castilla*, vol. 1 (1977), pp. 292-3, 296.

See also Chapter 23 below for Enrique's 'my own heart' statement. Enrique's younger brother Fernando of Antequera (b. 1380) married Leonor Urraca, countess of Albuquerque, whose father Don Sancho was one of the illegitimate Trastámara siblings, son of Alfonso XI and his mistress Leonor de Guzmán, and a younger brother of Enrique of Trastámara, king of Castile (d. 1379).

7. Guzmán, *Pen Portraits of Illustrious Castilians*, pp. 8, 12; Folger, *Generaciones y Semblanzas*, p. 187; and see also *Crónica del Señor Rey Don Juan, Segundo de Este Nombre, en Castilla y en León*, compiled by Fernán Pérez de Guzmán, amended by Lorenzo Galíndez de Carvajal (1779).

8. Francisco de Paula Cañas Gálvez, 'Don Sancho de Castilla (1363– 1371): Apuntes Biográficos de un Hijo Ilegítimo de Pedro I', *Mundos Medievales, Espacios, Sociedares y Poder,* vol. 2, pp. 1133-4; García Rey, 'La Famosa Priora Doña Teresa de Ayala', pp. 747-8. Sancho's mother was Pedro the Cruel's mistress Isabel de Sandoval, and he was born in Almazán in September 1363: *Crónicas de los Reyes de Castilla ... por D. Pedro López de Ayala*, p. 570; Cañas Gálvez, pp. 1126-7; Verardo García Rey, 'La Famosa Priora Doña Teresa de Ayala' p. 710.

9. García Rey, 'La Famosa Priora Doña Teresa de Ayala', pp. 751-4 (*como aquella que amo en mi coraçón*).

10. Francisco de Paula Cañas Gálvez, ed., *Colección Diplomática de Santo Domingo el Real de Toledo I: Documentos Reales (1249-1473)* (2010), pp. 148-50; María del Pilar Rábade Obradó, 'Religiosidad y Memoria Política: Las Constituciones de la Capilla de Pedro I en Santo Domingo el Real de Madrid (1464)', *En la España Medieval,* 26 (2003), pp. 229-30, 235; Surtz, *Writing Women in Late Medieval and Early Modern Spain*, pp. 41-2. Juan, son of Pedro the Cruel and Juana de Castro, was re-interred in Santo Domingo el Real after his daughter Costanza became prioress there in 1442 (*Crónicas de los Reyes de Castilla ... por D. Pedro López de Ayala*, p. 571), and in 1877 his remains were moved to Seville Cathedral. Juan was born in early January 1355 nine months after his parents' wedding ceremony, at almost exactly the same time that his famous maternal aunt Inês de Castro was assassinated in Portugal on 7 January 1355, and in the same year that his half-sister Duchess Isabel of York was born as well.

Chapter 14: Two Queens and a Poet

1. Anne of Gloucester's entry in the *ODNB* says (without citing a source) that her wedding to Thomas Stafford took place at Pleshey in June 1391. Marie de Coucy's husband Henri's paternal grandmother Yolande of Flanders, dowager countess of Bar, was still alive when her great-grandson was born, and died in 1395.
2. *Anglo-Norman Letters and Petitions from All Souls MS 182*, ed. Mary Dominica Legge, nos. 297, 307, pp. 360-61, 372-3.
3. Tiago Viúla de Faria, 'From Norwich to Lisbon: Factionalism, Personal Association, and Conveying the *Confessio Amantis*', *John Gower in England and Iberia: Manuscripts, Influences, Reception*, ed. Ana Sáez-Hidalgo and R. F. Yeager (2014), pp. 131-3, 136-8.
4. Earenfight, *The King's Other Body*, pp. 21, 23. Berenguela of Castile was the eldest child of Alfonso VIII of Castile (d. 1214) and Eleanor of England (d. 1214), daughter of Henry II and Eleanor of Aquitaine, and sister of Richard Lionheart and King John. One of Berenguela's younger sisters was the famous Blanche of Castile (1188–1252), queen of Louis VIII of France and mother of Louis IX, and also regent for and adviser of her underage son.
5. See Fernão Lopes and Derek W. Lomax, eds., *The English in Portugal, 1367–87: Extracts from the Chronicles of Dom Fernando and Dom João* (1988). The 'tenacious ruler' quotation is from Brian A. Catlos, *Muslims of Medieval Latin Christendom, c. 1050–1614* (2014), p. 169.
6. TNA E 41/202, E 40/5925; *Issues of the Exchequer*, ed. Devon, p. 252.
7. *CPR 1391–96*, p. 13.
8. *CPR 1391–96*, p. 34; *Oeuvres de Froissart*, ed Lettenhove, vol. 14, pp. 3, 378, 380-81, 388.
9. Robert's entry in the *ODNB*.
10. *CPR 1389–92*, p. 407.
11. *CPR 1391–96*, pp. 393, 716; *CPR 1396–99*, pp. 12, 109, 581.
12. *CPR 1391–96*, pp. 620, 667.

Chapter 15: A Young Widow and a Visit to Hungary

1. According to Douglas Richardson's *Plantagenet Ancestry: A Study in Colonial and Medieval Families* (2004), p. 334, Joan and Robert

married before 30 September 1390, but it is impossible to follow Richardson's source for this statement. The National Archives website says that the couple married in March 1392, G.L. Harriss's *Cardinal Beaufort: A Study of Lancastrian Ascendancy and Decline* (1988), p. 6, says they were betrothed in 1386 and married in 1392, and Joan Beaufort's entry in the *Oxford Dictionary of National Biography* also states that she married in 1392. The National Archives website, describing an extant roll of Gaunt's accounts, says that Joan is called 'Beaufort' up to March 1392 in the roll and 'Ferrers' afterwards: https://discovery.nationalarchives.gov.uk/details/r/c36349b9-701c-4cb2-94b3-96329c78ebed, accessed 28 November 2021. For the jousting in France, see *Oeuvres de Froissart*, ed. Lettenhove, vol. 14, pp. 414, 416.

2. *Gaunt's Register 1379–83*, no. 1029. Anthony Goodman (*My Most Illustrious Mother*, p. 6), states that Robert Ferrers was 'much older' than Joan, which he was not; the age difference was about six years at most and perhaps only two or three. Robert was said to be either 8 or 10 years old at his father's inquisition post mortem in May/July 1381: *CIPM 1377–84*, nos. 346-9.
3. *CFR 1377–83*, p. 260; *CIPM 1377–84*, nos. 346-9.
4. *CIPM 1405–13*, nos. 821-24.
5. Elizabeth married John, Lord Greystoke (b. *c.* 1389/90) and had twelve children, and Mary married her stepbrother Ralph Neville, one of the sons of Joan Beaufort's second husband from his first marriage, and also had children of her own.
6. *CIPM 1399–1405*, nos. 158, 164-5; *CCR 1399–1402*, pp. 261, 453; *CFR 1399–1405*, p. 120.
7. *CIPM 1392–99*, nos. 907-19, is the IPM of Gilbert's father, giving Gilbert's age as 12 or 13 in 1396/97. He was certainly born after 14 September 1383 and was younger than his sisters Elizabeth and Mary: *CIPM 1377–84*, no. 1024, and see *CCR 1402–05*, p. 98.
8. *CIPM 1392–99*, nos. 196-239, 556-7.
9. *CCR 1392–96*, pp 38-40, 47-8; *CCR 1396–99*, p. 138; *CFR 1391–99*, p. 54.
10. *CPR 1391–96*, p. 203; Viúla de Faria, 'From Norwich to Lisbon' in *John Gower in England and Iberia*, pp. 133-4.
11. Duchess Isabel's will (in French) is now in the National Archives, TNA PROB 11/1/53. A much abbreviated English translation, which fails to mention any of the numerous bequests Isabel made to her

husband Edmund of Langley and has thus often led modern writers, including myself on previous occasions, astray as to the nature of their relationship, is in *TV*, vol. 1, pp. 134-5. For the 'crown of Spain', see T.B. Pugh, *Henry V and the Southampton Plot* (1988), pp. 125, 135, 165, 176 (I owe this reference to Brian Wainwright).

12. *CPR 1391–96*, pp. 384, 386, 483. Joan Holland's date of birth is not recorded, but her oldest sister Alianore I, countess of March, was born on 13 October 1370, her oldest brother Thomas, earl of Kent, on 8 September 1372, and her younger sister Alianore II, countess of Salisbury, on 29 November 1384. Other siblings were born in November 1374, April 1376 and January 1382 or 1383. See https://www.joh.cam.ac.uk/library/special_collections/manuscripts/medieval_manuscripts/medman/K_26.htm, accessed 19 October 2021.

13. Bretton Rodriguez, 'Competing Images of Pedro I: López de Ayala and the Formation of Historical Memory', *La Corónica: A Journal of Medieval Hispanic Languages, Literatures, and Cultures*, 45 (2017), pp. 88, 100-01; L.P. Harvey, *Islamic Spain, 1250 to 1500* (1990), pp. 204, 207, 214-15, 222.

14. Henry Charles Lea, 'Ferrand Martinez and the Massacres of 1391', *The American Historical Review*, 1 (1896), pp. 210-11.

15. Lea, 'Ferrand Martinez', pp. 212-20.

16. *Foedera 1373–97*, p. 764; *CPL 1362–1404*, pp. 294-5, 300, 489; *CPR 1391–96*, p. 363; *Diplomatic Correspondence of Richard II*, ed. Perroy, no. 199, pp. 144-5, and note on p. 244. John was at his Devon manor of Dartington on 21 October 1393, *CPR 1391–96*, p. 639.

17. Attila Bárány, 'King Sigismund and the "Passagium Generale" (1391–96)', *Conferinta Internationala Sigismund de Luxemburg*, ed. Florena Ciure and Alexandru Simon (2007), pp. 12-14.

18. *CPR 1399–1405*, p. 457, gives 2 July as the date of Mary's death, though Henry IV seems also to have marked the anniversary on 4 July; see his entry in the *ODNB*.

19. *Crónicas de los Reyes de Castilla Don Pedro, Don Enrique II, Don Juan I, Don Enrique III por D. Pedro López de Ayala*, pp. 561-4. For Pedro's seizure of el *Bermejo*, meaning 'russet' or 'the red one', see L.P. Harvey, *Islamic Spain, 1250 to 1500*, pp. 213-14. Another of Bermejo's large balas rubies was set into a decorative eagle which Pedro bequeathed to his eldest daughter Beatriz.

Chapter 16: A Scandalous Marriage

1. *CIPM 1418–22*, no. 149.
2. TNA E 42/19; E 40/2248.
3. TNA E 40/6964.
4. TNA C 1/68/40.
5. *CPR 1399–1405*, p. 435.
6. *Chronica Maiora*, trans. Preest, p. 295.
7. Cited in McHardy, *Reign of Richard II*, p. 310. Froissart claims that the countess of Derby was another of the ladies who angrily refused to acknowledge Katherine as duchess, but Mary de Bohun had died eighteen months previously (and had always been on excellent terms with Katherine anyway).
8. *CPR 1396–99*, p. 86.
9. *CPR 1396–99*, p. 127.
10. *CPR 1396–99*, p. 39.
11. Jonathan Sumption, *Divided Houses: The Hundred Years War III*, p. 834.
12. Carlier, 'Henri d'Oisy', pp. 1-2.
13. *CIPM 1399–1405*, no. 2.
14. *CPR 1399–1401*, p. 336; *Cardiff Records*, vol. 1, ed. J.H. Matthews (1898), pp. 31-2.

Chapter 17: The Extermination of Schismatics

1. *Anglo-Norman Letters and Petitions*, ed. Legge, no. 28, pp. 73-4.
2. *Collection of All the Wills*, pp. 118-19; *CIPM 1392–99*, nos. 798-849. Thomas's elder son and heir Thomas the younger was 24 going on 25 in 1397, his younger son Edmund was 14 or 15, and he had five daughters, including Alianore, countess of March, Joan, duchess of York, and Margaret, soon to become countess of Somerset by marriage to the now-legitimate John Beaufort.
3. *CPL 1362–1404*, pp. 294-5, 300.
4. *CPR 1396–99*, p. 149.
5. The house is often assumed to have been Coldharbour, also known as Pulteney's Inn, though Pulteney's Inn belonged to Richard, earl of Arundel; it is mentioned in his will of 1392 (*Collection*, p. 138, *mon houstel de Pulteney*).

6. *Chronica Maiora*, trans. Preest, p. 298; *Chronicque de la Traison et Mort de Richart Deux Roy Dengleterre,* ed. Benjamin Williams (1846), pp. 7-8, 127-30; *Chronicles of the Revolution, 1397–1400: The Reign of Richard II*, ed. Chris Given-Wilson (1993), pp. 94-5; Thomas of Woodstock's entry in the *ODNB.*

7. *Chronicles of the Revolution*, p. 103.

8. *CPR 1396–99*, p. 214; *Chronicles of the Revolution*, p. 116. The earl of Arundel's elder son Richard was his heir at the time of his execution, but Richard died sometime between 1397 and 1399, leaving his younger brother Thomas as the Arundel heir. See *TV*, vol. 1, pp. 129-34; *Collection*, pp. 120-44. The entry on the Patent Roll (p. 214) talks of the earl of Arundel's sons Richard and John, presumably an error for Richard and Thomas. The earl of Nottingham was the brother-in-law of the Arundel brothers, being the husband of their sister Elizabeth.

9. *Chronicque de la Traison et Mort*, p. 11: *ot le pris pour la mieulx dancant.* On 4 November 1397, John Holland was staying in his London house after parliament ended, and presumably Elizabeth was there with him: TNA E 40/235. John referred to himself in this document as 'John de Holand, duke of Exeter, earl of Huntingdon, chamberlain of England'.

10. Jenny Stratford, *Richard II and the English Royal Treasure*, p. 95.

Chapter 18: Murder of a Royal Duke

1. *CIPM 1392–99*, nos. 1022-52; *CFR 1391–99*, p. 224; *CCR 1402–05*, p. 35; Given-Wilson, *Chronicles of the Revolution*, pp. 78-83; *PROME*, September 1397 parliament. The duke of Gloucester's confession, in English, appears in *PROME*.

2. *CCR 1396–99*, pp. 149-50, 157; *Foedera 1397–1413*, pp. 19, 20, 24; Sumption, *Divided Houses: The Hundred Years War III*, pp. 837-8, for Gloucester's speech.

3. *CPR 1396–99*, pp. 376, 384; TNA SC 8/221/11020.

4. *CIPM 1392–99*, nos. 196-239, 556-7; *CPR 1396–99*, p. 456; *CCR 1396–99*, p. 467.

5. Cited in Alastair Dunn, 'Richard II and the Mortimer Inheritance', *Fourteenth Century England II*, ed. Chris Given-Wilson (2002), p. 166; see also *CCR 1396–99*, p. 325, *CPR 1396–99*, pp. 374,

390, 401 etc. Anne Mortimer's date of birth is given in Dugdale, ed., *Monasticon Anglicanum*, vol. 6, p. 355 ('*Anna nata erat in die S. Johannis evangelistae, in natale Domini, anno regni regis Ricardi secundi xii*'). Roger's wife Alianore Holland, eldest daughter of the earl of Kent and niece of the earl of Huntingdon, was born on 13 October 1370: Douglas Richardson, *Magna Carta Ancestry: A Study in Colonial and Medieval Families,* pp. 195-6, and see https://www.joh.cam.ac.uk/library/special_collections/manuscripts/medieval_manuscripts/medman/K_26.htm, accessed 19 October 2021.

6. *CCR 1396–99*, pp. 291-2.
7. *PROME*.
8. *CCR 1396–99*, pp. 281-2; *Foedera 1373–97*, p. 532; *Anglo-Norman Letters and Petitions*, ed. Legge, no. 56, p. 104.
9. *CPR* 1396–99, pp. 420, 422, 439; *Foedera, Conventiones, Litterae et Cujuscunque Acta Publica*, ed. Thomas Rymer, vol. 8, 1397–1413, pp. 47-8, 51; Given-Wilson, *Chronicles of the Revolution*, p. 135.
10. *Chronicles of the Revolution*, pp. 105-6.
11. *CPR 1396–99*, p. 422; Jenny Stratford, *Richard II and the Royal Treasure*, p. 94. Philippa was not, as sometimes assumed, the person in charge of the young Queen Isabelle's household; this was the Lady de Courcy, given name Marguerite, not de Coucy. Richard ended up sending Marguerite de Courcy back to her native France in 1399.

Chapter 19: Two Deaths

1. Gaunt's will is printed in full, in the original French, in *Collection of All the Wills*, pp. 145-73, and also in *Testamenta Eboracensia, Or Wills Registered at York*, part 1, ed. James Raine (1836), pp. 223-39. A highly abridged English translation is printed in *TV*, vol. 1, pp. 140-45. The scribe who wrote down the will misdated it to 1397.
2. Eleanor's will is printed in full, also in the original French, in *Collection*, pp. 177-85; a much abridged version is in *TV*, vol. 1, pp. 146-9. The chronicle which states that she was buried in the London house of the Minoresses and died of grief, and that Humphrey of Gloucester died of plague, is *Johannis de Trokelowe et Henrici de Blaneforde, Monachorum S. Albani, Chronica et*

Annales, ed. Henry Thomas Riley (1866), p. 321. For Thomas of Woodstock's books, see Jeanne E. Krochalis, 'The Books and Reading of Henry V and his Circle', *The Chaucer Review*, 23 (1988), pp. 50-52.

3. Given-Wilson, *Chronicles of the Revolution*, p. 160.
4. *Chronicque de la Traison et Mort*, pp. 63-4, 215. Thomas Fitzalan had escaped from the custody of his brother-in-law Thomas Mowbray and fled abroad to join Henry of Lancaster and Archbishop Thomas Arundel, his uncle.
5. *Chronicque de la Traison et Mort*, p. 193.
6. *CPR 1399–1401*, p. 244.
7. *ANLP*, no. 287, pp. 347-8; Echevarría, 'Catalina de Lancaster, the Castilian Monarchy, and Coexistence', p. 193. Philippa referred to her brother as duke of Lancaster, so she must have sent the letter after her father Gaunt's death in early February 1399, but did not call him king, so must have sent it before late September that year.

Chapter 20: The Epiphany Rising

1. *ODNB*, entry for John Holland.
2. *Chronicles of the Revolution*, pp. 230-31, 235-6; Mortimer, *Fears of Henry IV*, p. 206.
3. *CCR 1399–1402*, p. 41.
4. *ANLP*, nos. 1, 62, 64, pp. 45-6, 110-15.
5. *Chronica Maiora*, trans. Preest, p. 317; *Chronicles of the Revolution*, p. 227.
6. The younger Holland's inquisition post mortem (*CIPM 1399–1405*, no. 1188), says that he died on 15 January, though according to the rolls of parliament, he might in fact have died as early as 9 January. *Johannis de Trokelowe*, ed. Riley, p. 320, says that the earls of Kent and Salisbury were executed in Cirencester.
7. *PROME*, January 1401 parliament, *le dit roialme de gentz d'autre lange enhabiter*.
8. *CPR 1399–1401*, pp. 188, 197, 223-4, 226.
9. *Issues of the Exchequer*, ed. Devon, pp. 278-9; *CPR 1399–1401*, pp. 387, 394, 435, 439.
10. *CPR 1399–1401*, pp. 197, 273.

Chapter 21: Elizabeth's Third Marriage

1. Cited in *CP*, vol. 5, p. 199 note f.
2. *CCR 1399–1402*, p. 78; *CPR 1399–1401*, p. 409.
3. *Issues of the Exchequer*, p. 278; Simon Walker, 'Janico Dartasso: Chivalry, Nationality and the Man-at-Arms', *History*, 84 (1999), pp. 37, 41-2.
4. A 'John Cornwaill, knight' who went to Gascony on the king's service in May 1388 has sometimes been identified as Elizabeth of Lancaster's future husband, though another 'John Cornewaille, knight' was named on the Patent Roll in February 1382 and November 1385, and might in fact be the man of this name who went to Gascony in 1388; perhaps this was John's father, John Cornwall Sr. It is often impossibly difficult to differentiate men who bore the same name. C 61/100, nos. 76.2, 81, available at gasconrolls. org (identifying 'John Cornwall' as the one who later married Elizabeth); *CPR 1396–99*, pp. 64, 91, 187, 516, and John's entry in the *ODNB* (Richard II's retention of John); *CPR 1381–85*, p. 133, and *CPR 1385–89*, pp. 43-4, 205 (the other John Cornewaille).
5. *CIPM 1392–99*, nos. 421-22, 1093; *CIPM 1399–1405*, nos. 31-8; *CIPM 1413–18*, nos. 190-94; *CIPM 1418–22*, nos. 443-6; *CFR 1391–99*, p. 254; *CPR 1396–99*, p. 516. Various inquisitions state that Philippa's eldest daughter Elizabeth Sergeaux was 30 or 33 in 1400, so she was born in the period 1367–70, and gave birth to Thomas Marny on 6 or 7 February 1393. Philippa Arundel's mother Sybil (b. *c.* early 1330s) was the daughter of William Montacute, earl of Salisbury (1301–1344); Philippa's father Sir Edmund Arundel was born *c.* 1326 as the only child of Richard, earl of Arundel from his first marriage to Isabella Despenser, a great-granddaughter of Edward I. Edmund Arundel was made illegitimate when his parents' marriage was annulled at the end of 1344, and his much younger half-brother Richard, b. *c.* 1347, was the earl of Arundel's heir when he died in January 1376. Edmund's daughters Philippa, Elizabeth and Katherine were his heirs.
6. *CCR 1396–99*, pp. 268, 321, 371; *CPR 1396–99*, pp. 550, 559; TNA SC 8/249/12422. On 20 September 1398 during John's brief marriage to Philippa, Richard II granted him the marriage rights of his two unmarried Sergeaux stepdaughters, Alice and Joan.

With their older sisters Elizabeth Marny and Philippa Pashley, the two were the Sergeaux heirs after their brother died in June 1396. John arranged Alice's marriage to Guy St Aubyn before January 1400, and after Guy's death she married the earl of Oxford. *CFR 1391–99*, p. 291; TNA SC 8/213/10650; *CIPM 1399–1405*, nos. 31-8. John was not mentioned in Philippa's inquisition post mortem, most probably because he had no right to hold any of her lands by the 'courtesy of England', as they had no children together.

7. Barker, *Agincourt: The King, the Campaign, the Battle*, pp. 158, 161.
8. *CP*, vol. 5, p. 253.
9. *CPR 1396–99*, p. 436 (keeper of the peace); *CPR 1402–05*, p. 94 (Gaunt).
10. *CPR 1399–1401*, p. 241. Dartington was one of the manors later assigned to Elizabeth in dower: *CIPM 1399–1405*, no. 1005.
11. See *ODNB*, 'Cornewall, John, Baron Fanhope, d. 1443'. It is impossible to follow the *ODNB*'s source for the statement about young John's date of birth and baptism, and it seems odd that if the king was his nephew's godfather, young John was not named after him.
12. Edward Hol(l)and is in *CPR 1416–22*, p. 201. John Cornwall's youngest stepdaughter Joan Sergeaux also died that year, on 31 July, a few weeks after his third stepdaughter Alice St Aubyn proved her age and left his wardship. *CIPM 1399–1405*, no. 37 (Joan); *CIPM 1413–18*, no. 59 (Richard Holland's death). Alice Sergeaux St Aubyn was born on 1 September 1384; *CIPM 1399–1405*, no. 312, and *CFR 1399–1405*, pp. 73, 100-1.
13. *CPR 1401–05*, p. 282; TNA SC 8/331/15675.
14. *CPR 1399–1401*, pp. 201, 206, 241, 348, 483; *CPR 1401–05*, p. 386, etc; *A Descriptive Catalogue of Ancient Deeds*, vol. 2, no. B.2009; *CIPM 1399–1405*, no. 1188; Stratford, *Richard II and the English Royal Treasure*, p. 121.

Chapter 22: The Coucy Sisters' Dispute

1. *CIPM 1413–18*, no. 184.
2. *ANLP*, no. 225, p. 291; the index ascribes this letter to Constance.

3. *CIPM 1399–1405*, nos. 123-89; *CCR 1402–05*, p. 35 ('Monday after the Assumption, 1 Henry IV'). In June 1400, Joan had a guardian called Robert Riketon, which in this context probably means someone appointed to look after her legal interests: *CCR 1399–1402*, pp. 161, 164.

4. W. Dugdale, ed., *Monasticon Anglicanum*, vol. 4, p. 141 (Walden Abbey Cartulary); *CIPM 1418–22*, nos. 308-22, 779-87.

5. Isabel being professed as a nun on 23 April 1402 is in *CIPM 1399–1405*, no. 125; her being placed in the convent as an infant is in *CPL 1398–1404*, p. 385; Henry IV's granting of a favour is in *CPR 1401–05*, p. 248; Gaunt's bequest to the Minoresses is in *Collection of All the Wills*, p. 153; Constance and Thomas's doorway is in *CPL 1398–1404*, p. 544 (though it is likely, given the Gloucester-de Bohun family's close connection to the convent, that the 'earl of Gloucester' mentioned was an error for 'duke of Gloucester' and meant Thomas of Woodstock); the mention of the abbess Margaret Holmystede is in *Calendar of Wills Proved and Enrolled in the Court of Husting, London*, ed. R.R. Sharpe (1890), vol. 2, 1358–1658, p. 382; Marion Charteseye is in *Calendar of Wills Proved*, vol. 2, p. 331; Isabel of Gloucester being the abbess around 1421/22 is in Henry Fly, 'Some Account of an Abbey of Nuns', p. 105; and her legal action is in *London Possessory Assizes: A Calendar*, ed. Helena M. Chew (1965), no. 230. Edmund Stafford, presumably with Anne of Gloucester, was at Stafford Castle on 6 September 1400, in London on 16 February 1401, and at Stafford on 4, 8 and 12 June and 1 and 4 July 1401. *CPR 1401–05*, pp. 270, 308, 311, 378-9, 382, 423; TNA C 146/2213.

6. Carlier, 'Henri d'Oisy', pp. 110, 157-8. The son and heir of the duke of Orléans was Charles of Angoulême (b. November 1394), who as a child in June 1406 married his first cousin Isabelle de Valois (b. November 1389), daughter of Charles VI and widow of Richard II of England. Charles of Angoulême became both a father and a widower in September 1409, still only 14 years old , when Isabelle died after giving birth to their daughter Jeanne.

7. *The Parliament Rolls of Medieval England,* ed. Brand, Curry, Given-Wilson, Horrox, Martin, Ormrod and Phillips (2005), January 1401 parliament.

8. *CPR 1399–1401*, p. 528.

9. *CPR 1399–1401*, pp. 197, 273, 528.
10. Earenfight, *The King's Other Body*, pp. 25, 27; García Rey, 'La Famosa Priora Doña Teresa de Ayala', p. 772. Doña María of Castile's wetnurse was Juana de Zúñiga, wife of the mayor of Burgos in northern Castile, and her tutor or governess was Inés de Ayala, another member of the Ayala family; Earenfight, p. 27.
11. Catalina's daughters María and Catalina of Castile both married their first cousins, the brothers King Alfonso V of Aragon, b. 1396, and Enrique of Aragon, b. 1400.
12. *CFR 1399–1405*, pp. 159-60, 201-2. In or soon after April 1401, Thomas Arundel, archbishop of Canterbury, went in person to the convent of the Minoresses in London to ascertain whether Isabel of Gloucester was living there of her own free will, and discovered that she was. A letter of Pope Boniface IX on the matter stated correctly that Isabel's late mother Eleanor de Bohun (1366–1399) was Archbishop Arundel's niece (Eleanor's mother Joan, dowager countess of Hereford, was the archbishop's older sister), but claimed incorrectly that all of Isabel's siblings were dead. Archbishop Arundel was concerned 'lest the duke [of Gloucester]'s inheritance devolve to strangers'. *CPL 1398–1404*, pp. 385, 387.
13. *CPR 1401–05*, pp. 270, 304, 367, 385.
14. *CIPM 1422–27*, no. 369. Edmund Stafford was at Thornbury in Gloucestershire, one of Anne's manors, on 1 January 1403: *CPR 1401–05*, pp. 307, 382. Presumably she was also there.
15. Anne Stafford married firstly Edmund Mortimer (1391–1425), earl of March, with whom she had no children. She married secondly Elizabeth of Lancaster's son John Holland (b. 1395), and gave birth to their son and John's heir, Henry Holland, on 27 June 1430. *CIPM 1442–47*, nos. 531-43.
16. Luís de Cacegas and Lucas de Santa Catharina, *Primeira Parte da História de S. Domingos, Particular do Reino e Conquistas de Portugal* (1866), vol. 2, p. 312. The year previously, King João had created his illegitimate son Dom Afonso (b. 1377) count of Barcelos, and arranged Afonso's marriage to Beatriz Pereira de Alvim. Afonso and Beatriz's daughter Isabel (b. 1402) would marry her half-uncle, Queen Philippa and King João's second youngest son Dom João (b. 1400).

17. Antonio Henrique R. de Oliveira Marques and S.S. Wyatt, *Daily Life in Portugal in the Late Middle Ages* (1971), pp. 211, 221.
18. *si jeo faille de Messe, jeo en orroie demeyn diaux*: *Livre de Seyntz Medicines: The Unpublished Devotional Treatise of Henry of Lancaster*, ed. E.J. Arnould (1940), pp. 22-3; Henry of Grosmont, First Duke of Lancaster, *Le Livre de Seyntz Medicines: The Book of Holy Medicines*, ed. and trans. Catherine Batt (2014), pp. 92-3.

Chapter 23: Queen Catalina's Son

1. Gemma Hollman, *Royal Witches: From Joan of Navarre to Elizabeth Woodville*, p. 46. For Edmund Lebourde, who was raised in London and joined the Church in 1411/12, see Mortimer, *Fears of Henry IV*, pp. 356, 372, 442.
2. Mortimer, *Fears of Henry IV*, pp. 246-7, 356.
3. Anne's dower from her marriage to Edmund is in *CCR 1402–05*, pp. 212-15, 218, 237-40, 260-61, and her income is given in the *ODNB* entry for her second husband William Bourchier. Stafford's IPM is in *CIPM 1399–1405*, nos. 804-53; his and Anne's son and heir Humphrey Stafford was 'aged one year on 15 August last' on 26 September 1403. Henry IV's grant to Joan Beaufort is in *CPR 1401–05*, p. 251, and see also *CIPM 1392–99*, nos. 10-24.
4. *CIPM 1399–1405*, nos. 1003-5; *PROME*, parliament of January 1404; and see also *CPR 1385–89*, pp. 494-5.
5. *ODNB*, 'Cornewall, John, Baron Fanhope (d. 1443)'. As always with the *ODNB*, a list of sources is provided at the end of the biography, with no indication given as to which source relates to which statement; it is therefore impossible to determine which primary source reveals that Elizabeth gave birth to a son in February 1405.
6. *Medieval Iberia: Readings from Christian, Muslim, and Jewish Sources*, ed. Constable and Zurro, p. 438; Echevarría, 'Catalina de Lancaster, the Castilian Monarchy, and Coexistence', pp. 105-6; García Rey, *La Famosa Priora Doña Teresa de Ayala*, p. 739; Francisco de Asís Veas Arteseros, *Itinerario de Enrique III* (2003), p. 429.
7. Asís Veas Arteseros, *Itinerario de Enrique III*, p. 429; Echevarría, 'Catalina de Lancaster, the Castilian Monarchy, and Coexistence', pp. 106-7 (Catalina also wrote to Teresa as *muy cara e muy amada*

madre); Cañas Gálvez, 'Don Sancho de Castilla', p. 1134 note 58, *muy cara e mucho onrrada e muy deseada tia señora e madre, vuestra fija*. Queen Catalina's brother-in-law Don Fernando of Antequera also politely addressed Teresa and María de Ayala as his aunts, though the familial relationship was much more distant: García Rey, 'La Famosa Priora Doña Teresa de Ayala', pp. 756-8.

8. *Medieval Iberia: Readings*, ed. Constable and Zurro, pp. 438-9; Echevarría, 'Catalina de Lancaster, the Castilian Monarchy, and Coexistence', pp. 106-7.
9. Surtz, *Writing Women in Late Medieval and Early Modern Spain*, p. 42.
10. *Medieval Iberia: Readings*, p. 439.
11. Asís Veas Arteseros, *Itinerario de Enrique III*, p. 436. At the end of her husband's reign, Catalina's *mayordomo mayor* or high steward was Gómez Suárez de Figueroa, lord of the town of Feria 100 miles north of Seville, and her cupbearer was Diego Fernández: Asís Veas Arteseros, *Itinerario*, pp. 334, 418, 425, 476, 492.

Chapter 24: An Illegitimate Daughter and an Unlicensed Marriage

1. TNA SC 8/216/10782.
2. Edmund's proof of age gives his date of birth as 6 January 1382 (in the Hampshire village of Brockenhurst, in the New Forest), whereas the inquisition post mortem of his older brother Thomas gives 6 January 1383: *CIPM 1399–1405*, nos. 974-80. Rather confusingly, the proof of age was taken on 22 May 1404, gives Edmund's date of birth as 6 January 1382, and then states 'he is therefore aged twenty-one'. According to Psalter K.26 now in the library of St John's College, Cambridge, Edmund was born on 9 January 1382: https://www.joh.cam.ac.uk/library/special_collections/manuscripts/medieval_manuscripts/medman/K_26.htm, accessed 19 October 2021.
3. *CPR 1401–05*, p. 478. Another issue is the medieval habit of dating the new year from 25 March rather than 1 January, which perhaps goes some way to explaining the confusion over Edmund's correct year of birth.
4. Alianore's claim is in *PROME*, January 1431 parliament, and also in *The Statutes of the Realm*, vol. 2 (1816), pp. 269-72. Edmund was a keen jouster, like his late uncle John Holland, earl of Huntingdon:

among other examples, in or soon after April 1407 he competed against the Scottish earl of March. *Calendar of Documents Relating to Scotland 1357–1509*, no. 730. His marriage to Lucia (d. 1424), who like Constance was some years his senior, was under discussion by Easter 1406, which perhaps provides a *terminus ad quem* for his relationship with Constance: Karl Wenck, 'Lucia Visconti, König Heinrich IV. von England und Edmund von Kent', *Mittheilungen des Instituts für Österreichische Geschichtsforschung*, 18 (1897), pp. 113-15.

5. *Monasticon Anglicanum*, ed. William Dugdale, vol. 2 (1846), p. 62 (*Et postea domina Constantia nupta erat domino Thomae comiti de Arundell, de qua genuit filiam nomine Elianoram*).

6. Edmund and Roger Mortimer, and their older sister Anne, later countess of Cambridge, were the children of Edmund Holland's eldest sister Alianore (1370–1405).

7. TNA SC 8/231/11526 (the queen's petition to her husband to be granted Constance's lands until her son Richard came of age, dated 23 February 1405); *CCR 1401–05*, pp. 435-6; *CCR 1405–09*, p. 207; *CPR 1401–05*, p. 496; *CPR 1405–08*, pp. 4, 107.

8. Carlier, 'Henri d'Oisy', p. 110.

9. *CPR 1401–05*, pp. 391, 480; *CCR 1402–05*, pp. 334-5, 441-2.

10. Constance married secondly Sir John Grey, son and heir of Reginald, Lord Grey of Ruthin, and gave birth to her son Edmund Grey, later earl of Kent, on 26 October 1416.

11. *Complete Peerage*, vol. 10, p. 235 note h. Richard de Vere married Alice St Aubyn née Sergeaux, stepdaughter of Elizabeth of Lancaster's third husband John Cornwall and widow of Guy St Aubyn, in or before the summer of 1407; their eldest son John de Vere, earl of Oxford, was born in April 1408.

12. *CPR 1405–08*, p. 97.

13. *CIPM 1399–1405*, nos. 13-15 (Bartholomew was 'thirty and more' and 'of full age' in June 1400; *CIPM 1405–13*, nos. 640-2, 736-9 (IPMs of Bartholomew and his widow Idonea); *Complete Peerage*, vol. 2, pp. 246-8.

14. *CP*, vol. 2, p. 248, saying he was 'scarcely sixteen' on 28 May 1420 when his father died; William's IPM of October/November 1420 gives Henry's age then as 'sixteen and more'. Henry was possibly named in honour of the king, and perhaps was Henry IV's godson.

15. *ODNB*, William Bourchier entry; *Issues of the Exchequer*, ed. Devon, p. 311. Confusingly, the payment to William for travelling to Denmark states (*Issues*, p. 311) that he was to 'treat with Isabella, Queen of Denmark, for a marriage to be had between Lord Henry, Prince of Wales, and the daughter of Philippa, Queen of Denmark'. The name 'Philippa' must be a clerical error, and the name 'Isabella' is also an error. The girl whose marriage to the prince of Wales was under discussion was Katharina of Pomerania (b. *c.* 1390), daughter of the duke of Pomerania and Maria of Mecklenburg-Schwerin, herself the daughter of Ingeborg of Denmark, who had died back in 1370. Katharina's brother Erik of Pomerania married Henry IV's daughter Philippa of Lancaster. At Easter 1415, Henry V sent William Bourchier to Paris 'to confer with and treat with the French king [Charles VI] upon certain secret articles and matters': *Issues of the Exchequer*, pp. 340-41.
16. *CPL 1404–15*, p. 140.

Chapter 25: Queen Philippa and an Arundel Marriage

1. Earl Thomas's father Richard, earl of Arundel (executed by Richard II in 1397), was a brother of Mary and Eleanor de Bohun's mother Joan and of Archbishop Thomas Arundel, and his mother Elizabeth de Bohun (d. 1385) was a sister of Mary's father Humphrey (d. 1373).
2. Manuela Santos Silva, 'O Casamento de D. Beatriz (Filha Natural de D. João I) com Thomas Fitzalan (Conde de Arundel) – Paradigma Documental de Negociação de uma Aliança', *Problematizar a História: Estudos de História Moderna e Homenagem a Maria do Rosário Themudo Barata*, ed. Ana Maria Leal de Faria and Isabel Drumond Braga (2007), p. 78, estimates Beatriz's date of birth as perhaps 1380. Thomas himself had an illegitimate son named John, though whether he was born during Thomas's marriage to Beatriz or before they wed is unknown. Beatriz was perhaps infertile, as she and Thomas were to have no children in the ten years of their marriage. See *Register of Henry Chichele, Archbishop of Canterbury 1414–1443, Volume II: Wills Proved Before the Archbishop or his Commissaries*, ed. E.F. Jacob and

H.C. Johnson (1937), pp. 72, 77 (*Johan nostre fitz'*/'*Iohannis filii mei*). Henry IV had given Thomas permission to 'marry whom he please' on 3 July 1403 not long before the battle of Shrewsbury, where Thomas fought for him against the Percys and alongside Edmund Stafford, though the king managed to persuade Thomas to marry a Portuguese bride in his own interests rather than the earl's: *CPR 1401–05*, p. 242.

3. *Royal and Historical Letters During the Reign of Henry the Fourth*, ed. Francis Charles Hingeston, vol. 2, pp. 83-102.
4. Santos Silva, 'O Casamento de D. Beatriz', p. 87 note 45.
5. Thomas's letter is printed in the original French in Edward Blore, *The Monumental Remains of Noble and Eminent Persons* (1826), p. 5. The book dates the letter to 1405, but Thomas himself dated it to the seventh regnal year of Henry IV, which ran from 30 September 1405 to 29 September 1406, and he had not yet married Beatriz in June 1405. His will is in *Register of Henry Chichele*, vol. 2, pp. 71-8.
6. Cañas Gálvez, 'Don Sancho de Castilla', pp. 1133-4; Louise Mirrer, 'Leonor López de Córdoba and the Poetics of Women's Autobiography', *Mester*, 20 (1991), pp. 9-10; Surtz, *Writing Women*, p. 42. Martín López de Córdoba, a supporter of Pedro the Cruel, was executed by Pedro's half-brother and usurper Enrique of Trastámara in 1371, even though Enrique had promised to protect Martín and his family. Leonor spent the next few years of her life imprisoned. Another master of the Order of Calatrava was Don Diego García de Padilla (d. 1368), brother of María de Padilla, and Duchess Costanza of Lancaster's uncle.
7. Folger, *Generaciones Y Semblanzas: Memory and Genealogy*, p. 64; Guzmán, *Pen Portraits of Illustrious Castilians*, p. 12.
8. Surtz, *Writing Women*, pp. 42-3; Echevarría, *Catalina de Lancaster*, pp. 137-9; David Nirenberg, *Neighboring Faiths: Christianity, Islam, and Judaism in the Middle Ages and Today* (2014), p. 71.
9. Earenfight, *The King's Other Body*, p. 24.
10. García Rey, *La Famosa Priora Doña Teresa de Ayala*, pp. 747-9, 763, 772.
11. See Joan's entry in the *ODNB*; the source cited is British Library Cotton MS Vespasian F.xiii.

Chapter 26: Queen Philippa's and Queen Catalina's Diplomacy

1. *CIPM 1405–13*, nos. 991-4; *CPR 1396–9*, p. 583; *CPR 1399–1401*, p. 273; *CPR 1401–05*, p. 484; *CPR 1405–08*, pp. 297, 299, 311, 314.
2. *CIPM 1405–13*, nos. 1044-53. In Maud's IPM, the Rutland jurors were confused about the countess's identity, and wrongly named her as the daughter of an 'Elizabeth', perhaps confusing her mother Maud of Lancaster with her much older half-sister Elizabeth de Burgh (1332–1363), duchess of Clarence. Her heir was named as one Robert Willoughby, apparently in error. Maud's identity as the daughter of Sir Ralph Ufford (d. 1346) and Maud of Lancaster, dowager countess of Ulster (d. 1377), and niece of both Robert Ufford, earl of Suffolk (d. 1369) and Henry of Grosmont, first duke of Lancaster (d. 1361), is not in doubt: see *CPR 1345–48*, p. 449.
3. *Foedera 1361–77*, pp. 983-5 (text of the 1373 Treaty of Windsor); *Foedera 1397–1413*, pp. 561-7 (text of the 1408 Franco-Castilian treaty); Given-Wilson, *Henry IV*, pp. 344-5 (safe-conducts and Anglo-Portuguese and Anglo-Castilian relations).
4. César Olivera Serrano, *Beatriz de Portugal. La Pugna Dinástica Avís-Trastámara* (2005), p. 130.
5. Santos Silva, 'Felipa de Lancáster, la Dama Inglesa', pp. 214-15; *trabalhava muito com elle que ouvese boa paaz e amizade com dom Joham Rey de Purtuguall, casado com sua irmã.*
6. Santos Silva, 'Felipa de Lancáster', p. 216.
7. Diana Pelaz Flores, 'Queenly Time in the Reign of Juan II of Castile (1406–1454)', *Queenship in the Mediterranean: Negotiating the Role of the Queen in the Medieval and Early Modern Eras*, ed. Elena Woodacre (2013), pp. 169-90; Santos Silva, 'Felipa de Lancáster', p. 217. Catalina of Castile married Infante Enrique of Aragon, and Duarte of Portugal married Infanta Leonor of Aragon; Juan II of Castile married his first cousin María of Aragon (b. 1403), daughter of Fernando of Antequera, though after her death in 1445 he married his second wife, Philippa of Lancaster's granddaughter Isabel of Portugal the younger (b. 1428).
8. *CPL 1404–15*, p. 412.

9. Earenfight, *The King's Other Body*, p. 24. King Joan of Aragon (d. 1396) was married to Yolande de Bar, sister-in-law of Marie de Coucy, countess of Soissons.
10. *CPL 1404–15*, pp. 247, 462.
11. *CPL 1417-31*, pp. 494, 571, and see Robert's entry in the *ODNB*.

Chapter 27: The Claiming of Castile

1. *Foedera 1397–1413*, p. 729; Jean-Christophe Cassard, 'Tanguy du Chastel, l'Homme de Montereau', *Le Trémazan des du Chastel: du Château Fort à la Ruine*, ed. Yves Coativy (2004), p. 88 note 20, p. 90.
2. James Hamilton Wylie and William Templeton Waugh, *The Reign of Henry V*, vol. 1 (1914), p. 3; William A. Shaw, *The Knights of England*, vol. 1 (1970), p. 129; *ODNB* for the snow.
3. *CIPM 1413–18*, nos. 278-9, 632; *CCR 1413–19*, pp. 133-4, 175; *CPR 1413–16*, pp. 192-3, 263; Northamptonshire Archives W(A) box 1/parcelXI/no. 5/d. The *Complete Peerage*, vol. 4, p. 282, claims wrongly that Richard died on 7 October 1414, following the Tewkesbury Abbey chronicler, though it does not cite the source (*Monasticon Anglicanum*, vol. 2, p. 62).
4. *CPL 1404–15*, pp. 128-9. Eleanor was probably the eldest Neville child, and born *c.* 1397; she married in July 1411 and her sister Katherine married John Mowbray in January 1412, suggesting that Eleanor was older (unless perhaps they were twins). The Tewkesbury Abbey chronicler says that Eleanor was the eldest Neville daughter, though wrongly calls her Elizabeth: *Monasticon Anglicanum*, ed. Dugdale, vol. 2, p. 62. On the other hand, the fact that Katherine bore the name of her grandmother Katherine Swynford might indicate that she was in fact the eldest daughter. Eleanor Neville Despenser later married Henry Percy (b. 1393), second earl of Northumberland, whose mother was Philippa of Clarence's eldest child Elizabeth Mortimer. (b. 1371)
5. Cited in Olivera Serrano, *Beatriz de Portugal: La Pugna Dinástica*, pp. 158-60, 165. Leonor later married Queen Catalina's nephew, Queen Philippa's son Duarte I of Portugal.
6. TNA SC 8/103/5145. In the petition Edmund calls himself 'duke of York', a title he received in August 1385, so it must have been

issued sometime between then and Isabel's death in December 1392. Unfortunately the petition is extremely faded and much of it is unreadable.

7. *Crónicas de los Reyes de Castilla ... por D. Pedro López de Ayala*, ed. Amirola, vol. 1, pp. 366-7, 558-70, *'fijo o fija'*.

8. Philippa's mother Joan, Lady Mohun, née Burghersh (*c.* early or mid-1320s–1404), was in charge of Catalina of Lancaster's household during Catalina's childhood.

Chapter 28: Death of a Queen

1. *CP*, vol. 6, p. 196, and Richardson, *Magna Carta Ancestry*, p. 283, for the date of the Ferrers/Greystoke marriage.

2. Earenfight, *The King's Other Body*, p. 27.

3. *Crónica da Tomada de Ceuta por el Rei D. João I Composta por Gomes Eanes de Zurara*, ed. Francisco Maria Esteves Pereira (1915), pp. 138-40.

4. *Crónica da Tomada de Ceuta*, ed. Pereira, pp. 125-6; Edgar Prestage, *The Portuguese Pioneers* (1966), p. 22.

5. Taylor, *Isabel of Burgundy*, p. 29; Santos Silva, 'Portuguese Household of an English Queen', pp. 283, 285; Echevarría, 'Catalina de Lancaster, the Castilian Monarchy, and Coexistence', p. 193.

6. Jessica Barker, *Stone Fidelity: Marriage and Emotion in Medieval Tomb Sculpture* (2020), pp. 135-7.

7. *CPL 1404–15*, p. 457.

8. William's entry in the *ODNB*.

Chapter 29: Joan Beaufort and Margery Kempe

1. Wylie and Waugh, *Reign of Henry V*, vol. 3, pp. 9-15; *CIPM 1418–22*, no. 149. John was granted 100 marks a year during his minority, 'for his maintenance': *CPR 1413–16*, p. 136.

2. *Monasticon Anglicanum*, ed. Dugdale, vol. 2, pp. 62-3.

3. *PROME*, January 1401 parliament; *Statutes of the Realm*, vol. 2, pp. 125-8; *diversi perfidi et perversi cujusdam nove secte*.

4. Goodman, *My Most Illustrious Mother*, pp. 13-14; Joan's entry in the *ODNB*; *The Book of Margery Kempe*, trans. Barry Windeatt (2005), p. 16. Margery, herself illiterate, dictated her book to a scribe and did not write it herself.

5. Mortimer, *Fears of Henry IV*, pp. 45-6, 220, 309.
6. Goodman, *My Most Illustrious Mother*, pp. 12-13; Krochalis, 'The Books and Reading of Henry V', p. 65; *Testamenta Eboracensia*, vol. 2 (1855), pp. 13-15; Joan's entry in the *ODNB*. Goodman, p. 21 note 37, citing *CCR 1401–05*, p. 470, points out that the squire John Morton had known Joan and her late husband Ralph Neville since at least 1404.
7. Mortimer, *Fears of Henry IV*, p. 46.
8. Francisco de Paula Cañas Gálvez, *El Itinerario de la Corte de Juan II de Castilla (1418–1454)* (2007), p. 167.
9. Cited in Juan Luis Carriazo Rubio, *La Casa de Arcos entre Sevilla y la Frontera de Granada (1374–1474)* (2003), p. 104.
10. Earenfight, *The King's Other Body*, p. 27.
11. See https://dbe.rah.es/biografias/18350/teresa-de-ayala, accessed 19 December 2021.
12. María del Pilar Rábade Obradó, 'Religiosidad y Memoria Política', p. 240.
13. *Medieval Iberia: Readings*, p. 439.
14. Juan II's ultimate heir was his daughter from his second marriage to Isabel of Portugal: Enrique IV's much younger half-sister Isabel la Católica, queen-regnant of Castile and queen-consort of Aragon, who was not born until April 1451 when Juan was 46. Isabel of Portugal, queen of Castile, was the daughter of Dom João of Portugal, son of Philippa of Lancaster, and Isabel la Católica was descended from John of Gaunt and the English royal family via both her parents. Her youngest daughter Catalina (b. 1485), presumably named after her great-grandmother, Catalina of Lancaster, is better known to history as Katherine of Aragon, first wife and queen of Henry VIII.
15. *CIPM 1418–22*, nos. 278-80.
16. Carole Rawcliffe, *The Staffords, Earls of Stafford and Dukes of Buckingham 1394–1521* (1978), pp. 14-16; *CPR 1422–29*, p. 542; *PROME*, May 1421 parliament.
17. *CP*, vol. 2, p. 248.

Chapter 30: The Infant King

1. *ODNB*.
2. *CIPM 1418–22*, nos. 431-2. Nor is there anything particularly useful about Henry's age in the chancery rolls. He was later count of Eu,

inheriting his father's title, and in 1462 was made earl of Essex as well: *CChR 1427–1516*, p. 184.

3. *ODNB*, citing TNA C 115/K2/6682, folio 129r, for Anne's correspondence with John Wyche. For Anne's will, see also below.

4. For this research on Isabeau, contradicting the older view of her as seen in e.g. Rosemary Hawley Jarman's novel *Crown in Candlelight*, see Rachel Gibbons, 'Isabeau of Bavaria, Queen of France (1385–1422): The Creations of an Historical Villainess', *Transactions of the Royal Historical Society*, 6th series, 6 (1996), and Tracy Adams, *The Life and Afterlife of Isabeau of Bavaria* (2010), especially pp. 231-3.

5. Michael Stansfield, 'John Holland, Duke of Exeter and Earl of Huntingdon (d. 1447) and the Costs of the Hundred Years War', *Profit, Piety and the Professions in Later Medieval England*, ed. Michael Hicks (1990), pp. 108-9; Juliet Barker, *Agincourt: The King, the Campaign, the Battle*, pp. 161-2, 372. Barker, pp. 361-2, points out that John Holland served Henry V in France with 'a courage and distinction beyond his years', and was rewarded in 1416 by receiving his father's earldom of Huntingdon.

6. Barker, *Agincourt*, p. 159.

7. *ODNB*, entries for Richard of York, Ralph Neville and Joan Beaufort.

8. Ralph's will is printed in Latin in *Wills and Inventories Illustrative of the History, Manners, Language, Statistics etc of the Northern Counties of England, from the Eleventh Century Downwards*, part 1, ed. James Raine (1835), pp. 68-74; see also *CIPM 1422–27*, nos. 643-4, *CCR 1422–29*, p. 325, and Goodman, *My Most Illustrious Mother*, p. 10. Joan's brother Thomas Beaufort, duke of Exeter, made his will in Latin on 29 December 1426, and died two days later. He left Joan 'a book called Tristram' (*'unum librum vocat Tristram'*): *Collection*, pp. 250; *TV*, pp. 207-11. Sometime before 15 February 1404, Thomas had married Margaret Neville of Hornby, an heiress in Lincolnshire and Yorkshire, who was born *c.* 1384/85; she was 'aged twenty-eight and more' in May 1413. They had no surviving children; they did have a son named Henry, but he died childless in his father's lifetime. At Thomas's inquisition post mortem held between March and May 1427, his heir was named as his and Joan's nephew John Beaufort (*c.* 1404–1444), earl and later duke of Somerset. *CPL 1398–1404*, pp. 621, 626-7; *CIPM 1413–18*,

no. 30; *CFR 1430–37*, p. 138; *CIPM 1422–27*, nos 791–804. Thomas was buried with his wife at the abbey of St Edmunds in Suffolk, and his remains were discovered and examined on 20 February 1772; his hair was said to be 'of a fine brown colour': *Complete Peerage*, vol. 5, p. 204 note c.

9. Shaw, *Knights of England*, vol. 1, pp. 130-31; *PROME*, February 1426; *ODNB*.
10. *CCR 1422–29*, pp. 238-40, 246-8, 348.
11. *CCR 1422–29*, p. 247; *CPR 1399–1401*, p. 149; *CPR 1401–05*, p. 493; *CIPM 1422–27*, no. 643.
12. *London Possessory Assizes*, no. 230.

Chapter 31: The Last Granddaughters

1. Elizabeth of Lancaster's IPM is in *CIPM 1422–27*, nos. 610-16; the duchess of York's will, in French, is in *Collection*, pp. 224-8. Duchess Philippa's mother Joan, Lady Mohun, formerly in charge of Catalina of Lancaster's household, also lived to a ripe old age.
2. *PROME*, May 1432 parliament.
3. An abstract of John's will is printed in English translation in *Early Lincoln Wills: An Abstract of All the Wills and Administrations Recorded in the Episcopal Registers of the Old Diocese of Lincoln, 1280–1547*, ed. Alfred Gibbons (1888), pp. 166-7; a more abbreviated abstract is in *TV*, p. 246.
4. *CIPM 1442–47*, nos. 201-2; https://www.british-history.ac.uk/vch/beds/vol3/pp268-275, accessed 18 November 2021.
5. *Collection*, pp. 282-9. Beatriz died in 1439 and was buried with her first husband Thomas, earl of Arundel, in Arundel, where their effigies can still be seen; Beatriz's effigy wears a horned headdress of astonishing width.
6. *CIPM 1422–27*, nos. 639-54; *CIPM 1427–32*, no. 314; *ODNB*, entry for Ralph Neville, second earl of Westmorland. Ralph the younger's mother was Alianore or Eleanor Holland (b. 1384), one of the many children of Richard II's half-brother the earl of Kent, and a niece of Elizabeth of Lancaster's husband John Holland.
7. *ODNB*, entry for Ralph Neville, second earl of Westmorland.
8. Salisbury's inquisition post mortem is in *CIPM 1427–32*, nos. 462-85.

9. Hugh Bicheno, *Battle Royal: The Wars of Lancaster and York, 1440–1462* (2015), pp. 96-7; *ODNB*, entry for Ralph Neville, first earl of Westmorland (with the Ross quote); *CPR 1429–36*, pp. 595-6; *CCR 1429–35*, p. 67.
10. *Collection of All the Wills*, pp. 278-80; *Register of Henry Chichele*, vol. 2, pp. 596-7; *CIPM 1437–42*, nos. 238-40; *CCR 1422–29*, pp. 332, 335, 358. Humphrey Stafford, earl of Stafford, later became the first duke of Buckingham, and married Joan Beaufort's daughter Anne Neville. On his death in 1460, his heir was his young grandson Henry Stafford, executed by Richard III in 1483.
11. Amin, *The House of Beaufort: The Bastard Line that Captured the Crown*, p. 196.
12. *CIPM 1437–42*, nos. 513-19; *CFR 1437–45*, p. 164: the writ to hold Joan's IPM was issued on 16 November 1440, three days after her death.
13. Joan's will is printed in the original Latin in *Historiae Dunelmensis Scriptores Tres, Gaufridus de Coldingham, Robertus de Graystanes, et Willielmus de Chambre*, ed. James Raine (1839), pp. cclviii-cclx. Her son William Neville married Joan Fauconberg, heir to her father Thomas, Baron Fauconberg (d. 1407).
14. Goodman, *My Most Illustrious Mother*, p. 15.
15. *CPR 1436–41*, p. 137.

Bibliography

Primary Sources

Adae Murimuth Continuatio Chronicarum, ed. E.M. Thompson (1889)

Anglo-Norman Letters and Petitions from All Souls MS 182, ed. Mary Dominica Legge (1941)

The Anonimalle Chronicle 1333 to 1381, ed. Vivian Hunter Galbraith (1927; reprinted with minor corrections 1970)

The Antient Kalenders and Inventories of the Treasury of His Majesty's Exchequer, three vols., ed. Francis Palgrave (1836)

The Book of Margery Kempe, trans. Barry Windeatt (2005)

The Brut or the Chronicles of England, parts 1 and 2, ed. F.W.D. Brie (1906–8)

Calendar of Ancient Petitions Relating to Wales, ed. William Rees (1975)

Calendar of the Charter Rolls, two vols., 1341–1417 and 1427–1516 (1916)

Calendar of the Close Rolls, twenty-one vols., 1349–1447 (1906-37)

Calendar of Documents Relating to Scotland, vol. 4, 1357–1509, ed. Joseph Bain (1888)

Calendar of Entries in the Papal Registers Relating to Great Britain and Ireland: Papal Letters, six vols., 1342–1447, ed. W.H. Bliss, C. Johnson and J.A. Twemlow (1897–1912)

Calendar of Entries in the Papal Registers Relating to Great Britain and Ireland: Petitions to the Pope, one vol., 1342–1419, ed. W.H. Bliss (1896)

Calendar of the Fine Rolls, twelve vols., 1347–1452 (1921–39)

Calendar of Inquisitions Miscellaneous (Chancery), two vols., 1308–77 (1916)

Calendar of Inquisitions Post Mortem, eighteen vols., 1347–1447 (1916–2009)

Calendar of the Patent Rolls, twenty-one vols., 1354–1441 (1907–1909)

Calendar of Select Plea and Memoranda Rolls of the City of London, three vols., 1323–1412, ed. A. H. Thomas (1926–32)

Calendar of Wills Proved and Enrolled in the Court of Husting, London, ed. R.R. Sharpe, vol. 1, 1258–1358, and vol. 2, 1358–1688 (1889-90)

The Chronica Maiora of Thomas Walsingham, 1376–1422, ed. Richard Barber, translated David Preest (2005)

The Chronicle of Adam Usk, 1377–1421, ed. Chris Given-Wilson (1997)

The Chronicle of Geoffrey le Baker of Swinbrook, ed. Richard Barber, trans. David Preest (2012)

Chronicles of the Revolution, 1397–1400: The Reign of Richard II, ed. Chris Given-Wilson (1993)

Chronicon Angliae, ab Anno Domini 1328 usque ad Annum 1388, ed. Edward Maunde Thompson (1874)

Chronicon Galfridi le Baker de Swynebroke, ed. Edward Maunde Thompson (1889)

Chronicon Henrici Knighton, vel Cnitthon, monachi Leycestrensis, two vols., ed. J.R. Lumby (1889–95)

Chronicque de la Traison et Mort de Richart Deux Roy Dengleterre, ed. Benjamin Williams (1846)

Chroniques de London, ed. J.G. Aungier (1844)

Colección Diplomática de Santo Domingo el Real de Toledo I: Documentos Reales (1249–1473), ed. Francisco de Paula Cañas Gálvez (2010)

A Collection of All the Wills Now Known to be Extant of the Kings and Queens of England, Princes and Princesses of Wales, and Every Branch of the Blood Royal, ed. John Nichols and Richard Gough (1780)

Crónica del Señor Rey Don Juan, Segundo de Este Nombre, en Castilla y en León, compiled by Fernán Pérez de Guzmán, amended by Lorenzo Galíndez de Carvajal (1779)

Crónicas de los Reyes de Castilla desde Don Alfonso el Sabio hasta los Católicos Don Fernando y Doña Isabel, ed. Cayetano Rosell, vol. 2 (1877)

Crónicas de los Reyes de Castilla Don Pedro, Don Enrique II, Don Juan I, Don Enrique III por D. Pedro López de Ayala, ed. Don Eugenio de Llaguno Amirola, vol. 1 (1779)

Bibliography

Crónica da Tomada de Ceuta por el Rei D. João I Composta por Gomes Eanes de Zurara, ed. Francisco Maria Esteves Pereira (1915)

A Descriptive Catalogue of Ancient Deeds, six vols., ed. H.C. Maxwell Lyte (1890–1915)

The Diplomatic Correspondence of Richard II, ed. Edouard Perroy (1933)

Early Lincoln Wills: An Abstract of All the Wills and Administrations Recorded in the Episcopal Registers of the Old Diocese of Lincoln, 1280–1547, ed. Alfred Gibbons (1888)

English Historical Documents, vol. 4, 1327–1485, ed. A.R. Myers (1969; reprinted 1996)

Eulogium Historiarum Sive Temporis, vol. 3, ed. Frank Scott Haydon (1863)

Excerpta Historica, Or, Illustrations of English History, ed. Samuel Bentley (1831)

Expeditions to Prussia and the Holy Land Made by Henry, Earl of Derby (Afterwards King Henry IV) in the Years 1390–1 and 1392–3, Being the Accounts Kept by his Treasurer for Two Years, ed. Lucy Toulmin Smith (1894)

Foedera, Conventiones, Litterae et Cujuscunque Acta Publica, ten vols., 1327–1441, ed. Thomas Rymer (1821–29)

The Gascon Rolls Project (1317–1468), at www.gasconrolls.org

Henry of Grosmont, First Duke of Lancaster, *Le Livre de Seyntz Medicines: The Book of Holy Medicines*, translated with notes and introduction by Catherine Batt (2014)

Historia Vitae et Regni Ricardi Secundi, ed. George B. Stow (1977)

Historiae Dunelmensis Scriptores Tres, Gaufridus de Coldingham, Robertus de Graystanes, et Willielmus de Chambre, ed. James Raine (1839)

Issues of the Exchequer; Being a Collection of Payments Made Out of His Majesty's Revenue, From King Henry III to King Henry VI Inclusive, ed. Frederick Devon (1837)

Jean Froissart: Chronicles, translated and edited by Geoffrey Brereton (1968)

Johannis de Trokelowe et Henrici de Blaneforde, Monachorum S. Albani, Chronica et Annales, ed. Henry Thomas Riley (1866)

John of Gaunt's Register, vol. 1, 1371–1375, ed. Sydney Armitage-Smith (1911)

John of Gaunt's Register, vol. 2, 1379–1383, ed. Eleanor C. Lodge and Robert Somerville (1937)

Knighton's Chronicle 1337–1396, ed. Geoffrey Haward Martin (1995)

Life-Records of Chaucer, Parts I-IV, ed. Walford D. Selby, F.J. Furnivall, Edward A. Bond and R. E.G. Kirk (1900)

Livre de Seyntz Medicines: The Unpublished Devotional Treatise of Henry of Lancaster, ed. E.J. Arnould (1940)

London Assize of Nuisance 1301–1431: A Calendar, ed. Helena M. Chew and William Kellaway (1973)

London Possessory Assizes: A Calendar, ed. Helena M. Chew (1965)

Memorials of London and London Life in the XIIIth, XIVth and XVth Centuries, ed. H.T. Riley (1868)

Memorials of the Order of the Garter from Its Foundation to the Present Time, ed. George Frederick Beltz (1841)

Monasticon Anglicanum, ed. William Dugdale, six vols. (1846)

The National Archives: C (Chancery), DL (Duchy of Lancaster), E (Exchequer), SC (Special Collections)

Oeuvres de Froissart, ed. Kervyn de Lettenhove, twenty-five vols. (1867–77)

The Parliament Rolls of Medieval England, ed. Brand, Curry, Given-Wilson, Horrox, Martin, Ormrod and Phillips (2005)

Polychronicon Ranulphi Higden, Monachi Cestrensis, vols. 8 and 9, ed. Joseph Rawson Lumby (1882–86)

Records of the Borough of Leicester, vol. 2, 1327–1509, ed. Mary Bateson (1901)

Recueil de Lettres Anglo-Francaises, 1265–1399, ed. F.J. Tanqueray (1916)

The Reign of Richard II from Majority to Tyranny 1377–1397, ed. A.K. McHardy (2012)

Register of Edward the Black Prince Preserved in the Public Record Office, ed. M.C.B. Dawes, parts I-IV (1930–33)

Register of Henry Chichele, Archbishop of Canterbury, 1414–1443, Volume II: Wills Proved Before the Archbishop or his Commissaries, ed. E.F. Jacob and H.C. Johnson (1937)

Royal and Historical Letters During the Reign of Henry the Fourth, King of England and France and Lord of Ireland, Vol. II, A.D. 1405–1413, ed. Francis Charles Hingeston (reprinted 1964)

The Statutes of the Realm, vol. 1, 1100–1377, and vol. 2, 1377–1509 (1810–16, reprinted 1965)

Testamenta Eboracensia: A Selection of Wills from the Registry at York, parts 1 and 2, ed. James Raine (1836-55)

Testamenta Vetusta: Being Illustrations from Wills, vol. 1, ed. Nicholas Harris Nicolas (1826)

Thomae Walsingham, Quondam Monachi S. Albani, Historia Anglicana, ed. Henry Thomas Riley, vol. 2 (1864)

The True Chronicles of Jean le Bel, 1290–1360, ed. and trans. Nigel Bryant (2011)

The Westminster Chronicle 1381–1394, ed. L.C. Hector and B.F. Harvey (1982)

Wills and Inventories Illustrative of the History, Manners, Language, Statistics etc of the Northern Counties of England, from the Eleventh Century Downwards, part 1, ed. James Raine (1835)

Selected Secondary Sources

Adams, Tracy, *The Life and Afterlife of Isabeau of Bavaria* (2010)

Amin, Nathen, *The House of Beaufort: The Bastard Line that Captured the Crown* (2017)

Asís Veas Arteseros, Francisco de, *Itinerario de Enrique III* (2003)

Bárány, Attila, 'King Sigismund and the "Passagium Generale" (1391–96)', *Conferinta Internationala Sigismund de Luxemburg*, ed. Florena Ciure and Alexandru Simon (2007) [page numbers not available]

Barker, Jessica, *Stone Fidelity: Marriage and Emotion in Medieval Tomb Sculpture* (2020)

Bicheno, Hugh, *Battle Royal: The Wars of Lancaster and York, 1440–1462* (2015)

Blore, Edward, *The Monumental Remains of Noble and Eminent Persons, Comprising the Sepulchral Antiquities of Great Britain* (1826)

Bradford, Ernle, *A Wind From the North: The Life of Henry the Navigator* (1960)

Cacegas, Luís de, and Lucas de Santa Catharina, *Primeira Parte da História de S. Domingos, Particular do Reino e Conquistas de Portugal*, vol. 2 (1866)

Calmet, Augustin, *Histoire Ecclésiastique et Civile de Lorraine*, vol. 2 (1728)

Cañas Gálvez, Francisco de Paula, 'Don Sancho de Castilla (1363–1371): Apuntes Biográficos de un Hijo Ilegítimo de Pedro I', *Mundos Medievales, Espacios, Sociedares y Poder: Homenaje al Profesor José Ángel García de Cortazar y Ruiz de Aguirre,* University of Cantabria (2012), vol. 2, pp. 1125-36

Cañas Gálvez, Francisco de Paula, *El Itinerario de la Corte de Juan II de Castilla (1418–1454)* (2007)

Carlier, Jean-Joseph, 'Henri d'Oisy, Fragment d'Études Historiques', *Mémoire de la Société Dunkerquoise pour l'Encouragement des Sciences, des Lettres et des Arts* (1858), pp. 1-167

Carriazo Rubio, Juan Luis, *La Casa de Arcos entre Sevilla y la Frontera de Granada (1374–1474)* (2003)

Cassard, Jean-Christophe, 'Tanguy du Chastel, l'Homme de Montereau', *Le Trémazan des du Chastel: du Château Fort à la Ruine*, ed. Yves Coativy (2004)

Castor, Helen, *Joan of Arc: A History* (2014)

Catlos, Brian A., *Muslims of Medieval Latin Christendom, c. 1050–1614* (2014)

Cowling, G.H., 'Chaucer's Complaintes of Mars and of Venus', *The Review of English Studies*, 2 (1926), pp. 405-10

Dunn, Alastair, 'Richard II and the Mortimer Inheritance', *Fourteenth Century England II*, ed. Chris Given-Wilson (2002), pp. 159-70

Earenfight, Theresa, *The King's Other Body. María of Castile and the Crown of Aragon* (2010)

Echevarría Arsuaga, Ana, *Catalina de Lancaster: Reina Regente de Castilla, 1372–1418* (2002)

Echevarría Arsuaga, Ana, 'Catalina de Lancaster, the Castilian Monarchy, and Coexistence', *Medieval Spain: Culture, Conflict, and Coexistence: Studies in Honour of Angus McKay*, ed. Roger Collins and Anthony Goodman (2002), pp. 79-122

Estow, Clara, *Pedro the Cruel of Castile 1350–1369* (1996)

Estow, Clara, 'Royal Madness in the Crónica del Rey Don Pedro', *Mediterranean Studies*, 6 (1996), pp. 13-28

Green, Mary Anne Everett, *Lives of the Princesses, From the Norman Conquest*, vol. 3 (1851)

Flórez, Enrique, *Memorias de las Reynas Catholicas: Historia Genealogica de la Casa Real de Castilla y de León, Todos los Infantes, Trages de las Reynas en Estampas, y Nuevo Aspecto de la Historia de España*, vol. 2 (1770)

Fly, Henry, 'Some Account of an Abbey of Nuns Formerly Situated in the Street Now Called the Minories in the County of Middlesex, and Liberty of the Tower of London', *Archaeologia*, 15 (1806), pp. 92-113

Folger, Robert, *Generaciones Y Semblanzas: Memory and Genealogy in Medieval Iberian Historiography* (2003)

García Rey, Verardo, 'La Famosa Priora Doña Teresa de Ayala (su Correspondencia Íntima con los Monarcas de su Tiempo)', *Boletín de la Real Academia de la Historia*, 96 (1930), pp. 685-779

Geaman, Kristen L., 'A Personal Letter Written by Anne of Bohemia', *English Historical Review*, 128 (2013), pp. 1086-94

Geaman, Kristen L., 'Anne of Bohemia and her Struggle to Conceive', *Social History of Medicine*, 27 (2014), pp. 1-21

Gibbons, Rachel, 'Isabeau of Bavaria, Queen of France (1385–1422): The Creations of an Historical Villainess', *Transactions of the Royal Historical Society*, 6th series, 6 (1996), pp. 51-73

Given-Wilson, Chris, *Henry IV* (2016)

Goodman, Anthony, *John of Gaunt: The Exercise of Princely Power in Fourteenth-Century Europe* (1992)

Goodman, Anthony, *'My Most Illustrious Mother, the Lady Katherine': Katherine Swynford and her Daughter Joan* (2008)

Harriss, G.L., *Cardinal Beaufort: A Study of Lancastrian Ascendancy and Decline* (1988)

Harvey, L.P., *Islamic Spain, 1250 to 1500* (1990)

Hollman, Gemma, *Royal Witches: From Joan of Navarre to Elizabeth Woodville* (2019)

Jolly, Margaretta, ed., *Encyclopedia of Life Writing: Autobiographical and Biographical Forms* (2013)

Krochalis, Jeanne E., 'The Books and Reading of Henry V and his Circle', *The Chaucer Review*, 23 (1988), pp. 50-77

Lea, Henry Charles, 'Ferrand Martinez and the Massacres of 1391', *The American Historical Review*, 1 (1896), pp. 209-19

Lopes, Fernão, ed. by Derek W. Lomax and R.J. Oakley, *The English in Portugal, 1367–87: Extracts from the Chronicles of Dom Fernando and Dom João* (1988)

Marques, Antonio Henrique R. de Oliveira and S.S. Wyatt, *Daily Life in Portugal in the Late Middle Ages* (1971)

Mirrer, Louise, 'Leonor López de Córdoba and the Poetics of Women's Autobiography', *Mester*, 20 (1991), pp. 9-18

Mortimer, Ian, *The Fears of Henry IV: The Life of England's Self-Made King* (2007)

Mortimer, Ian, 'Richard II and the Succession to the Crown' in his *Medieval Intrigue: Decoding Royal Conspiracies* (2010), pp. 259-78

Nirenberg, David, *Neighboring Faiths: Christianity, Islam, and Judaism in the Middle Ages and Today* (2014)

Olivera Serrano, César, *Beatriz de Portugal. La Pugna Dinástica Avís-Trastámara* (2005)

Ormrod, W. Mark, *Edward III* (2011)

Ormrod, W.M., 'Edward III and his Family', *Journal of British Studies*, 26 (1987), pp. 398-422

Palmer, J.J.N., 'The Historical Context of the "Book of the Duchess": A Revision', *The Chaucer Review*, vol. 8. No. 4 (1974), pp. 253-61

Payling, S.J., 'The Economics of Marriage in Late Medieval England: The Marriage of Heiresses', *Economic History Review*, 54 (2001), pp. 413-29

Pelaz Flores, Diana, 'Queenly Time in the Reign of Juan II of Castile (1406–1454)', *Queenship in the Mediterranean: Negotiating the Role of the Queen in the Medieval and Early Modern Eras*, ed. Elena Woodacre (2013), pp. 169-90

Pérez de Guzmán, Fernán, *Pen Portraits of Illustrious Castilians* (2003)

Pohl, John, and Garry Embleton, *Armies of Castile and Aragon 1370–1516* (2015)

Prestage, Edgar, *The Portuguese Pioneers* (1966)

Pugh, T.B., *Henry V and the Southampton Plot* (1988)

Rábade Obradó, María del Pilar, 'Religiosidad y Memoria Política: Las Constituciones de la Capilla de Pedro I en Santo Domingo el Real de Madrid (1464)', *En la España Medieval*, 26 (2003), pp. 227-61

Rawcliffe, Carole, *The Staffords, Earls of Stafford and Dukes of Buckingham 1394–1521* (1978)

Rodrigues Oliveira, Ana, 'Philippa of Lancaster: The Memory of a Model Queen', *Queenship in the Mediterranean: Negotiating the Role of the Queen in the Medieval and Early Modern Eras*, ed. Elena Woodacre (2013), pp. 125-44

Richardson, Douglas, *Magna Carta Ancestry: A Study in Colonial and Medieval Families* (second edition, 2011)

Richardson, Douglas, *Plantagenet Ancestry: A Study in Colonial and Medieval Families* (2004)

Rodriguez, Bretton, 'Competing Images of Pedro I: López de Ayala and the Formation of Historical Memory', *La Corónica: A Journal of Medieval Hispanic Languages, Literatures, and Cultures*, 45 (2017), pp. 79-108

Santos Silva, Manuela, 'O Casamento de D. Beatriz (Filha Natural de D. João I) com Thomas Fitzalan (Conde de Arundel) – Paradigma Documental de Negociação de uma Aliança', *Problematizar a História: Estudos de História Moderna e Homenagem a Maria do Rosário Themudo Barata*, ed. Ana Maria Leal de Faria and Isabel Drumond Braga (2007), pp. 77-91

Santos Silva, Manuela, 'Felipa de Lancáster, la Dama Inglesa que fue Modelo de Reginalidad en Portugal (1387–1415)', *Anuario de Estudios Medievales*, 46 (2016), pp. 203-30

Santos Silva, Manuela, 'The Portuguese Household of an English Queen: Sources, Purposes, Social Meaning (1387–1415)', *Royal and Elite Households in Medieval and Early Modern Europe, More Than Just a Castle*, ed. Theresa Earenfight (2018), pp. 271-87

Shaw, William A., *The Knights of England*, vol. 1 (1970)

Silva, Amélia Maria Polónia da, 'D. Filipa de Lencastre: Representações de uma Rainha', *Actas do Colóquio Comemorativo do VI Centenário do Tratado de Windsor*, ed. Manuel Gomes da Torre (1988), pp. 297-313

Stansfield, Michael, 'John Holland, Duke of Exeter and Earl of Huntingdon (d. 1447) and the Costs of the Hundred Years War', *Profit, Piety and the Professions in Later Medieval England*, ed. Michael Hicks (1990), pp. 103-18

Stansfield, Michael M.N., 'The Hollands, Dukes of Exeter, Earls of Kent and Huntingdon, 1352–1475', Oxford University DPhil thesis (1987)

Steer, Christian, "For Quicke and Deade Memory Masses': Merchant Piety in Late Medieval London', *Medieval Merchants and Money: Essays in Honour of James L. Bolton*, ed. Martin Allen and Matthew Davies (2016), pp. 71-89

Stratford, Jenny, *Richard II and the English Royal Treasure* (2013)

Suárez Fernández, Luis, *Historia del Reinado de Juan I de Castilla*, two vols. (1976–7)

Sumption, Jonathan, *Divided Houses: The Hundred Years War III* (2011)

Surtz, Ronald E., *Writing Women in Late Medieval and Early Modern Spain* (2016)

Taylor, Aline S., *Isabel of Burgundy: The Duchess Who Played Politics in the Age of Joan of Arc, 1397–1471* (2001)

Tuck, Anthony, 'Richard II and the House of Luxemburg', *Richard II: The Art of Kingship*, ed. Anthony Goodman and James Gillespie (1999), pp. 205-29

Valdaliso, Covadonga, 'Las Mujeres del Rey don Pedro de Castilla de J.B. Sitges desde una Perspectiva de Género', *Investigaciones Feministas*, 1 (2010), pp. 213-26

Viúla de Faria, Tiago, 'From Norwich to Lisbon: Factionalism, Personal Association, and Conveying the *Confessio Amantis*', *John Gower in England and Iberia: Manuscripts, Influences, Reception*, ed. Ana Sáez-Hidalgo and R. F. Yeager (2014), pp. 131-8

Walker, Simon, 'Janico Dartasso: Chivalry, Nationality and the Man-at-Arms', *History*, 84 (1999), pp. 31-51

Warner, Kathryn, *John of Gaunt: Son of One King, Father of Another* (2022)

Warner, Kathryn, *Philippa of Hainault: Mother of the English Nation* (2019)

Warner, Kathryn, *Richard II: A True King's Fall* (2017)

Wells-Furby, Bridget, 'Marriage and Inheritance: The Element of Chance in the Development of Lay Estates in the Fourteenth Century', *Fourteenth Century England X*, ed. Gwilym Dodd (2018), pp. 113-32

Wenck, Karl, 'Lucia Visconti, König Heinrich IV. von England und Edmund von Kent', *Mittheilungen des Instituts für Österreichische Geschichtsforschung*, 18 (1897), pp. 69-128

Wogan-Browne, Jocelyn, "*Cherchant toute Egypte pour les bons homes*': Philippa de Vere (1367–1411) and Her Book', *People, Power and Identity in the Late Middle Ages: Essays in Memory of W. Mark Ormrod*, ed. Gwilym Dodd, Helen Lacey and Anthony Musson (2021), pp. 227-45

Wylie, James Hamilton, *History of England Under Henry the Fourth*, vol. 4 (1898)

Wylie, James Hamilton, and William Templeton Waugh, *The Reign of Henry V*, three vols. (1914–29)

Index

Women appear under their maiden names; only a person's highest title is given.